AIDS in
Latin America

AIDS in
Latin America

Tim Frasca

First published in 2005 by
PALGRAVE MACMILLAN™
175 Fifth Avenue, New York, N.Y. 10010 and
Houndmills, Basingstoke, Hampshire, England RG21 6XS
Companies and representatives throughout the world.

PALGRAVE MACMILLAN is the global academic imprint of the Palgrave Macmillan division of St. Martin's Press, LLC and of Palgrave Macmillan Ltd. Macmillan® is a registered trademark in the United States, United Kingdom and other countries. Palgrave is a registered trademark in the European Union and other countries.

ISBN 1–4039–6944–2 hardback

Library of Congress Cataloging-in-Publication Data

AIDS in Latin America / by Tim Frasca.
    p. cm.
Includes index.
ISBN 1–4039–6944–2
    1. AIDS (Disease)—Latin America. I. Title.

RA643.86.L29F73 2005
362.169′9792′0098—dc22   2005043131

A catalogue record for this book is available from the British Library.

Design by Newgen Imaging Systems (P) Ltd., Chennai, India.

First edition: September 2005.

10 9 8 7 6 5 4 3 2 1

Printed in the United States of America.

TO

Miguel Gacitúa
(1964–1996)

A Lost Friend

Contents

Acknowledgments

The Ford Foundation through Program Officer Gaby Oré provided essential financial support for my endeavors; both she and Mireya Díaz often surprised and inspired me with their confidence in the final product. I hope they will not be disappointed. Many people assisted me along the way, often interrupting their busy lives to provide contacts and even an office or an overnight sofa, including Alejandro Brito and Cecilia Araneda in Mexico, Laura Asturias in Guatemala, Mario Pecheny in Argentina, Carlos Cáceres and Mirtha Bravo in Peru, Nigel Celestine in Trinidad and Fernando Seffner in Brazil, to name only a few.

Laetitia Atlani enabled me to see an earlier stage of the social response to HIV/AIDS in several countries of the former Soviet Union when she hired me to consult on a UN Development Programme project in Russia, Kazakstan and Kyrgyzstan in the mid-1990s. Her determination to see the people of those countries reap the benefits of good care and prevention programs was an inspiration to persist under adversity and to acquire deeper knowledge of human and institutional dynamics.

Elena Droguett, Jimmy Esparza and Myriam Lillo of the CIPRESS Foundation in Santiago supported my efforts by reminding me that you cannot please all of the people all of the time and by believing that my vision of AIDS work was valid, even correct, and ought to be preserved. Deborah Meacham kept me aware of the debates and projects taking place among women in Latin America concerned with gender and health issues and kindly suggested that I was not crazy.

Frans Mom of the Dutch development agency HIVOS provided an incomparable model of critical support by showing me how to recognize human imperfections and still support the urgent work that only imperfect human beings can carry out. Lezak Shallat provided invaluable help in thinking through and editing early drafts.

The real architects of this book, however, are the many people who told me their stories, not all of which are included. To thank them on this page is small reward for sharing their intimacy; I only hope I was a good listener.

Introduction

On a pleasant spring day in November 1998, some one hundred people paraded along a circuitous route through downtown Santiago in one of the first demonstrations by people with HIV and their supporters to demand access to the new life-saving antiretroviral drugs. The existence of these triple-combination drug treatments had been announced two years earlier at the Vancouver International AIDS Conference, although the news of the discoveries had trickled back to Santiago very slowly, in part due to the inexperience and sketchy English-language skills of the Chilean community delegates invited to attend. Chilean authorities, like those in many countries of the region, dawdled and dissembled on the chances that any of the several thousand citizens needing these therapies would get them in time to save their lives. Ministry officials never quite closed the door on the idea, nor did they commit the government to shouldering the considerable expense; eventually they would offer *some* drugs to *some* people. The event was deadly serious and at the same time brash and festive as the crowd surged occasionally into the street, then back onto the sidewalk to let cars pass, weaving past Santa Lucía hill—at other times one of the city's main gay cruising areas—en route to the La Moneda presidential palace.

After ten years of engagement with the AIDS issue, I was struck by the laughter and even optimism that rippled through the crowd. Although in the early 1990s we regularly mobilized five hundred people to the candlelight memorial marches in May to remember the dead and denounce discrimination, those events were grim affairs, and people with an HIV diagnosis usually preferred to melt discreetly into the crowd. This time the demonstration was explicitly *of* and *by* them. People joked and jostled each other, mocked their friends' clothes and welcomed unexpected allies, such as a newly posted United Nations' agency representative just becoming familiar with the AIDS issue. All this occurred even though the sallow complexions and emaciated frames of several of the participants showed that they needed an answer fast.

In fact, I was shocked to realize that I had not recognized two of the young fellows walking right next to me due to their poor physical condition, despite having known them very well nearly a decade before. At that time I had tried hard to interest both of them in our AIDS prevention activities aimed specifically at gay men or at least persuade them to say that they would incorporate well-known precautions into their sexual repertoire. To see them so obviously sick was a reminder of how meaningless information about health risks can be to people trying to live their lives and find happiness, love or satisfaction in their own ways.

Both these guys, in their late twenties or early thirties, came from the vast, working-class sectors of Santiago, now a city of six million inhabitants, and had had to make their way in the gay demimonde without the advantages of ready cash, education or middle-class refinements. Instead, they had relied on their youthful appeal to meet partners, make friends and defy the built-in limitations of their origins. Now, fighting for survival, they had shed any lingering fears of family rejection or neighborhood embarrassment to take a public stand on what was the central issue of their lives.

We whooped and hollered our way down past the statue of Salvador Allende toward the Finance Ministry and were finally halted by police while the leaders took advantage of the negotiations to stretch out our raucous presence downtown and attract media coverage. Those passersby who took interest in the event were sympathetic, and later on the evening news officials looked uneasy admitting that the government had no plans to save the lives of those protesting because it would cost more money than it was willing to spend. Despite the immediate failure, we felt the action to be a success. The momentum created by the humanitarian appeal favored our demands that the Chilean state provide access to the new AIDS medicines to everyone who needed them.

By 2003 the government was providing nearly universal coverage for those who met certain clinical criteria. Today, despite some bureaucratic delays, most everyone covered by the public health system in Chile—70 percent of the populace—can get the minimum antiretroviral treatment for HIV infection. Not surprisingly, mortality rates have dropped sharply.

But as that scene in downtown Santiago replayed itself in my mind over the succeeding months and years, I asked myself how the AIDS issue had narrowed from the intense debates we had generated in the late 1980s on sexual culture and sex education, health services, human rights and social exclusion, how the epidemic had returned instead to the white-smocked sphere of the sexually transmitted infection clinic and the hospital. Instead of a challenge to hundreds of years of sexual hypocrisy and a call to guide youth in managing sexuality for their own well-being and fulfillment, AIDS was steadily evolving back to its initial status as an issue for doctors to resolve with their patients. The government, paralyzed by right-wing opposition to universal sexuality education, had retreated to largely voluntary sex-ed programs, complemented by focused interventions for gay men and commercial sex workers that were far removed from the public gaze. The Chilean state had been shamed into fulfilling its responsibility to provide treatment and care for the sick, a role that ironically was less controversial than taking the necessary steps to prevent its citizens from acquiring the disease in the first place. Although HIV already had had a profound affect throughout Latin America in the areas of sexuality, medicine and public health, its radical, subversive edge, its innovative spirit and potential to engender lasting institutional changes were in doubt. As AIDS is a dynamic, rapidly changing epidemic, this loss eventually may be quite costly. Not everyone who marched through downtown Santiago that day survived the wait for access to the life-saving treatments. Not everyone watching from the sidelines will avoid acquiring HIV.

As the new clinical focus around AIDS presented less of a challenge to public sexual mores, conservative critics lost interest in the issue and shifted their attention to holding the line against divorce (legalized in Chile only in 2004) and against the legalization of emergency contraception. The community groups that once had clashed bitterly with the government were now partners in administering the enormous streams of AIDS project funding pouring in from overseas. Public opinion was satisfied that the many people living with AIDS, whose dramatic stories had illustrated the treatment-access battles, were now getting what they needed. For many observers, AIDS as an issue of social concern, controversy, even of human suffering was pretty much over.

The reality is not quite as cheerful, as people compelled to bombard their bodies with the powerful anti-HIV medicines know: side effects, long-term consequences, constant clinical tests and monitoring, worries about viral rebound, not to mention the complications for sexual expression, childbearing, family relations, disclosure on the job or at school. For many people HIV has been downgraded to the status of a "chronic" condition, but this is far from saying it is no big deal. Infections continue to climb in most countries, and improved survival rates mean that the burden of the disease to governments and societies is steadily increasing. In the United States a certain "AIDS fatigue" has settled in as the epidemic falls more heavily on poor and minority communities and as more and more medical costs are shifted onto bankrupt states.

So the sudden calm did not necessarily mean that the original thorny issues around the AIDS epidemic had gone away. Regular epidemiological announcements from the Chilean government continue to describe a worrisome increase in HIV infection among married women, a consistent regional tendency that reflects deep-seated structural and gender inequities for which no credible and realistic policy has yet been devised. Universal coverage for the costly drugs is sustained in Chile by a temporary influx of foreign funding, outlays that eventually must be assumed by the state as the patient load steadily rises. Even the issue of prevention among gay men, who presumably are more aware of the problem and more attuned to the risks, is far from resolved; given the high rates of seroprevalence in gay enclaves around the region—often in the range of 12 to 15 percent—the chances of sexually-active gay youngsters acquiring HIV during their lifetimes remain extremely high. Even in the wealthier countries of the North, gay-community prevention initiatives are facing increasing doubts about the efficacy of their programs, given not only the evolving epidemic but even the notion of gay "community" itself.

In short, treatment advances have not solved the AIDS drama. But overlaid on the agitation around HIV/AIDS persist echoes of the age-old dynamic of charity, in which the sick or infirm present their sorrows and the healthy respond with succor; the medical breakthroughs reinforced this paradigm even though the activist vigor of those living with HIV and AIDS contradicted it. A charitable approach to social ills is particularly strong in the Latin American context, where destitution and hunger have always been part of the landscape along with handouts as an expression of Christian pity. A Catholic sisters' center for AIDS babies in Santiago hums along, and the special Catholic AIDS clinic that once promised "death with dignity" for those felled by the disease has branched out to fill its empty beds with cancer patients now that HIV no longer provides dying victims with the previous velocity.

As an epidemic transmitted mainly through sexual relations, AIDS forced Latin American societies to become open to public discourse over matters previously restricted to the private sphere, to nuance, secrecy and considerable hypocrisy. African and now Asian countries face similar obstacles in dealing with HIV and sexuality, but Latin America had two additional aggravating factors: the relative preponderance of homosexual relations as the transmission route and the heavy influence of the Catholic church—often an ally in the fight against military rule—now led by the Vatican's increasingly militant obscurantism with regard to sex. On the positive side, the protagonism of people living with HIV/AIDS and the broad social support that emerged in response to the abuses they suffered shook up clinical practice and the long-standing notion of the "patient" as a passive receptor of orders and instructions. The gradual realization that stigma and discrimination are public health issues and directly affect individuals' physical, as well as psychological, well-being further removed the debate about public health policy from the exclusive hands of doctors and placed it on the political agenda. Early on, women, defenders of human rights, and gay men were almost thrown together as allies because they realized that their adversaries—recalcitrant governments, obscurantist social and religious tendencies and scapegoating political culture—were largely the same. Finally, the advent of the antiretroviral treatments for HIV in the mid-1990s and the sustained battle to force often reluctant public health systems to provide them was a landmark in citizen demands for accountability.

These achievements were hard-won. AIDS arrived in Latin America some years after its appearance in the United States and Africa, and this slight delay could have given our governments and societies an advantage in mounting an effective response. But for the most part, the benefits of the early warnings were wasted. Despite knowing the identity of the infectious agent, how to detect it, its modes of transmission and the prevention strategies most likely to work with different population groups, government authorities, news media, churches and even grassroots organizations often committed the same errors as their northern counterparts had done: They ignored the epidemic, scoffed at the possibility that it would worsen or affect them, responded inappropriately, ignored key transmission routes, discriminated against people with HIV, reinvented the wheel, used failed educational methods or fell back on moralistic campaigns that were ineffective and counterproductive. These early mistakes were devastating to the lives and health of many people.

The countries of Latin America faced broadly similar epidemics, originating nearly always among homosexually-active men. (Only in Argentina and to a lesser extent Brazil was intravenous drug injection a significant early factor.) The infection rates usually crept upward fairly slowly; this tendency gave the authorities an excuse to believe that their countries were different, that things would not be so bad there; often they noted that there were no gay bathhouses or other supposedly essential elements of an AIDS epidemic. "This isn't Uganda," one smiling health official told me in the late 1980s, implying that his citizens had nothing to fear due to their superior moral habits and modern health system.

However, notwithstanding many similarities among countries in the region, the story of HIV/AIDS in each is unique to its political and cultural contexts, economic conditions and recent histories. In some cases, health ministries, social organizations and people with HIV/AIDS generated dynamic and creative strategies to address prevention and care issues; in other countries the response started out well and stagnated. A few barely got off the starting block. These variations are the subject of this book, as told by activists, doctors, government officials, reporters and the army of volunteers and sympathizers who drove the early efforts and scored important successes.

At the same time, further progress is not guaranteed. Now that medicines are available to treat HIV, the complex issues surrounding the epidemic, including sexuality, tend to get lost. The alliance between feminists or women's health activists and other affected groups is, in my view, more rhetorical than real. Many prevention and support initiatives have been invented and are now standard practice in many countries, but they have created their own constituencies and interest groups resistant to change and innovation. In addition, Latin America suffers from a set of chronic ailments that make the AIDS epidemics affecting each country potential disasters on a much broader scale. Distribution of wealth and income is more unequal on this continent than anywhere else on earth, with the richest quintile (20 percent) of the population receiving on average twenty times more than the poorest. (The ratio in the industrialized world is eight to one.) These income disparities are comparable only to those of Africa, even though per capita income in Latin America is twice as high.

Not surprisingly, economic inequality is accompanied by political instability throughout the region. Just in the first half of the current decade, the presidents of Ecuador, Peru, Argentina and Bolivia have been chased out of office before ending their terms. Brazil passed the presidential sash from one elected chief executive to another in 2003 for the first time in forty years. Central American countries such as El Salvador, Honduras, Nicaragua and Guatemala face the same entrenched social problems that plunged the region into civil wars during the 1970s and 1980s. Despite its oil wealth, Venezuela experienced a coup d'état in 2003, and Colombia long ago slid off the map as a humanitarian disaster with the second-largest internally displaced population in the world (after Angola). AIDS, which still challenges governments and health systems even in the wealthiest countries of the North, presents these struggling states with issues more easily postponed until later. They do so at their peril.

In 1988 I attended a meeting of a newly established AIDS prevention project in a barren office set up on the ground floor of a crumbling adobe structure a dozen blocks from downtown Santiago. I had been in Chile as a freelance journalist for five years watching the progress of the movement to the military dictatorship headed by the notorious Augusto Pinochet. (A few months later—in October 1988—Pinochet's defeat in a national plebiscite on his continued rule was a turning point in the fight to restore democracy.) In trips back to the United States, I could see the worrisome spread of AIDS among friends and acquaintances and knew that the bad news would reach Chile sooner or later. The preexisting gay-rights organizations and the new AIDS projects that were springing up in the major cities of the United States had no counterpart where I was living, and for years there was nowhere to offer to help out as a volunteer.

Chile under military dictatorship might not seem a likely choice for someone seeking to live outside his country of origin, but for me it had unusual attractions. The fight against military rule was extraordinarily gripping while at the time most attention in the United States was concentrated on Nicaragua and El Salvador, whose wars were a political focus of the Reagan years. As a result, freelance reporting work was plentiful, and I often hustled interviews for television crews, filed to National Public Radio or the BBC, *The Christian Science Monitor* or the London *Independent*, as well as specialized magazines and the few papers in San Diego, Fort Lauderdale or Chicago that would take articles from overseas.

As the country was trying to rediscover its political voice, gay Santiago was emerging from the shadows as well. The gay bars operating under the dictatorship were reminiscent of the pre-Stonewall era in the United States where petty harassment was common but the spirit of camaraderie and bohemian glee was unmatched. In a society that controls everything and randomly criminalizes private life, even bar-hopping felt subversive. The two bars I patronized had marked political tendencies: the more elegant, middle-class club attracted a snooty, conservative crowd that sympathized with the dictatorship although less for ideological motives than in the spirit of social climbing. The ratty downtown disco featured topical drag shows in which "policewomen" would chase lumpen "housewives" protesting against the generals and beat them with plastic batons before breaking into a lip-sync chorus of a timely love ballad, such as "Odiame" ("Hate Me"). If the owners did not pay off the right officials, the show might be interrupted by a raid, and the whole bar crowd would end up at the stationhouse until 7:00 A.M. Dupont Circle seemed dull by comparison.

In addition, people went out of their way to meet me and practice their English. Instead of the typical long nights nursing a drink in D.C., a trip to Santiago's clandestine gay clubs in the 1980s guaranteed entry into a tight social circle in which no one, least of all a *gringo*, would be left out. Although I later realized that much of the cordiality was related to my passport rather than my modest attractions, I also made real friends who are still part of my life. Six months into my stay, I had a *pareja* (partner) of my own and even less inclination to leave. Six years later, he would be one of the first people in Chile to die of AIDS.

As the political narrative wound down toward the end of the 1980s with the slow withdrawal of the armed forces to their barracks, my time in Chile seemed to be coming to a similar conclusion. But the AIDS epidemic revived all the reasons I had had for going there and for staying: an obvious need, a role I was equipped to play, and passion. Despite the frightening and tragic events occurring around us during the dictatorship, one often felt that participation was simply impossible to avoid. Likewise in the case of HIV: Something had to be done although we had no idea what. But we had to do it; no one else would. It was as simple as that.

My visit to the embryonic AIDS awareness group led me over the next twelve years to become intimately involved in the construction of Chile's response to the HIV/AIDS epidemic. From 1993 to 2000 I served as the first AIDS organization's director. The achievements of that isolated group were remarkable for its time and conditions; with better preparation, insights and the right support, we could have done much better.

Superficially at least, my status as a foreigner was a nonissue throughout my years in Chile; my colleagues and friends very cordially used to insist that I not use the third person when referring to Chileans, but instead say "we." After five years on a temporary visa, noncitizens can obtain permanent resident status, which carries with it all legal and civil rights, including the right to vote (but not run) in elections. I took this as an invitation to participate socially and politically on equal terms with full citizens. Furthermore, Chileans do not particularly resent gringos individually even when they dislike them politically. I probably felt more uncomfortable about it than anyone else and at first resisted taking a leadership role.

But there were advantages in not being part of the Chilean class and social structure in which individuals are acutely aware of the roles they are expected to play. For example, when we began to receive telephone calls from panicked gay men who had just had their HIV-positive diagnosis tossed at them in an envelope, I proposed that we do the testing and counseling ourselves. My colleagues at first thought the idea insane: We were neither doctors nor psychologists. Once we inaugurated the service, our volunteer staff plunged in enthusiastically and realized that they had skills and insights the college-trained professionals lacked. It sometimes took an outsider to redefine the limits of what was possible.

Eventually, however, I became a dissident within the Chilean AIDS movement. The research that went into this book was made possible when I decided to resign from my position as director of the organization we had founded in the late 1980s. I had two main reasons for leaving: first, I felt that the old guard with whom I had built the organization did not share my vision of the entity as a social service provider for people with HIV, capable of filling in the gaps that neither the public health system nor the HIV-positive groups could provide.

The concept of AIDS service organizations, as they are known in the developed world, has little meaning in Latin America. There are few resources from state or local government to tap, but people living with HIV and AIDS have just as many needs as their counterparts in London or Chicago, if not more. A group such as ours, using its base as a prevention entity with an innovative approach to the ongoing epidemic, could have generated support to provide those kinds of services to a shifting client population. But that would have required an organization willing and motivated to convert itself into a social service organization rather than a gay-oriented, sexual health promoter. My attempt to redefine the organization in these terms culminated with the appointment of an older woman to a newly created post; her anecdotes precede many chapters throughout the text as testimony to the kinds of services that I still believe should form the core of a second-generation response to AIDS.

However, that decision stirred deep resistance, as did my second program priority: to expand our AIDS work toward women and connect it with sexual rights and reproductive health issues in alliance with feminists and women health activists. One reason for the very lukewarm success of early attempts to introduce nationwide sexuality education in Chile as part of a comprehensive AIDS strategy is that the epidemic did not break out of the confines of the early epidemiological patterns despite steady alarms about heterosexual and perinatal (mother-to-child) infections. The prospect of an African-style epidemic sweeping through straight families was particularly daunting partly because nebulous populations such as "heterosexuals," either male or female, are far more difficult to reach in programmatic terms. Although commercial sex workers or gay men can be found in certain venues, approached by their peers and theoretically educated about the wisdom of avoiding HIV, the "general public" is too vast and too diverse for these tactics. Concern about the rising rates of HIV infection in women often run up against the thorny and largely unanswered question of what can be done to avoid it, especially given the recognition that deep-seated habits of discrimination and inequality weaken women's capacity to avoid risk. One approach I favored was to open up a gradual dialogue to see how the lessons we had learned in dealing with homosexual transmission might be applicable, or not, to the primarily heterosexual majority.

But that vision failed as well, and I believe that the logical gay-feminist alliance that should have emerged around the HIV epidemic is generally lacking throughout the region. Unwilling to dedicate the bulk of my energies to a bureaucratic war of attrition with my erstwhile best friends, I chose to resign my post. The women's program I had established was dismantled a few months later and has not been replicated in the years since. My doubts and skepticism throughout these country-based narratives no doubt are influenced by my surprise at finding the AIDS community I had grown up with so rigidly determined to defend its time-honored ways even if those activities and programs were making less and less sense with the passage of time.

AIDS hit Latin America at a unique moment. During the late 1960s and 1970s, virtually the entire continent was in the grip of military dictatorships, setting back or wiping out mass social movements that once had promised profound structural change and a better life for the majority. In Brazil in 1964, Bolivia in 1971, Uruguay and Chile in 1973 and Argentina in 1976, uniformed strongmen swept into power on a wave of counterrevolution fanned by the traditional economic and political elites, often with the approval or active complicity of the United States. The Nicaraguan revolution of 1979 broke the pattern but provoked a new era of U.S. intervention that worsened civil and regional wars in El Salvador, Honduras, Guatemala, Nicaragua and even touching peaceable Costa Rica.

Reactionary dictatorships were not seen as problematic for the United States in the cold war-obsessed Reagan era. Jeane Kirkpatrick, the notorious Georgetown University academic who would later become Reagan's Ambassador to the United Nations, wrote in her famous essay "Dictatorships and Double Standards" that the United States did not need to concern itself with "human rights" or other limp-wristed holdover issues from the Carter era. Trying to recover from the skepticism of the post-Vietnam years and relegitimize the projection of American power worldwide, Kirkpatrick saw reactionary dictatorships in places like Argentina or Indonesia—or Iraq—as less problematic than communist countries because under American influence these police states eventually would evolve into liberal, capitalist democracies while left-wing revolutions would lead to congealed, pro-Soviet totalitarian regimes that would last for decades. Kirkpatrick thus provided the intellectual ammunition to justify Reagan's decision to turn a benign, blind eye on torture and political murder at the exact moment when fascist death squads roamed the Salvadoran countryside massacring peasants.

But Reagan's enthusiastic military campaigns in Central America relied on the rhetoric of democracy for their justification. As a result, it became increasingly uncomfortable for the U.S. government to tolerate de facto, authoritarian states anywhere in the region. Reagan himself once lumped Chile, Paraguay, Cuba and Nicaragua together as "entrenched dictatorships," which made it hard for his representatives to show sympathy for one while arming guerrilla movements against the other.

By the mid-1980s the United States had rediscovered the virtues of democratic rule on the continent, and official policy shifted to the promotion of prompt transitions. In the Chilean case, the Reagan Administration took a dim view of Pinochet's attempts to cling to power until the end of the century and worked to ensure a fair vote in Chile's 1988 plebiscite on his rule, helping to prevent an attempt to rig the vote when it became apparent that he had lost. The Argentine junta already had collapsed after its ill-advised war against Great Britain over the Falkland/Malvinas Islands; earlier, Brazil and Uruguay had pushed out their military regimes. Even the forty-year Stroessner kleptocracy in Paraguay finally collapsed in 1989. Throughout the continent the recovery of democracy reawakened people's suppressed hopes for a better deal in life, for governments that would attend to their needs, reduce the endemic inequality and curb corruption.

As several of those quoted in this book note, the new, more representative governments sometimes recognized AIDS as an issue that the new democracies had to address. But there were dangers as well. The earliest popular reactions to the disease, based on fear and alarm, drew heavily on the habits of repression and victimization that had been inculcated in them during the recent police states whose National Security Doctrine taught people to believe in the "enemy within," the Marxist subversive eager to seize their property and enslave them. Repression was justified in the name of the security of the majority or the "survival of the nation," and many citizens were willing to believe in this menace and the need for drastic measures. HIV easily could have become the new invasive agent, requiring drastic measures against "carriers" to protect the rest of society, or perhaps "the body politic."

Military regimes in Latin America always enjoyed at least a degree of popular support. Consider the enthusiasm that greeted Alberto Fujimori in Peru when he dismantled the judiciary in 1992, closed Congress and slaughtered supposed guerrilla sympathizers in the countryside. Americans who find it difficult to understand sympathy for the generals should ask themselves how long after the events of September 11, 2001, President Bush waited to suspend the right of habeas corpus, and how much resistance to this measure—essential for any police state—emerged from the opposition Democrats.

Given this context, AIDS could have opened the way for repressive measures, rather than a humane public health approach based on individual rights and solidarity. As described in chapter 8, on Chile, such measures were tested in the waning days of military rule there. Throughout the early 1990s, the Cuban approach of quarantining people with HIV or AIDS drew wistfully admiring glances from many commentators, especially right-wing politicians who otherwise had nothing good to say about Fidel Castro. When AIDS appeared, public discussion of the issue inevitably included anxious parents complaining that concern about the rights of people with AIDS was all very well but that "the rights of the majority" to be protected from them also should be considered. Human beings are quick to suggest that threats to their well-being be eliminated at whatever cost, and the rights or comforts of others are rarely a central concern.

It is to the credit of Latin American societies that overtly reactionary measures by governments were largely avoided. Raids on gay bars or bordellos to track down the early cases of HIV infection were relatively rare. Even the traditional contract tracing used to pursue the chain of syphilis or gonorrhea infection quickly proved impractical or controversial: unlike those diseases, HIV had no cure, and given the heavy predominance of homosexual transmission, health personnel often found that their efforts to follow up with sexual partners of those infected met with violent hostility, even threats.

Instead, the earliest cases often stimulated solidarity and concern among people who had not previously worked together. Calls for a humane approach to combat stigma, firings, expulsions from school and shunning by families and to insist on proper health services often garnered support from human rights figures, medical personnel, churches, women's groups and other public actors as the epidemic slowly emerged as not merely a medical but a profoundly political affair. Unfortunately, these campaigns often remained in the realm of good intentions; the social movements were not always able to enforce non-discrimination in education and the workplace, and the use of HIV screening for employment continues in many countries to this day, despite formal prohibitions of the practice.

It is axiomatic in the AIDS field today that the epidemic was never simply or even primarily a disease and could never be handled exclusively by doctors. Gay subcultures or commercial sex venues were not places where white-shoed nurses or traditional health promoters were likely to feel welcome or to know how to behave. Medical professionals, accustomed to receiving patients and instructing them on the treatments to follow, were at a loss when faced with the complexities of people's sexual behaviors.

Similarly, given the extreme paucity of a clinical response in the early years, when patients could be offered only prophylaxis against certain infections and eventually palliative care to ease their pain and suffering, prevention and solidarity were the first priorities because doctors and health services had little to offer. At the same time, people receiving the HIV diagnosis faced multifaceted disasters in their lives, which often had little to do with their physical state. Alarm among relatives often led to subtle discrimination, isolation or shame; many people suffering from AIDS were hidden away while neighbors were told that the diagnosis was cancer or leukemia. Employers promptly dismissed people found or suspected to be HIV-positive, and university students were pressured to withdraw. "Social death" was the term coined in Brazil to describe these nonclinical manifestations of the deadly effects of the virus in a society plagued by ignorance and selfishness. Once again, the medical professions were largely helpless to address these circumstances.

Churches often played a positive role in combating manifestations of the deadly role of prejudice in the AIDS epidemic, including Catholic churches, despite their simultaneous and highly damaging resistance to sex education or sexual autonomy. More comfortable with traditional charity in ministering to the sick, churches and religiously inspired individuals sometimes urged their congregations to overcome their fears and learn about the disease rather than treat people with HIV as modern lepers. As AIDS became a more common ailment, some employers reacted with humanitarian concern and used the discovery of an HIV-positive employee as a chance to educate their workers.

But Catholicism in Latin America has changed markedly since the days when priests were encouraged to promote social justice and hope for the downtrodden in this life rather than the next. Instead of resistance to police states and the "preferential option for the poor" endorsed in the late 1960s and 1970s by Latin American bishops, the current emphasis from Rome is on resistance to sex. Bishops routinely suggest that only anti-abortionist politicians can receive the votes of the faithful, and sexuality education and reproductive health services are constantly an arena for ecclesiastical grandiloquence. HIV prevention campaigns that include condom promotion systematically are attacked by Catholic spokespeople, exercising a subtle influence even on people who defy these teachings. As mentioned above, divorce was legalized in Chile only in 2004 after ferocious Catholic opposition, and even public discussion of abortion—prohibited in all cases without exception—is utterly taboo there.

AIDS also aggravated the chronic dysfunctions of public health systems in Latin America, which typically provide services to the majority of the population although private doctors and clinics also exist for those who can pay. These state-run systems nearly always are underfunded and plagued with problems of bureaucracy, shortages and poor quality care. They are sometimes ill-equipped to respond to any sort of new demands and tend to be highly sensitive to Catholic dogma on birth control and reproductive health issues.

In fact, the historic shortcomings of these systems have stimulated moves to privatize more and more health services. According to neoliberal orthodoxy, reducing the central government's role will improve the efficiency of health care by introducing the disciplines of the for-profit marketplace. These tendencies have powerful backers in governments and among economic elites although medical professionals tend to resist, arguing that health care is not comparable to other "products." However, the complexities of the debates often leave users confused and sidelined from the struggle over the future of health care throughout the region. AIDS had an important impact on this debate in Brazil; activists resisted the World Bank's early emphasis on cost-effectiveness and defended the humanitarian aspects of providing drug treatments. In other countries the HIV drug-access issue remains separate from the privatization debates.

Homosexual rights have made important strides in the wake of the AIDS epidemic, particularly in the realm of public opinion. But legal advances lag far behind. Although Chile decriminalized sodomy in 1999, gay couples have little recourse for protecting their joint possessions in the event of the death of one partner. All too often relatives seize the property along with the funeral arrangements.

Today, twenty years after the HIV/AIDS epidemic appeared in the region, more resources are flowing into Latin America than ever before. Brazil, Argentina and Chile provide nearly universal access to HIV medicines and have ample programs for prevention and care, funded either by their governments or by international agencies. The Global Fund to Fight AIDS, Tuberculosis and Malaria is pouring millions of dollars into country projects to stem the growing infection rates and alleviate human suffering. In many countries knowledgeable activists are pushing treatment, care and prevention issues with varying degrees of success. There is a potentially felicitous combination of grassroots capacity, funding and political recognition of the importance of avoiding Africa's fate with regard to AIDS.

Nevertheless, shortfalls of resources are not always the only or even the main obstacle. Even when governments can provide life-saving prevention education or essential medicines to their citizens at minimal cost, they often do not. Political will and a commitment to serve the needy is as important, and as often absent, as money. Prevention initiatives that require facing the uncomfortable realities of human sexual activity and thus entail a political cost are extremely easy to resist, delay or shelve. Price reductions for drugs do not mean governments will buy them; offers of assistance also must be taken up by health administrators eager to save lives. As is clear from a steady reading of the Internet news from countries of the region, all too often these conditions are not present.

Finally, grassroots organizations also cannot escape the critical microscope. Social movements face a treacherous moment in their evolution as the pressure to institutionalize and professionalize clashes with the desire to retain the movement's mystique and idealism. Empowerment of individuals is easily confused with empowerment of the groups they purportedly represent; the two are not equivalent. As seen in the chapters that follow, some governments resist and battle civic organizations; others subcontract them. Neither approach is problem-free;

increased funding solves some problems, but it creates others. AIDS organizations did a lot to raise the alarm and challenge official negligence, stigma and discrimination. But as Ramón's story, which follows, illustrates, they do not necessarily know how to help people in need.

Efforts to slow down the epidemic and alleviate the sufferings of people dealing with the disease still face the tough issues of influencing sexual culture and attending to people's health, including preventive services; in these areas Latin America shows no sign of resolving its endemic structural weaknesses. If AIDS is or could soon be a chronic, manageable disease, it must form part of the continent-wide debates on health sector reform and creeping privatization and address the long-standing problems of how to provide medical care through overburdened, inefficient or bankrupt health systems.

Therefore, the story of AIDS in Latin America can be seen in terms of the glass-half-full, glass-half-empty conundrum. Chilean officials often played the game in a slightly perverse way, contrasting the country with Peru or Guatemala when celebrating its modernity and prosperity, then shifting to comparisons with France or Taiwan when pressed to spend some of this money on AIDS. For countries as well as individuals, there is indeed room for both self-congratulation and self-criticism, and this volume is written in that spirit. If AIDS is not to fade back into the permanent crises of Latin American societies, an understanding of the strengths and weaknesses of what we have achieved so far is required, free of triumphalism, oversimplification or dogma.

The chapters gathered here do not pretend to be definitive reviews of the state of the AIDS epidemics in each country or of the efforts of the people engaged in addressing them. For that reason, I have avoided accumulating dates, reconstructing the often-conflicting histories of relations between governments and non-governmental organizations (NGOs) and NGO intramural relations, naming all the key actors or reviewing epidemiological statistics and tendencies aside from presenting the barest minimum of data in a table at the beginning of each chapter, where I also have included certain anecdotes from our work. While they do not always bear directly on the narratives or the reflections that flow from them, I believe they ground the abstractions about policy and history in the realities of people's lives and suggest the many ways that HIV requires subtle and creative responses that are not well captured by reviews of epidemiology or the fight for treatment access.

My original idea was to find a variety of people who had joined HIV/AIDS work in Latin America and tell their stories. However, shortly after setting out with that project in mind, it became clear that most people's motivations were quite similar, even if their experiences were not. Individuals were drawn to the issue due to personal proximity, knowing someone with HIV, being gay, having gay friends or because they acquired the virus themselves; out of general human sympathy; as a result of their medical studies; or because they were inspired to combat the discrimination and stigmas that accompany AIDS. Instead, in the narratives of people closely engaged in AIDS-related work, I sought to capture something about them and their country that illustrated what was different or characteristic of the response that grew out of that particular soil, the unique and subtle ways each country or locality left its stamp on the individuals, organizations and activities that formed the AIDS universe there. Their interlocking tales eventually became the subject of these chapters. In shaping them, I undoubtedly misread some aspects and take sole responsibility for errors of fact or judgment.

The countries visited were selected for different reasons. Chile, Peru and Argentina are neighbors and have recognizable similarities in the way AIDS was handled, although the differences are also immense. Brazil, which occupies fully half the continent, broke ground by showing that a country with enormous inequalities and severe poverty still could create a coherent, humane response and give the lie to the "we-cannot-afford-it" argument. Central America's experience was remote from us in the Southern Cone countries but offered interesting contrasts, especially due to Costa Rica's role as the island of gay tolerance in the area, its early and sophisticated NGO activities and the many spin-offs it generated around the isthmus. Mexico was important to include for its proximity to the United States and leadership of the first regional networks. Trinidad and Tobago, the site of a conclave of the official coordinating body of people with HIV/AIDS, the Global Network of People Living with HIV/AIDS, was added to explore the reality of the Caribbean island states, usually lumped together with Latin America in international structures despite the linguistic and epidemiological distances.

The chapters concentrate heavily on gay-oriented prevention projects and their issues. As the history to date of AIDS in Latin America is heavily populated with gay and other homosexually active men both as activists and as victims, it should come as no surprise that they appear frequently here. Despite worrisome tendencies throughout Latin America, heterosexual transmission of HIV infection at the devastating levels seen in Africa has not yet occurred there, with the partial exception of some Caribbean countries. This may change, and it behooves us to ask whether the necessary lessons have been well learned and whether the needed alliances among gays, feminists and health professionals have been constructed to address this shifting landscape.

Two Lives

T he following stories are composites, but all the incidents related in them are real. The ages, social circumstances, employment and other details of the lives described are typical of those acquiring HIV infection in Latin America during the 1980s and 1990s.

Ramón

When the armed forces took control of the government and shut down the capital city, Ramón was just old enough to realize that something dangerous was occurring. No one close to him suffered reprisals from the new regime, but everyone had to adapt to the new conditions, including considerable hardships for working families such as his. Ramón's parents were apolitical and struggled to pay off their tiny home in a poor but not destitute part of town; being home-owners made them feel "middle-class," and they had certain sympathies for the military regime. Ramón learned to avoid political topics and largely accepted the generals' explanations of what was happening in his country.

Most of his teenage years were spent socializing in cramped, private parties around the neighborhood, sometimes lasting to dawn because of curfew restrictions. Newspapers and broadcast media were tightly controlled, and the most common link with the outside world were reports about movie stars or rock bands whose records could be heard on local radio stations. Some of these groups seemed wildly extravagant, and Ramón found the stories of their drug habits and other escapades exciting and a bit shocking.

But as the military's grip on power weakened during the 1980s, Ramón found he was also losing his center of gravity in an important area of his own life: sex. His peers had frequent dates, and some already were sleeping with their girlfriends. But he was disturbed by the feeling that he was not like the rest. One night he was intrigued by a sensationalist TV program showing secret meeting places among homosexuals in a downtown park. He felt vaguely disturbed by the program and shortly thereafter wandered down to the park in a state of anxious curiosity.

There Ramón found other men who had little to say and pressured him into sex. He was eager to meet guys like himself and had a lot on his mind, but he often went along with the sex, somewhat clumsily and uncomfortable with the hurried atmosphere and the dangers of muggings or police. Finally he met someone who offered to take him to one of the discreet clubs that were tolerated by the military government.

In the club Ramón found himself thrust into an unimagined, semiclandestine world of men with an entirely separate code. They touched each other, danced together and sometimes introduced other men as their *parejas* (partners). He made friends and read the roughly produced pamphlets and foreign magazines they showed him, including references to "gays," and was profoundly mortified when, following Spanish orthography, he pronounced it "guise" and became the butt of a huge joke.

Being a newcomer and barely nineteen, Ramón was popular in the gay scene and often invited to drinks. He met dozens of people and was charmed by an architect who lived in a fine apartment in a section of town that was inaccessible to most people of Ramón's social class. But after two or three sexual encounters, the architect made excuses and did not return his phone calls.

He continued to visit the bar every Saturday and never left until the 6:00 A.M. closing time, usually quite drunk. After the disappointment with the architect and several one-night stands, Ramón began to feel uneasy about the "gay" scene. His parents wondered about his sudden burst of social activity and the frequent calls from his new friends. He enjoyed the sex, which was abundant, but never understood why his lovers always disappeared after a week or two. One afternoon in a particularly blue mood, he met a fellow riding a bicycle. By now he had learned how to recognize his peers. They spoke, exchanged telephone numbers and began to see each other.

Carlos was twenty-seven and a civilian employee of the police department. He said he was looking for a serious relationship and demanded absolute sexual fidelity. Carlos looked down on the city's gay nightclubs as decadent and superficial, although he and Ramón occasionally went together for lack of alternatives. Sex between them was spectacularly successful; Ramón fell in love and began to spend every weekend at his new boyfriend's downtown flat.

After several months of virtual cohabitation, Ramón and Carlos decided to visit a gay organization in a commercial sector near several warehouses. The group said its mission was prevention of the new disease—AIDS—but the meeting felt more like the gay parties they sometimes attended in private homes. The business meeting consisted of long arguments about whether gay rights or AIDS education should be the group's priority. Ramón found the debate impossible to follow, and Carlos said it was a "catfight among queens."

The night they visited, a doctor explained how the HIV virus attached to cells that formed part of the immune system and also showed how condoms, which no one had ever seen before, prevented transmission. The meeting broke up around 10:30, but everyone lingered until the clubs opened at midnight. At the disco the AIDS group handed out condoms to everyone; most ended up tossed into a corner along with the empty beer cans.

Ramón and Carlos never discussed AIDS after that; after all, the few fellows they had heard of who had gotten it had traveled to Brazil or the United States. Or they were guys with multiple sex partners, regulars in the raunchy park scene or the saunas. Ramón, who had a steady and exclusive partner, felt those dangers were remote.

Meanwhile, he was having more and more problems at home. His mother insisted that Carlos, his downtown "friend," was not just a drinking buddy and demanded that he tell her the truth, which he denied. His older sisters were concerned, and his father hardly spoke to him. Increasingly, Ramón identified his life at Carlos's apartment as an island of security and stability in a hostile and uncomprehending world. He earned little at his job in a department store, but enough to go his own way. Eventually, he showed up at home only on rare weekends.

After a year Carlos and Ramón decided to move into a better apartment, and Carlos began the process of buying his own place through a government subsidy program even though as a single man with no dependents, he would have to wait three years for a contract. Ramón's future felt secure; he hardly went out to the gay nightspots anymore and lost contact with all his friends from his earlier, bohemian days.

That winter Carlos had a bout of flu that kept him away from work for a week, followed by a quick relapse when he tried to go back. When he felt short of breath one night, they took a taxi to the emergency room. Carlos turned out to have a light case of pneumonia and was put on intravenous antibiotics. As Ramón sat by him in the packed hallway, two night-shift nurse's aides walked by and snickered to each other.

After three weeks, Carlos had lost twenty pounds and looked sallow and drawn. His own family lived in a small town in the south and knew nothing of his life or his relationship. Carlos called Ramón his "roommate" and kept his hospitalization a secret.

Once winter was over, Carlos's health improved, but he did not gain back his normal weight. He began to have stomach problems and ate poorly. He also turned moody and preoccupied, and his jealousy worsened. He was angry if Ramón didn't arrive home promptly after work. "You're young and attractive, you'll find someone else you like better than me," he would say. They argued more, but Carlos always apologized and often said, "You're all I have in the world." Ramón visited his family infrequently and had little to say to them. His worries began to interrupt his sleeping patterns, and he was not getting on well at work. He also was drinking almost every night and tended to overdo it on weekends.

One day in early summer Carlos felt too weak to get out of bed. After three days Ramón insisted they see a doctor, who diagnosed lymphoma. He sat them both down and asked them if they had ever been tested for HIV. Ramón, shocked, heard nothing more of the conversation. Carlos did not refer to the issue and spoke optimistically of the doctor's explanation that the cure rate for his type of lymphoma was 80 percent.

Because their medical care was provided through the public health system, Carlos had to follow complicated paperwork to get tests and appointments. These errands often took days, and when Carlos felt too weak to stand in lines or make the inquiries, Ramón would ask for time off from work. Ramón's coworkers had met Carlos and already wondered if they were lovers. Rumors immediately circulated that both had AIDS, and Ramón's supervisor cooled to him.

Meanwhile, Carlos had taken a lengthy sick leave from his job, and there were increasing signs that he would not get it back. The police department often investigated its employees and did not tolerate homosexuality, at least officially. The two men's household budget was in crisis, and without a solution of some sort they would have to give up the apartment. Ramón's income would only cover a room in one of the warrens of downtown passageways, with a shared bathroom and little privacy. They took the money out of their housing account and gradually spent it.

Over the next six months Carlos was hospitalized four more times. Ramón never brought up the issue of HIV, but he knew the truth. He realized they had stopped having sex even before Carlos's illnesses, with no explanation. When they were out of money, Ramón found them a room in a shared apartment with another gay couple. He went back to the AIDS organization they had visited the year before and asked to speak to someone confidentially. The conversation did him good, and the people were sympathetic but had very little concrete to offer.

In the hospital Carlos received decent care, and the attending physician was young and did his best. But there were few clinical options. In addition, the infectious disease unit had complex restrictions on visitors, and the windows were covered with wire screens. To communicate, Ramón sometimes had to shout from outdoor stairway while other visitors stared. Meanwhile, some medical staff shunned them: the older nurses and auxiliaries would push Carlos off on the lower-ranking newcomers. One day, when they came back for a checkup, the guards' cubicle was full for a shift change, and the guard on duty phoned inside to say "two sisters" were on their way while the rest celebrated the joke. Ramón was furious, but Carlos refused to complain. He had become more and more detached and insisted that Ramón not leave him for a moment.

At their downtown lodgings, the other residents were upset that someone who might have AIDS was sharing their bathroom and pushed for the pair to leave. Carlos hid the situation from his family, but a married sister came to town and realized he was seriously ill. She quickly told the rest of the family, and his mother made a surprise visit. They were polite to Ramón but did not include him in their hushed conversations. However, they would show up unannounced and give him instructions about Carlos's care.

Suddenly Carlos's condition deteriorated severely. The doctors diagnosed toxoplasmosis and said it could be fatal. His sister checked him into a hospital close to her home without telling Ramón. Meanwhile, he was laid off from his department store job and had to return to live with his parents. The next few weeks were a blur in his mind. Carlos's family took over and left him on the sidelines. He could visit Carlos in the new hospital, but all decisions were made by the sister. She moved Carlos's household possessions and promised to give Ramón the things they had bought together but never did. Even though they had had no religious practice, Carlos was visited by a priest and had Catholic symbols set up by his bed.

In the midst of his disorientation, Ramón went back to the AIDS organization and again was treated sympathetically. The atmosphere was festive, and people joked about having HIV themselves. He felt welcome, but the group had few resources and did not really know how to help him. He felt alienated from the happy-go-lucky gay patrons who said "living with HIV" instead of "AIDS patients" and seemed more interested in seducing him than hearing about his troubles. "There's always hope," one said brightly, and left him alone.

One volunteer suggested he visit an HIV mutual support group that met in a hospital. He went and enjoyed finally being able to talk about everything that was happening to him. The meeting was run by a social worker who responded to each person's story with a set of suggestions and concluded with an upbeat speech.

Finally Carlos died. Several relatives came by to accompany his mother at the wake. Some greeted Ramón warmly; others were distant. At the funeral he sat with two friends in a back row. When he went back to the hospital for some final paperwork, the nurse at the HIV unit said, "You're probably positive too, so you'd better come back for your test."

His own illness was much more rapid. After an outbreak of Kaposi's sarcoma, the doctor told him it could affect the internal organs and kill him within three months. He fell into a profound depression and did not resist the bout of pneumonia that followed. Ramón was twenty-three when he died.

Amanda

By the 1980s, more and more women in Amanda's country were holding
down jobs even while raising a family. She bucked her parents' skepticism
and worked her way through an accounting degree at a private institute.
Her longtime boyfriend supported her decisions and never pressured her to
stay at home, even after she unintentionally got pregnant shortly after their
marriage. They moved in with his family, where a grandmother and a maid
could watch the child during the day. Amanda wished that labor laws would
have given her more than ninety days of maternity leave, but the wild fluctua-
tions in the country's economy and the sudden bouts of inflation meant that
no one could give up their second income.

Amanda came from a conservative, middle-class professional family that
had sent her to Catholic girls' schools run by nuns and had kept her and her
sisters on a tight leash during adolescence. Respect and polite behavior were
high ideals in their social circle, and children, especially girls, were taught to
be pleasant, cordial and soft-spoken, to learn domestic skills and head straight
for the kitchen when visiting other homes. Her brothers' teenage friends were
allowed to visit only when a parent was at home to chaperone. To Amanda,
her family's way of life seemed harmonious and perfect. She and her sisters
made their own clothes and splurged on CDs of their favorite pop stars but
gave their parents no cause for concern. Her elder sister married a prosperous
businessman and moved to the capital after a spectacular wedding.

Amanda had met her husband through her studies and was a virgin when
they married. She had little notion of sex until then and was unimpressed
by it. "I don't know what all the big deal is," she confided to a girlfriend soon
after, which caused them both to collapse in giggles. After she became pregnant, she barely noticed that the frequency of sex with her husband dropped
off sharply. Her husband was a good provider and left most decisions to her,
although she disliked it when he worked late or wandered off by himself
on weekends. He was reserved and did not have much to say to her sisters'
husbands, often staying home instead of joining the constant round of family
birthdays, christenings and graduations. They had a second child and managed
to prosper modestly on the two incomes.

As a busy, working mother, Amanda had more than enough to keep her occupied and felt comfortable with her routine. She ran the household, helped the children with their schoolwork and visited her parents or her in-laws every weekend. For summer holidays they would combine resources for a beach rental and fill it with cousins, nephews, nieces and the children's friends. She liked to go to Sunday mass on occasion but did not participate in the church's other activities.

When pregnant with their third child, Amanda was called in by her longtime obstetrician for a special meeting. Expecting to be told to prepare for another cesarean, she almost forgot to go to the appointment. At the doctor's office, the secretary stared at her oddly. Her doctor was abrupt: You have HIV, she said, so I cannot be your physician anymore or attend the birth. You will have to go to the public hospital. Amanda had no idea what she was talking about. When the doctor spelled out the diagnosis, Amanda said it was impossible, a mistake. Upon learning that the disease was transmitted through sex or blood, she thought of the difficult birth of her previous child and assumed there had been a transfusion. "What will happen to my baby?" she asked, but sensed they just wanted her to leave as soon as possible. The entire story remained unreal; she fell into a dreamlike state that caused her to take the wrong bus home.

After a week of barely sleeping and an increasing sense of panic, Amanda confided in her closest sister, who promised to tell no one. Amanda's main fear was how her husband would react. That weekend, no one came to the regular Sunday gathering at her parents' house, and Amanda's children had to play by themselves. Finally she blurted out the news to her husband, who said nothing and put his head in his hands.

At the public hospital, Amanda was humiliated and stunned to join homosexuals and sex workers in the waiting room and to see how sick some of them were. She waited four hours for her first appointment and was told by the midwife that a short drug regimen would reduce the probability of HIV transmission to her baby from 30 percent to 10 percent. When she asked if her husband should come in for a test, the medical staff looked at each other until one replied, "Haven't you talked it over with him?"

Despite the promises of confidentiality, Amanda soon realized that all her siblings and their families knew of her situation. One sister continued to phone and visit, but other relatives declined her invitations. Eventually her mother called her on the telephone crying and demanding to know everything. The two of them made an appointment to visit one of the specialized organizations dealing with the illness.

At the headquarters they were again uncomfortable to see so many homosexual men but were received and counseled by a woman. They had coffee, wept and related all their terrors and disorientation. They leafed through pamphlets and medical guidebooks. In one of them, Amanda saw references to "cotrimoxazol" and "acyclovir," which sounded vaguely familiar. They were invited to a meeting to hear about the new HIV therapies that had just been discovered and tested, which were very promising. Worried about keeping the situation a secret, the counselor advised them to say they were attending for a brother or uncle and that no one would be surprised.

Back home, Amanda opened her husband's closet and found the drugs she had just read about. He admitted that he had known about his own diagnosis for over a year and was too ashamed and terrified to tell her. He said he had had extramarital affairs and refused to provide any details. Amanda felt that her life had collapsed in front of her eyes. She asked for a medical leave from work, often barely dragging herself out of bed by noon. She called the counselor from time to time but could not imagine how to continue. Finally she agreed to go to an evening meeting of people with HIV but without speaking about her own situation.

At the mutual aid group, nine-tenths of the people were young, unmarried men. One young woman spoke of her HIV diagnosis and said her boyfriend was completely unfazed by the situation and supported her completely. The other described their problems at work, how to keep the secret, which family members to confide in. They compared notes about health services. Amanda felt relieved for the first time in weeks and decided to share her story with the group, especially her fears for her young children. They were sympathetic and let her ramble on for over half an hour. She took down two telephone numbers and felt a glimmer of optimism.

Shortly afterward, her husband fell seriously ill. She had nearly stopped talking to him, but suddenly she felt a wave of rage against him and rushed to the hospital. "You ruined my life!" she screamed at him. "I hope you die!

Make it quick!" Then she felt guilty and apologized, sobbing uncontrollably. The nurses brought her to their lounge and gave her a cup of tea while the other hospital staff stared and whispered among themselves.

At the public hospital Amanda was told she would have top priority for getting the new treatments but that the government had not decided to start providing them. Political pressure was needed, they said, and no one could do it better than a married woman with children. Amanda was dumbfounded at the idea of making her situation public and told them no. But she was feeling more energetic and ready to fight to survive.

Her husband, however, needed the triple therapy immediately or faced a grim prognosis. They had a good income but would need to spend over half of it on the drugs, which had to be bought directly from the pharmaceutical company. Amanda negotiated the purchases, got a discount and set up the dosing schedule. Her husband was depressed and refused to take responsibility for his treatment unless she reminded him. In addition, his constant absences were putting his job in jeopardy.

Little by little, Amanda became involved in the self-help groups springing up around the city, participated in their fund-raising activities and attended their informational seminars. She felt glad to have a weekly opportunity to talk about her situation openly instead of keeping everything to herself. She complained about her husband's passivity and shared her sense of outrage at the unfairness of what had happened to her. But the groups sometimes struck her as infantile; the gay fellows seemed more interested in their love affairs and sometimes made inappropriate jokes about dying. In addition, regular members often stopped coming, and only weeks or months later would she learn that they were dead.

Her best friend in the group was the cheerful young woman who had come with her boyfriend. One day the boyfriend disappeared without a word and never showed up again. Her friend later confided that she had a new partner and did not tell him about her HIV status.

The government programs based in each city hospital were soon overwhelmed with HIV patients, with more showing up every week. Amanda and her friends realized that only political agitation would stir the government to spend the money necessary to save their lives. Once again she was asked to take a prominent role, to show that married women with children—not just gay men—were among the people living with HIV. She agreed to attend meetings in the ministry but would not go public. "You have supported me more than my family," she said to her group, "but I can't make my children deal with this." She began to read medical journals and patient magazines produced in Spanish outside the country to understand the confusing array of possible treatment regimes.

At the hospital Amanda felt she was getting special treatment as a leader of the patient group. While the others waited hours for their appointments, she was shown in immediately to see the doctor. One day he said to her, "I have good news. We have the antiretrovirals for you. But don't tell anyone else: there aren't enough to go around." When she hesitated, the nurse added: "You can do a lot if you're in good health. If you get sick, you won't be any use to the organization." She agreed.

A city-wide coalition of all the hospital-based groups was now meeting every week, but Amanda could rarely attend. The Friday-night meetings lasted for hours and never began before 8:30; she would have to take a bus after midnight and walk home alone from the bus stop. The gay delegates even scheduled workshops for Sunday afternoon, the only time she had with her children and for family visits. At the same time, she realized that many important decisions were being made and that international agencies were interested in supporting the incipient patients' movement with funds. Sometimes they insisted on including women participants, and Amanda would be recruited. Representatives of the older AIDS nongovernmental organizations often courted her to warn her away from the other groups or individuals as unreliable or not really interested in people with HIV. "I don't know whom to trust," she lamented to her mother.

Meanwhile, her family budget was cracking under the strain of the costs of her husband's medication. Because he was covered by private health insurance, he had no access to the government drug programs. Amanda heard about a parallel market for AIDS medicines and made arrangements to buy some at a significant savings. She met the vendor at a park and realized the drugs came from the same hospital where she received treatment. "Some people prefer the money to the health benefit," the middleman told her. "If they get sick later, they can start taking it." She was appalled at the feeling that she was doing something illegal. The drug middleman refused to give his name.

Amanda's worst fear was for the HIV status of her children. Although they had always been healthy, she did not trust her husband's version of his extra-marital relationships and so did not really believe he had acquired the infection recently. She sought counseling at the various organizations but did not feel anyone really appreciated her situation. The other mothers at the hospital finally agreed to accompany her to the testing appointment. Two of her children were negative; the youngest had a positive test for HIV.

Upon receiving that result, Amanda lost all her fear and hesitation about going public. He'll face discrimination later anyway, she thought, so better to meet it head-on. She agreed to participate in a television show about people with HIV wearing a wig and dark glasses, but her coworkers recognized her anyway, confirming their suspicions. As a public spokeswoman, she was invited to a training seminar in another country and learned how to organize a news media campaign. She enjoyed the ambience of solidarity and continued to receive offers of assistance for herself and her family. She was promptly invited to two more international seminars and asked to be on an advisory committee for an international donor agency beginning to fund HIV-related projects.

When her baby began to have health problems, Amanda enrolled him in a special treatment program in a local hospital. One day in the waiting room, a nun told her that if the child became too much of a burden, the sisters could receive him in their home for HIV-positive minors and guarantee him the best and most up-to-date treatments. Amanda told her she could manage just fine, thanks anyway.

After this burst of activism and reorganization of her life, Amanda fell ill herself. The doctor told her it was probably HIV-related but aggravated by overwork. She was visited in the hospital by many of the gay fellows she had met in the groups and began to feel closer to them. They made her laugh and forget her troubles and played with her children when they came to see her. She realized that some of them knew her husband too and suspected it was not through seeing him in the hospital waiting room. Although they never discussed it, Amanda had concluded that her husband was probably homosexual and had married her in response to social pressures.

When school began the following year for her children, Amanda was shocked that her oldest was refused registration. Although school authorities denied it, she was certain it related to her HIV-status, which someone had leaked to the principal. She threatened a scandal, and city authorities found her a better school in a different neighborhood that would take the boy.

After recovering from her brief illness, Amanda cut back on her participation and left the main work to the fulltime activists who could travel to conferences and attend meetings frequently. She still went to the hospital support group, but the constant influx of new women with an HIV diagnosis and severe economic and family problems overwhelmed her. The AIDS drugs were becoming more and more available, but the single gay fellows seemed to recover their previous lives more quickly once the medical crises passed. She sympathized with the idea of forming a women-only HIV-positive group but decided to concentrate on her family responsibilities. Through a contact, her application for a subsidized mortgage was pushed quickly through the system. Today she is separated from her husband and lives with her three children and a dog. None of her neighbors know that she has HIV.

CHAPTER ONE

Peru: Testing, Testing

PERU	
Population	26.8 million
First reported case of AIDS	1983
Total estimated HIV infections	82,000
Male : female ratio	2.6:1
Estimated number of people needing antiretroviral treatment	11,000
Number receiving drugs in 2003	2,000
First AIDS prevention NGO established	1990
Adult women using birth control	50%
Gross domestic product (GDP) 2003	$61 billion
Per capita income (2003)	$2,150
Annual per-capita spending on health	$91
Unemployment rate	13.4%
Shining Path guerrilla insurrection launched	1980
Alberto Fujimori elected	1990
Palace coup by Fujimori, Congress closed	1992
Forced sterilization of an estimated 200,000 indigenous women in Peruvian countryside	1996–1998
Fujimori flees to Japan	2000
Estimated deaths during war with Shining Path	30,000
Reported political disappearances	3,140

The sophisticated use of peer educators to bring the AIDS prevention message to "hard-to-reach" groups dovetailed seamlessly into the construction of research cohorts to track the progress of the disease—but not to treat it.

June 24, 2001, 10:00 A.M.,
Swiss Pharmaceutical Building, Lima

"Hand in Hand with Our Doctors: First Steps Toward Living Well with HIV" read the announcement tacked on the bulletin boards both of Lima's AIDS prevention organizations and the many mutual support groups for people with HIV and AIDS that have mushroomed in tandem with the steady climb in HIV infections in the country, now estimated at over 80,000. The invitation called for HIV-positive *limeños* to gather on a June Sunday during the city's perpetually overcast but mild winter. The all-day meeting was to be held at the imposing Química Suiza (Swiss Pharmaceuticals, although the company has no connection to Switzerland) corporate headquarters just off the freeway, a well-known landmark in the La Victoria section of the city. A casual observer might surmise from the promotional flyers that people with HIV would come away from the miniseminar with useful information about how to pursue their desperate search for antiretroviral drugs—available in the rich countries or to those locals wealthy or connected enough to get them on their own, but light-years away from the capacity of the average Peruvian pocketbook.

As with any corporate office in Peru, security is overwhelming, even years after the last Shining Path (Sendero Luminoso) bombing. (A far more modest non-governmental organization that I had visited—engaged in nothing more controversial than condom marketing—sported closed-circuit television monitoring their parking spaces and back-door entrances.) The early arrivals loitered outside the gates topped with razor wire and peered through the safety glass into an empty guard booth: a few men in their twenties and thirties, a woman from the sponsoring pharmaceutical company trying to find someone on her cell phone, the ubiquitous taxi drivers who materialize out of nowhere at the vague prospect of a fare.

The late June 2001 seminar exactly coincided with a worldwide confab hosted by United Nations General Secretary Kofi Annan in New York, the General Assembly Special Session on AIDS, known as UNGASS, where delegates debated descriptions of "vulnerable groups" (the Taliban regime of Afghanistan, the Vatican and the Bush administration fought successfully to exclude mention of homosexuals, drug users and sex workers) and set the groundwork for the creation of the Global AIDS Fund. The fund has since amassed and committed more than $3 billion in response to the epidemic's fulfillment of the worst-case scenarios advanced by Jonathan Mann's Harvard-based AIDS think tank in the early 1990s, which once drew guffaws of disbelief at estimates of a possible 110 million AIDS infections worldwide.

At the time of the AIDS UNGASS, millions of Africans, Asians and Latinos with HIV, people like those attending the Lima educational meeting, were clamoring for access to the antiretroviral drugs that could extend their lives. As a result of their persistent demands to benefit from the scientific bonanza unveiled at the 1996 International AIDS Conference in Vancouver, some of them were slowly pushing past resistant local bureaucracies, underfunded governments and billionaire drug dynasties to get hold of them. However, many—and most in Peru—were still far from obtaining the AIDS-fighting medicines.

Due to the conflicting dates, the presidents of the two oldest and largest Peruvian organizations representing people living with HIV were at the New York meeting, and in their absence other collaborators were in charge. A guard eventually showed up, and two dozen early risers shuffled in. In the course of the morning, nearly a hundred people would filter into the meeting hall, mostly men but with an increasing presence of women and couples, reflecting the slowly changing epidemiological pattern of HIV in Peru. A thinnish and bespectacled man with the pale complexion of Lima's European-origin minority announced the names of the doctors who would be presenting the morning's subjects and their topics: HIV transmission, basic prevention, drug regimen adherence. With attendees shifting nervously in their seats, the meeting got under way.

For this observer, the topics themselves were enough to raise an eyebrow: Did people with HIV in Peru really *not know* how HIV is transmitted, given that they had already acquired it? At this point in their lives, were lessons on primary prevention appropriate? Wouldn't they prefer to discuss, for example, the complexities of revealing one's HIV status to partners or managing sex with HIV-negative mates?

But these questions were miles off the agenda. Our meeting chairman outlined the rules of the sessions: "After the presentations, we will write our questions and turn them in," he stated in a peremptory tone, "because under no circumstances are we going to interrupt the doctors." Silence. In this grand drug-company seminar hall, patients will hear useful information presented by the expert physicians. Maximum deference will be today's byword. Do not interrupt.

The first doctor, a cordial woman of about forty-five, her glasses resting on her bosom and her thick black hair held in place with a barrette, began the lessons by outlining the main "risk groups," a concept rejected by AIDS activists since the 1980s. A long list of these supposed groups appeared on an overhead projector: "promiscuous people," prostitutes, drug users, people with multiple partners. Oddly enough, given the overwhelmingly gay audience, homosexuals are not included on the list. During her presentation, the doctor almost managed to mention them in the newly coined euphemism, "men who have sex with men," but stumbled badly in her obvious embarrassment.

The AIDS 101 presentation droned on, deadly boring for anyone minimally familiar with the material and frankly irritating for even the novice activists who had graduated from the simplistic anti-"promiscuity" models of the early years to more nuanced views of sexual behavior. Finally, the pièce de résistance: strict exhortations to follow the doctor's instructions about when to take your dosages of Crixivan, azidothymidine (AZT) or nevirapine, the importance of regular meals for some medicines, the empty-stomach rule for others.

As the technical data rolls along like a river, I ask myself if anyone in the room is going to stand up and say, "Thank you, Madame Doctor, that is very interesting information, but do you have any advice as to how in the name of Jesus are we to get our hands on the medicines in the first place since they cost approximately eight times our monthly salaries?" A quick glance around the room, however, confirmed by a whispered conference with Hernán Gonzales sitting next to me, makes depressingly clear that no one is going to pose a challenging question, much less turn this polite assemblage into anything remotely resembling a confrontation. In cultural terms, it would simply look rude—after all, the doctors have been kind enough to take time out on a Sunday to instruct us.

Furthermore, one could easily surmise the type of reaction these apparently logical questions would generate from the doctors and stern NGO leaders: those not simply shocked would argue that drug access is another issue, a separate discussion, suitable for another time, another place. "Political" matters should be handled elsewhere, whereas today's gathering deals with "information" and "technical" questions. And heaven forbid any suggestion that the kindly drug company sponsoring the affair should have ulterior motives beyond the continued well-being of all those present.

"People from the HIV-positive groups can describe all the difficulties they face," whispers Hernán, "but in general among the members, there isn't much militancy." The morning's presentations are finished, and we push back our chairs to form a circle. There is much nervous rustling and fidgeting, a sense of anticipation and quiet humility. A woman I interviewed two days before approaches me in hushed tones and asks if I can "lend" 10 soles (about $3) to one of her members for bus fare home. (The lone foreigner is easier to hit up than the drug company sponsoring the event.) I refuse. Lunch appears, amid a deathly silence, and I finally understand the dynamic of this event much better. Beyond the rhetoric, beyond the classes and flip charts and color slides, this outing means *food*. The Sunday seminar includes an indoor picnic, and in Lima, Peru, that alone guarantees a relatively docile quorum.

During lunch, the pharmaceutical sponsors pass out information sheets for those in attendance: how long have you known your status, which is your hospital, what are your address and telephone number. The company rep gathers up the data politely and carries the questionnaires upstairs. Data on one hundred future clients clamoring for drug purchases are now filed away safely.

Peru's response to HIV has been surprisingly enlightened, considering the country's enormous social problems, the lingering effects of the ruthless guerrilla war launched by the Shining Path Maoists and the government's vicious response, which led to an estimated 30,000 deaths and another 3,000-plus political disappearances. Despite a powerful Catholic establishment, first grassroots organizations and soon after health officials themselves approached the AIDS epidemic with surprising openness to adult sexual activity, including commercial sex and homosexual subcultures. The ineffable Alberto Fujimori, who dismantled Peru's republican institutions, ruled as a dictator during the 1990s when the epidemic was incubating and later fled to Japan to escape prosecution on corruption charges, once inaugurated a continent-wide AIDS and sexually transmitted disease conference by promoting condom use from the pulpit of the city's main cathedral. By contrast, Chile's socialist-led coalition government would never dream of defending its supposedly similar program with such bold symbolism, nor would the local Catholic establishment let the government hear the end of it. Fujimori's appointee for the AIDS post, Dr. Jorge Sánchez, was not only a skilled innovator who put hundreds of AIDS prevention educators on the streets, he was also openly gay.

In short, the country's record in the early years bears respectable comparison with the efforts of wealthier countries with far less crushing poverty and political upheaval. Despite its chronic hardships and supposedly conservative Catholic and indigenous cultures, Peru is superficially at least a remarkably broad-minded place, capable of celebrating in stride an openly gay and HIV-positive TV actor, Ernesto Pimentel, as well as bad-boy talk-show host and author Jaime Bayly who encourages speculation about his presumed bisexual adventures. Its gay nightlife is dusk to dawn and not for the fainthearted. And in my nosing around the AIDS-related organizations and Health Ministry initiatives, I found a surprising number of people and resources dedicated to promoting safe sexual practices among the typically hardest-hit populations, the more down-and-out transvestites, gay guys in the outlying shantytowns and the hordes of young people, male and female, engaged in prostitution. At first glance, it all appeared far too good to be true and quite uncharacteristic for a country in such notoriously bad shape.

I am particularly curious about how things have played out in Peru because my own AIDS-related experience in Chile could easily have taken place there instead. Back in the late 1980s, when I was freelancing from Santiago and loitered regularly at the United Press International offices, a job opened up at UPI in Lima, and my roommate, another journalist kicking around South America, was offered it and left. Had it been me instead, no doubt I would have met and begun to circulate among the early gay activists concerned about AIDS and joined in the construction of that first, tentative response, just as I did farther south.

There are plenty of recognizable parallels between the two countries' responses to AIDS, but many contrasts as well, some no doubt due to historical accident and the play of personalities, but many others related to Peru's traumatic politics over the last twenty years, its brutal class divisions and the crushing weight of its citizens' struggle for survival.

As is often the case in Latin America, the origins of Peru's response to AIDS can be traced to the early, seat-of-the-pants efforts by Lima's gays to sound an alert about the epidemic among their friends. Despite the advance notice filtering in from the more mature epidemics in Europe and the United States, almost all governments in the region and certainly most news media reacted in the usual unenlightened ways, the former downplaying the dangers while the papers sounded scandalous and counterproductive alarms or dug out true-life horror stories for their "impact" value.

Several veterans of this period recall that gays in Peru's Health Ministry pushed the envelope on what was clearly a gay epidemic and won considerable leeway, probably because no one else wanted to deal with the problem. Governments and civic groups alike often missed the political implications of AIDS and the measures it eventually would entail. Our first community AIDS forum in Chile in 1991 was held in the auditorium of the Catholic University in Santiago; by the time we were ready for a second event, six months later, the church hierarchy had registered the issue as a hot potato and vetoed any involvement that was not strictly controlled by its official charity, Caritas.

As Aldo Araujo, at the time of our interview president of the Lima Homosexual Movement (MHOL), one of the oldest gay-rights groups on the continent, recalls:

> At a certain point we obtained some condoms. Then the AIDS and Sexually Transmitted Diseases Control Program was formed in the Health Ministry. We're talking about '86, '87. MHOL also participated in its creation, by invitation.

By government invitation?

> By invitation of some friends inside (laughs).

Unlike in other countries, where gay men would seek allies among key health authorities with whom to push their issues, in Peru relatively uncloseted gay men *were* the key health authorities. "They led the program," says historian Jorge (Tito) Bracamonte, another veteran of MOHL and other groups. "They weren't just brought into it; they ran it." Unsurprisingly, they were discreet at first about what they were doing. Araujo recalls:

> AIDS at first only had repercussions in the government because of the in-house gays, whom we will not mention by name for obvious reasons. They still work there. But their concerns made it possible to put this together.

Eventually an openly gay doctor became the director of the program. To my knowledge, only Brazil can boast a similarly daring, early use of gay collaborators in prominent positions from the first days of the epidemic.

Just as in the United States, gays took interest in the AIDS issue out of identification with it, a useful by-product of the otherwise damaging "gay leprosy" and "pink plague" propaganda pouring out of local news media. MHOL's members, mostly professionals from Peru's elite, were attuned in part due to their links with foreigners and trips outside the country. These links also made them the first victims. Araujo says:

> Beto Montalvo, the actor [*and first president of MHOL*], died of AIDS in 1989, he and other people who had been close to him. Being from the theater world, he traveled to New York. He got sick without telling anyone. We began to realize something was going on with him; the diseases he began to have were the same ones the papers mentioned.

As was common everywhere, the first attempts among gays to teach each other about the virus were didactic and unsophisticated. Araujo continues:

> We had to learn how to use condoms. There were lectures and all the rest. We made photocopied flyers about AIDS and the condom and passed them out, of course without the focus groups that you have now, without information. Nice drawings and nothing fancy. They were warnings.

He adds that they also didn't work.

We had an AIDS help-line here to talk about AIDS, and two guys, both named César, answered the calls. I was with the president and secretary [*of MHOL*] in Norway talking about the AIDS project. We get a call, and they were crying and saying, Look, César is sick. Both Césars are sick. Imagine, what are we going to do now? We were devastated; they were great kids.

While the first pioneers were trying to gain sophistication and experience about prevention initiatives, the nefarious particularities of HIV sabotaged the simple, first-wave solutions. The virus's long incubation period quickly facilitated infection while consciousness-raising efforts moved glacially into first gear.

Inexorably, AIDS infiltrated MHOL and shaped its political mandate. But illness and deaths in themselves did not clarify what role a gay-rights group should play in a public health crisis affecting its purported beneficiaries. Debates soon erupted. Often in Latin America, AIDS groups emerged together with gay-rights groups, and some activists eager to promote sexual emancipation explicitly felt constrained by the AIDS issue. Most often each went its own way; by contrast, MHOL managed to incorporate the epidemic into its gay mission. Araujo continues:

We saw that we could not medicalize ourselves as an institution. We could have doctors and a very small clinical service, those of us who had initiated the AIDS work. But it could not be the central focus of the institution. We deal with human rights; within that is health, but not just health.

Another early president of MHOL, Julio Gilvonio, puts it this way:

MHOL first had been formed to defend civil rights, but within these rights is also the right to life and to be informed, and this led us to rethink the role of the institution a lot.

This vision curiously takes a subtle distance from U.S.-style multicultural-ist, identity politics, despite MHOL's class and personal links to the developed world. Instead, it positions gays rather closer in spirit to the inclusive demands of Peru's dispossessed classes. As Araujo says:

> This complaint doesn't come just from a separate group, but rather from everyone; to be included within the whole. As you can see, now we are more included, seems to me.

This perspective suggests a link with MHOL's beginnings in the intellectual middle classes inspired by left-wing ideas. Araujo mentions Amnesty International, university circles and the political parties as if the founders' discourse were still closely associated in their minds with other emancipation movements, just as during the early gay-lib years in the United States when those pioneers still felt inspired by feminist militance, blacks battling for civil rights, or even Vietnamese Marxists. Despite their ties with first-world gay groups and venues, the Peruvian gay pioneers were able quickly to identify and articulate the underlying political implications of AIDS for their own country, facing a sharply different socioeconomic and cultural reality. The paragraphs just cited could easily serve as a rights framework for gay-oriented AIDS work even today, more than fifteen years later.

But despite this foresight, the response to AIDS would eventually fragment, and the gay movement's role in defending sexual emancipation within the HIV epidemic would be somewhat neutralized. In addition, the gay rights/AIDS prevention split reemerged, albeit in a different form.

Jorge "Tito" Bracamonte is perhaps typical of a generation of gay activists in Peru who came of age in that crucial period. Bracamonte is a forty-something historian who returned to Peru after finishing a doctorate in Mexico. His speech is unhurried, respectful and deliberate, and he appeared mildly shocked at the sorts of brusque comments that erupted from Chileans or the declamatory Argentines at the social sciences congress where we met. Tito was widely known in Lima's gay nightspots, and his steady, slightly paternal demeanor was a magnet for several timid, clearly smitten youths.

Notwithstanding his gently self-confident personal and political narrative, Tito's insertion in activist circles is both remarkable and emblematic of how Peru remains an anomalous case. In fact, the mere survival of MHOL, one of the earliest expressions of Latino gay consciousness, is an extraordinary achievement in itself.

Tito believes gay advocacy in Peru remains weak and poorly thought out, and he clearly hopes to close the gaps by pushing academic circles, including his own, to address these issues, as would be considered quite normal in most developed countries. His collection of essays by various authors, *De Amores y Luchas: Diversidad Sexual, Derechos Humanos y Ciudadanía*, (*Loves and Struggles: Sexual Diversity, Human Rights and Citizenship*) combined history, anthropology, sociology and activism, touching only lightly on the AIDS phenomenon in the context of a much longer and broader narrative. However, his journey to what in other countries might be a simple and logical combination of roles has been marked by zigzags and considerable trauma. Bracamonte explains:

> I was a university student, very involved politically but also eager to get a solid [*academic*] grounding, which I realized I needed to develop a critique of the existing state of affairs. It was interesting because from a gay perspective I could also understand more subtly, I believe, different forms of discrimination. So my previous phase as a leftwing militant enabled me to develop certain skills, organizing. I could turn my university experience and my political work to good account within what was the gay movement, not just in MHOL.

An admirable and perhaps unremarkable ambition, but in Peru these were not unremarkable times. Bracamonte came of age in the 1980s, just as the conflict with Shining Path was reaching its violent climax. Nonetheless, he plunged into gay-rights agitation where his beliefs and his sexual identity could be synthesized.

Despite his activism, Tito gives the impression of someone not particularly eager to expose his personal affairs to public gaze. But in the spirit of *consecuencia*, of being ready to act in accordance with one's beliefs, he had steered closer and closer to mixing intimacy and militancy and to constructing the conceptual bridges between his party's commitment to the poor and dispossessed and his own sense of exclusion, not of a material nature but nonetheless impossible to ignore. He says:

> ... after having begun timidly to collaborate with MHOL and the issue of human rights from a gay and lesbian perspective—

Why timidly?

> Timidly because I was more involved with a left-wing political party and with university political activism. So it meant directing, now, some of my work—as well as some fear, I have to admit, to be openly gay, especially as I had party responsibilities. I joined at a very young age but as a member of the (MHOL) council without being entirely convinced.

The mélange of elements must have felt strange for a young college student fully engaged in the radical political debates at San Marcos University in an atmosphere heady with the promise of rebellion and transformation. In the course of our interview, Tito mentioned the first time he and his friends set out to take the HIV test, the sad impact of the HIV-positive results received by a few, the special links to certain unique friends who shared this schizophrenic gay left-winger existence, jointly battling real demons on several simultaneous fronts.

Ironically perhaps, the advent of AIDS joined the strands of Tito's political ideals and his personal issues more neatly. Bracamonte continues:

> Then I got more involved with the problem of human rights and with the AIDS business when the entire movement turns its attention to it because it becomes a health problem that has to be faced immediately, no matter what. People need information, people have to know how to use condoms, that they are facing a grave risk if they don't use protection, and we have to say it. We have to—it couldn't be ignored.

MHOL was a particularly auspicious connection for these two issues and people like Tito who linked them ideologically.

> The generation before mine, the generation which founded MHOL in Lima, they were basically people coming from the left who leave the leftist

shop because in the end their issues were not picked up by those parties. In my case I still had the idea that social change was imminent, that's why we were very committed to the left.

Social change did in fact arrive, but not the sort that Tito and his friends were hoping for. When Shining Path mounted a serious challenge to the central government, the authoritarian response that followed had considerable popular backing: Fujimori, a political unknown, swept into office in the presidential election of 1990 and proceeded to dismantle any personal or institutional obstacle to his quasi-dictatorship, finally using the notorious 1992 palace coup to suspend the congress and take over the judicial branch, with merely pro forma objections from Washington and around the continent. With the ready pretext of the war against the Maoists, Fujimori unleashed a repression that did not confine itself to the *senderistas* or their ideological allies but rather swept across all social movements associated with leftwing politics. According to Bracamonte,

> What happened is that in 1992 I found myself at a terrible crossroads personally. I had invested in a lot of things, and they had all ended in failure, all the political violence and with friends dead. In the 1980s, Peru lived through a war, right? And in this war the loser in general terms was the social movement and very concretely the Peruvian left, which was totally decapitated. Not because it was involved with Shining Path but because the state systematically eliminated it, as well as due to its own limitations. So a lot of people from my generation paid the price.

Gay leaders, highly politicized and ideologically close to the left-wing movement, were felled from two directions.

> At least four people from my generation died in the political violence. Two of them involved with Sendero, and two other *compañeros* of mine killed by Sendero. That was a lot; then your friends whom you respect begin to die, the founders, dying of AIDS.

MHOL's innovations and later decline in the AIDS area is symptomatic of a gay-oriented social response to the epidemic that nonetheless could not put down the needed roots in the midst of such obstacles. Its story, I believe, says much about the nature of the AIDS services currently available, the prevention initiatives, the approach to testing and, indirectly perhaps, even the fight over access to medicines—in short, everything happening with regard to AIDS in Peru today.

Despite its obvious drawbacks, Peru's strict class consciousness paradoxically may have had certain beneficial effects on the early activism. Although in Chile few middle-class professionals were drawn to the gay-consciousness or AIDS-related initiatives, in Peru both were quickly dominated by educated volunteers. MHOL, the groundbreaking gay rights outfit, was historically an elite grouping, a fact that generated serious conflict once it began serving poor *limeños* in its HIV prevention programs. But its founders were recognizably capable of developing a theoretical underpinning for their movement and maintained close ties with gay groups and leaders in the United States and elsewhere, given their ability to travel and speak foreign languages. The importance of AIDS initiatives, which in Chile were left to our rather amateurish efforts, was quickly grasped in Peru, often spotted as prizes to be fought over. VIALIBRE, the first nonprofit to come together specifically to address the AIDS epidemic (its name means "free way" in Spanish), started out with a marked professional bias linked to clinical services, its administrator, Manuel Rouillon, recalls.

> They were doctors, sociologists, nutritionists, social workers, and the main thing was [*clinical*] care. From there came the idea that it should be not just a clinic but also prevention work, the idea that you have to work in both, and VIALIBRE opened up to prevention work.

While in Chile we were able slowly to develop a gay-oriented AIDS program, which eventually spun off an explicitly gay-rights group, the Homosexual Liberation Movement (MOVILH), in Lima clinicians and social scientists moved into the vacuum with dispatch to establish parallel health services and quickly incorporating the health ministry itself as well, where gays had high-level allies. By contrast, well-educated Chileans shunned our efforts for the most part, perhaps due to the less clearly defined class structure of the country.

They shuddered at our storefront offices and poor clientele in a grubby commercial part of the city; their Peruvian counterparts might well have taken similar conditions in stride, as no one could possibly mistake middle-class professionals for the supposed beneficiaries.

Although the privileged position of MHOL's founders as educated professionals no doubt facilitated their audacious beginnings and the strength of their early insights as a gay consciousness movement, class also quickly became an Achilles' heel. According to witnesses, class conflicts played out in two ways, the most evident of which was plain snobbery. Says Julio Gilvonio:

> So MHOL became popular, very well-known, but "popular" also means that the *cholito*, the dark-skinned guy, unemployed and all the rest of it, went there a lot. And we had a very distinct policy from the previous one, which was middle-class people, that we all went to the theater, to nice restaurants, had nice clothes. So the profile of the people coming to MHOL changed, and that was a problem.

Others considered that the opening to lower-class gay Peruvians watered down the group's capacities, although the incipient tension between a social movement and a technical service is evident as well. Says Luis Miranda, coeditor of the gay magazine *Rumbos*:

> I understand that MHOL started to decline because the people with more intellectual skills to manage things started to drop out, and people took over who didn't reach their level—very low, and everything fell apart. It became a social center, and its role with AIDS was reduced to the prevention hotline.

Bracamonte clearly felt at home with the new focus at MHOL, even if his was a minority view.

> By then we were handling AIDS as a health problem, but a health problem like all others in this country in which other variables are involved. In Peru people die of tuberculosis, but not middle-class or upper-class people. Something similar is happening with AIDS that should enable us to broaden

the idea of rights and the need for the state and its health services to include sectors that are marginalized for different reasons.

This identification with different types of marginalized persons, particularly the 70 percent majority of poor Peruvians, marks an important vein of AIDS-related activism, which is revealed again and again in ongoing work among gay men, sex workers and transvestites and more recently people living with HIV. Not everyone perceives the needs and the strategies in the same way, and important conflicts play out precisely in class terms. The issue is never far from the minds, if not the discourse, of the participants.

Naturally, this perspective quickly found a place within MHOL, and tensions arose as soon as the group set out to provide public services. President at the time, Gilvonio even dared to suspend certain collaborators for discrimination against these new participants, but the old guard overruled him. As a result, he left his position. A new vehicle was necessary, one of many that were emerging to complement, and eventually replace, MHOL itself. Says Bracamonte:

> We saw that MHOL wasn't aiming at the most vulnerable groups, you know, which were the sex workers, youth, adolescents. The institutional pretext in MHOL at that time was that we couldn't work with adolescents because we ran the risk up ending up in jail.

Rather than fight out the issue at MHOL, Bracamonte and others launched a separate initiative known as Germinal, which brought the prevention message out to the gritty gay street. The target beneficiaries were to be the young men working the sex trade in downtown Lima, with male clients.

It would be misleading to call these teens "hustlers" or male prostitutes, as those terms are understood elsewhere, because of the context of commercial sex in a city like Lima, where an enormous sector of the populace can barely guarantee its own basic survival. It may be hard to grasp, for people who have awakened sexually and romantically in more amiable circumstances, how naturally one may be drawn to attractive people who also can offer material rewards. Between one potential partner and another who can buy you lunch or give you a CD, scarcity may draw a subtly compelling distinction, to which not only adolescents may succumb. Hernán Gonzales, an early recruit to the Germinal experiment, explains:

> It's not the only option, but at least when you're young and you get involved in this [*gay*] world, it's the only one you see. Because people say to you, Ay, how handsome you are, how nice you are. You're the star for the moment, even more so if you realize that someone is taking you out in exchange [*for sex*]. So you say, Oh, great. You start growing into it, thinking a little further along. Why not ask them for money? But okay, it didn't just occur to us; we also did it because of what we saw and what some older people told us to do: Don't be a dope! You could get somewhere, you could be someone! So you grab onto that banner and you say, I'm the star here. On top of which in Peru work for young people is really—sometimes the sex trade provides you more benefits than a job.

The Germinal initiative, backed by foreign funding, broke free of MHOL and took the prevention and the gay-consciousness message to the skeptical youth of the hangouts in the Plaza San Martín and the Parque Universitario. Like many outreach programs, the founders of Germinal recognized that the particular form gay vulnerability took in their city was deeply related to the inevitable lure of sexual commerce for needy teens. The usual strategies—encouraging group solidarity or shared self-protective norms—would face special obstacles in such a mercantile environment.

Gonzales describes the dubious reaction of the denizens of these rough-and-tumble zones to the peer educators who at first were hardly their peers at all:

> The question among all the homosexuals downtown was: What do these people want? Do they want to study us, take advantage of us, take us somewhere and play musical beds, put us to use? I don't know—this was the question.

Distrust.

> Yes, total distrust from everyone. Because all of a sudden two strangers appear whom we've never seen before, more or less well dressed.

What are they doing here? Do they want to hire us? What do they want?

They didn't fit the typical client profile?

No, they didn't. Young guys, not bad looking.

In this difficult, wary environment, patient work, boosted by clearly ideological inspirations, paid off. Gonzales recalls:

> So, well, I went once to one of their meetings. I was surprised to find that there weren't just young gays there, but also heteros. And the dynamic was pretty friendly. There was no discrimination, once in a while from a partic-ipant, but not from the leaders. They tried to run things democratically, with respect. I liked their approach, and so I began to get closer to them. I starting participating more, inviting my friends, and we went to the monthly meetings Germinal would have with sometimes a hundred guys. Gays about 20 percent, queens another 10 or 15 percent. We felt it was a world, not a perfect world, but a world for us, an acceptable world. We contributed things. They encouraged us to produce a play, and we did.

By then the early, didactic approach had been superseded by more sophisti-cated methods and broader appeals. Germinal's founders knew enough to address the vivid experiences of these gay teens who often faced hostile family environments due to their sexual orientation and who moved naturally into hustling both to assert their identity and for survival. Gonzales says:

> They asked us what our concerns were when we were thirteen, fourteen years old, and we said we couldn't imagine telling our parents that we liked guys. They had taught us to want to marry a woman. How to say, Dad, I like the guy next door? And how to face the fact that once we say that, they throw us out?

Eventually the new recruits formed a movement of their own, and although both Germinal and the Azúcar Gonzales Movement have since disbanded, they left their mark on the AIDS ambiance. After being away for five years pursuing his studies, Bracamonte was pleasantly surprised to see these same early participants in charge of gay-oriented programs backed by the Health Ministry, producing research and writing about the issues as health promoters.

While this heady mix of trained activists and beneficiaries ripe for guidance and surprisingly quick to learn sowed important seeds for the future of HIV work, the cost was also considerable, as Pablo Anamaría, another early participant recalls:

> At first we took it [AIDS] as a joke, like something to scare us, to influence us, to restrict our freedom. We didn't take it too seriously. Even though— parenthesis—of the twenty guys from those days, only one is seronegative, I'm alive, and all the rest died.

Gonzalo Rey de Castro, one of the first people to acquire HIV in Peru and an early fatality, helped found VIALIBRE and generated groups known as GAMS (Grupos de Ayuda Mutua, or self-help groups) while the entity tried to establish a useful clinical service. VIALIBRE now occupies several buildings on Garibaldi Plaza in downtown Lima and has served thousands of people with HIV, saving them from the twelve stations of the public hospitals. The organization is the granddaddy of AIDS work in Peru and has managed not only to stay afloat financially but to stimulate or spawn other initiatives. In addition, during my interviews it drew remarkably little hostile fire from the other groups, an enviable position in the raucous AIDS NGO universe where sensibilities are usually worn on the sleeve. Early on Rey de Castro's group was tut-tutted by others around Latin America as too close to the Peruvian elite and too clinically focused. Nonetheless, it survives while others have passed into history.

Manuel Rouillon describes himself as a low-profile manager whose job was to manage the oversized egos of the volunteer medical professionals.

> I'm going to be completely frank with you. In VIALIBRE there were very enthusiastic young doctors, very enthusiastic, who although they did give their time to VIALIBRE, some hours per week, their future was not with the organization. They were focused elsewhere, or their work in VIALIBRE

opened up doors for them in bigger places. So that meant I had to push these folks, and it was a triple chore. It was pretty disastrous.

But in addition to offering clinical services, VIALIBRE plunged into prevention work, generated a volunteer base and won government contracts. Rouillon said the group earns half its operating expenses by charging clients on a sliding scale and from its research projects, although it still relies on international donor support as well. The outfit is a peculiar mix, with its patient services, its pharmacy, its participation in treatment-access initiatives, its history of prevention education and its support for mutual-support groups. In 2003 its director, Robinson Cabello, recognized that the concentration on medicines had sidelined prevention work while Rouillon expressed impatience with the frequent personal disputes and mistrust that characterized the larger NGO scene. But VIALIBRE is neither a clinic nor a think tank; nor is it a particularly overweening presence on the AIDS scene. Peru's brutal clarity about the realities of social class seems to have made it easier, ironically, for such an organization to spring up and thrive.

As in most of Latin America, HIV was concentrated among gay men in Peru in the first years but women and some straight men were also affected. Curiously, but perhaps not surprisingly, these cases attracted enormous interest and some theoretical sympathy especially when the woman or couple faced the possibility of an HIV-positive child. Generally speaking, however, these women faced the same abuse and discrimination as gay men; frequently it was directed at their children as well, even when they were free of infection. Although women's health advocates noted that the almost exclusive emphasis on men in relation to AIDS left out the complex issues of female vulnerability, in the early years the reproductive health field felt little urgency about the epidemic. Carola La Rosa works for a group called Population Programs Support (APROPO), a leader in social marketing of contraceptive devices.

When the AIDS problem arose, A.I.D. [*the U.S. Agency for International Development*] formed some working groups to see how it would be managed, but the nonprofits in family planning didn't want to have anything to do with AIDS or HIV or any of that. Why? Because for them AIDS was a homosexual disease, and family planning was prevention for families, for couples in a family, proper couples. I could see very clearly that the problem of AIDS was basically was about sexuality, and managing one's sexuality is not a monopoly of the nice married couple but can be lived in different ways. So A.I.D. asked us to consult with the government on their communications strategy, and we did.

Of course, policymakers and the broader population naturally paid more attention to heterosexual transmission because it touched them more closely. If straight couples could get HIV, then they and their supposedly heterosexual children could get it too. Many early prevention campaigns designed for communicating the facts about HIV to the general public focused almost exclusively on heterosexual transmission even when it was responsible for only a fraction of the epidemic. However, the early association in public consciousness of AIDS with homosexuality meant that these efforts usually were not very successful. Even today, after years of buzz about HIV, many countries still detect very low rates of condom use among heterosexual couples even when they are concerned about avoiding pregnancy and take other measures to do so.

When women did acquire the infection, the experience was often different in important ways. Sonia Borja led a group of women to set up their own HIV-positive group called Solas & Unidas (Alone & Together) after feeling dissatisfied with the mixed organization where she had started out her activism.

Our needs were different from those of the men. There were more and more HIV-positive women, but I asked myself, Why don't they come to the health workshops? We would talk to them and finally they would say, Look, Sonia, what I would spend in bus fare to get here is my bread money for tomorrow for my children. Just to give you one example. Because it's true, how can we give a workshop on nutrition if they can't buy any food? It didn't make sense. So we began to realize these women were widows and had children. It was very different from what the men experienced.

At the same time, these were the sorts of problems that were not easy to address in the kinds of AIDS-specific prevention interventions being developed for gay men or young people focused mostly on sexuality issues. But among one group of women the AIDS 101 model worked quite well: women in the commercial sex trade. Just like gay men or intravenous drug users, women selling sex could be approached by their peers and often were highly motivated to learn the practical information that AIDS educators wanted to give them. As a beleaguered and harassed group, they could use the natural solidarity or empathy that might exist to transmit health information and be believed in situations where medical personnel or formal health workers might be distrusted. And the whole process might well engender a different understanding of themselves and what their work meant. Aida Pacheco worked for a sex-worker information project run out of VIALIBRE in the 1990s and says she acquired a new outlook on the way she earned her living:

> A lot of the girls who work in the night clubs don't want to admit that they have sexual relations. Very few of them will be so uninhibited as to say, Yes, if the client pays well, I'll go with him. They don't want to categorize themselves as prostitutes—"I'm not that!" I'm not that way. I have to recognize that I am a sex worker and I have to live with that and accept it, just as later or tomorrow, maybe I'll decide to be a lawyer or start studying computer science. I just have to accept it straight out.

Sex-worker projects were common throughout Latin America, and there was even an attempt to constitute a sex-worker regional network based in Venezuela. The Chilean version, which began very early in the epidemic, seems to have been particularly successful, given the historically low rates of HIV infection in the world of female prostitution there. Of course, as a medical doctor from an international organization once quipped to us sardonically, it was almost predictable that the male-dominated health policy field would pay close attention to prevention among women in the sex trade. "After all," she said, "they use those services."

"Peer education" is now a standard component of AIDS prevention and care packages everywhere as educators consistently have seen that top-down, instructional approaches have little impact on behaviors, especially those related to sex. Instead, people from the target population itself are recruited as informal educators, trained and sent back into their usual environments. The approach seeks to create or reinforce group norms for the desired preventive measures, often using a group's natural cohesion in the face of social hostility, such as in the case of sex workers, drug users or gay youth. As a result, peer education projects also can have explicitly political ends as both health promoters and beneficiaries inevitably confront discrimination and abuse, often in the context of discussing negotiating skills or self-esteem issues. Or they can be narrowly focused on the informational content.

Given the diverse nature of what is loosely called the "gay" scene in Peru, where homosexual practices are not always linked to clearly defined sexual orientations, peer education implied real challenges. Says Alfonso Lescano, a veteran peer-education trainer for VIALIBRE:

At first, I had a hard time because I had a really mixed group, bisexuals, mostaceros [*straight-identified bisexual men*], transvestites, queens and guys you'd never take for gay. So trying to understand them here, some would be cutting up, others complaining, insulting each other—whenever you have gay people together in one place, they can't keep quiet.

In addition, many experts think bisexual practices are so widespread in Peru that it is virtually impossible to decide exactly who are MSM (men who have sex with men), to use the now-fashionable category. David Roca, coeditor of the gay magazine *Rumbos*, described one hilarious scene in a poor sector on the outskirts of Lima:

In the first meeting that the woman from PROSETSS [*the government AIDS program*] had with the guys who were going to be peer educators here, she asked them, 'Have any of you had homosexual relations?' And no one said anything. Finally one of them stood up and said, "Miss, we're all cacaneros here." And no one denied it.

A *cacanero* is a man who will engage in penetrative sex with a gay or transvestite—but only as the "active" or insertive partner and without assuming any homosexual identity. Peer educators like Lescano had to develop not only new knowledge but also an extraordinary sensitivity:

> One day I didn't know how to handle them, and I sat on this table and told
> them about my life and what had happened with my friend [*who had died*] and
> why I was motivated to do this work and what I felt at that moment, trying
> to lead them. And that they could educate other people. I think that's when
> things changed and that they felt they could somehow save lives, even just
> with words. And it was very moving because at the next meeting people had
> changed.

According to those involved, the gay-oriented peer education programs
bounced back and forth between Peru's Health Ministry and different NGOs
during the 1990s with a variety of groups marshaling educators and often
nongay collaborators to hit the streets and track down some of the most vulnerable residents of Peru's cities. Their tales are often inspiring: how they got over
their fears and prejudices, began to appreciate the unexpected depth and values
of diverse, often despised, people, or how their projects sensitized them to a
myriad of unsuspected dramas.

Outreach to street hustlers, transvestite sex workers and unemployed gay
youngsters in the outlying shantytowns often has been systematic in Lima, part
of large, peer-educator programs that have rotated from the Health Ministry to
the NGOs and back again, according to the exigencies of national politics,
NGO capacities, or the current state of intersectoral alliances. At least some of
this admirable work is surely constructed on these early experiences, along with
the lessons pouring in from around the world.

However, the combination of ideologically inspired activism and grassroots
empowerment is not so readily apparent in the later, more broadly based projects. Julio Chamochumbi told me about his participation in several of them
couched in technical language reflecting the takeover of the early activism by
social scientists, giving it a sharp epidemiological flavor and the impression that
the construction of research cohorts had become the top priority:

> We worked in a MSM institution, which means "men who have sex with
> other men." This was through the Health Ministry; we began in 1994 with

testing for STDs and HIV/AIDS. Then, we formed a group called ALASKA. This group was made up of many MSM people, with different sexual roles, let's say transvestites, gays, queens, buses [*straight-acting homosexual men*]. No one in this group was infected. It was the same as the ministry project: the objective was to see when they would get infected or might get infected, right? In the cohort.

The early impulse toward a movement to create consciousness around sexual emancipation nudged AIDS education into the realm of sexual and human rights, which implied a strategy of community- and organization-building and the empowerment of the actors involved. Peer education as a methodology was not just an efficient means to disseminate information but a vehicle for building a critical mass within this marginalized population, a horizontal approach to consciousness-raising and mobilization. These goals are quite different from putting together a sample population for the purposes of observing who gets a disease and then drawing epidemiological conclusions.

Therefore, the same projects or activities that on the surface are indistinguishable will have quite different emphases depending on who is executing them and with what in mind. For example, early prevention campaigns quickly learned not to rely on fear or didactic messages, but to appeal to individuals' desires and dreams. Says Julio Gilvonio:

The only way to motivate a gay guy to change some behavior is to make him see that he's having the time of his life and that he should make sure it stays that way, not scaring him. So the happier you are, the less you want to give that up.

Implicitly, these campaigns aimed at people's sense that they had the right to be happy—a radical notion—as well as other, more defensive rights. According to Julio Chamochumbi:

People have had their eyes opened a lot, they've been told: You don't have to demand a special law. The law is for everyone. What you have to do is respect it, make them respect the law with you. And a lot of people have realized this, especially now with the HIV business and the law on HIV.

By contrast, just as the early protagonism of MHOL faded, the approach edged toward utilitarian ends, often of an epidemiological nature, especially when the Health Ministry was the source of funding. This is particularly noticeable in the current approach to HIV testing.

For many gay men in those early days, getting tested meant a response—any response—to the epidemic. Without fully questioning or appreciating what they expected to gain from the experience, many, like Aldo Araujo, hurried to get the test as soon as it became available.

> I did it just because I had read where it said: get the test, and then we decided we're going to do it. It was a slew of people, a fad. We're going to find out if we have it, if we're bad off.

Araujo's reaction is a common one; people are anxious to get tested, often with the idea of "making sure" they are free of HIV. In our discussions some peer educators continued to use the term *descarte* (meaning "discard" or "elimination") to refer to testing that they promoted, which suggests, quite correctly, that people unconsciously assume that their test result will be negative.

But in Peru, testing from the beginning was linked to cohort studies of sample groups of individuals whose health history could be followed over a period of years, thereby charting the progress of the epidemic within that population. As Araujo recalled:

> Because they had to know who was sick. Because the person who did it at that time wanted to do a study because they had to know how the disease was evolving.

Although statistical data on disease progression is very important to health authorities and can be used to formulate policy, all too often in the case of HIV/AIDS it has been collected for its own sake. Luis Miranda explains:

> The Health Ministry and an NGO put together a campaign for behavior change for AIDS prevention, and the job was to go out and get people. They recruited people from the [gay] scene who could act as a bridge between the

ministry and those who went to discotheques and so forth. And they passed out condoms and talked a little about this. But the final objective was to recruit these people and take them to the ministry's clinics so they could be tested, and if they were negative, to form a follow-up group with free medical care so that they could study AIDS prevention in this small group. In the case of the positive tests, they didn't offer them much help.

The U.S. Naval Medical Research Institute Detachment (NAMRID), affiliated to the U.S. Navy, had offered to test people for HIV before any alternatives existed in the country. MHOL was the contact point and provided access to the test for its clients. But the foreign navy was hardly focused on the well-being of those who turned up HIV-positive.

Another indication of the displacement of the social movement by a sort of clinical sociology is the creeping elimination of the word *gay* in the AIDS field in favor of the epidemiological neologism, "men who have sex with men," or MSM (HSH in Spanish). This term was invented in an attempt to include the broad homoerotic behaviors that were not adequately covered by the identity-based term *gay* because, researchers rightly argued, plenty of men engaging in homosexual relations around the world do not see themselves as "gay" at all, or bisexual for that matter, especially if they are playing the "male" or insertive role sexually.

However, plenty of individual men from Singapore to Dar-es-Salaam and virtually all those actively dealing with HIV in homosexual circles very much do think of themselves as gay. Though behaviors may be important for statistics, they do not per se generate mobilization; these come from perceived shared needs, which sometimes give rise to shared identities. Replacing the term *gay* with *MSM* depoliticizes AIDS education while pretending to be more inclusive. It suggests that individual behaviors, not identities and certainly not social movements, are the key, in fact the only, issue.

With this constant pressure to remedicalize, even those organizations based by definition on gay identity become epidemiological agglomerates. Chamochumbi says:

Those of us who work with organizations, there are a lot that work with MSM. For example, we have the Pride Day, everyone gets together, mostly those of us in institutions who work in the same thing, we all know each other.

Over and over throughout my interviews with peer educators, it became clear that although they often had deep, personal motivations for carrying the prevention message into their communities and supporting their peers, institutionally they existed primarily to channel people into the testing services. According to peer educator Juan Carlos Mora:

> You have to contact people, talk about prevention and all that. We haven't gone into the field yet, but it's the work we're going to do, encourage people to make sure they're not infected, that they come back to the clinic every so often to make sure they haven't acquired it, and that they are careful in their sexual lives.

The push to test is so hegemonic that some peer educators complained that they did not know what to offer people who turned up with a positive result. Alfonso Lescanso explains:

> There was supposed to be a system of services for people with HIV, but the promoters didn't know. It wasn't even in the protocol. What happens if my promoters, at some point, saw that these people that they educated and took to do the test came out HIV-positive? What happened with them? A lot of the promoters who hadn't had contact with people felt, uh, now what?

Chamochumbi had similar misgivings:

> We don't do anything for people who are already infected. There are a lot in the hospitals abandoned completely by their families and friends, and it's a shame. They don't send them home because they have no place to go. And it's not just one case, there are a ton of them, and you go to those places, and everyone calls over to you and says, Hey, come here, come here.

Dr. Carlos Cáceres, a public health specialist at Lima's Cayetano Heredia University, confirms that in the early years, "virtually nothing was done about treatment, as if they assumed that in Peru treatment wouldn't happen." Instead, says Cáceres, "a good part of the funds went to building the research infrastructure, to put together a cohort or participate in vaccine tests." That was no doubt a worthy project but useless to those encouraged and pressured to find out if they had acquired HIV infection.

Needless to say, testing for HIV is not just, or even principally, a clinical procedure, and the meaning of the exam always will be quite different to health services and to the human beings undergoing it. The testing moment is critical for anyone engaged in behavior that puts them at risk for the infection and therefore a critical component of any coherent prevention strategy. Health systems operate under a different logic, that of finding out who is sick and treating them. But as a cognitive moment, a chance to reexamine what might be the eventual consequences of one's habits and to weigh the costs and benefits of continuing or modifying them, there is nothing quite like that week between the time one's blood is drawn and the appointment to get the results in an envelope. Not only can this opportunity easily be lost when testing services forget that they are dealing with people and their sexual and emotional experiences, but the experience can become a nightmare if handled badly, as peer educator Chamochumbi learned the hard way.

> That was a terrible week while I waited for the results. I had to take pills to sleep at night. A funny thing was that the counselor that afternoon spoke to me for more than half an hour without telling me my results, and I was ready to kill her. She said, Julio, you know what I told you the first time about if you're positive? And that if your first test is positive, that doesn't mean you're a carrier? And I said to myself, Uy! What's going on?! What's going on?! Then she said my test was negative. I talked about it with her later many times, and she said that was the counseling.

No doubt counseling has improved greatly since this extraordinary incident. But by the early 2000s, many if not most of Peru's gay peer educators existed in order to guarantee a steady flow of subjects for HIV testing as part of research cohorts. Furthermore, one longtime peer educator blithely told me that he continues to use HIV testing as his prevention strategy, getting tested "every three or four months," which presumably would be unnecessary if his own sexual practices remained within the guidelines he is promoting. If many of their clients do the same, *rather* than sticking to safe sex, obviously their training has not steered them to a more consistent course. But these subtleties seem not terribly pressing to the peer education scene among Lima's gays, encouraged on all sides to test, test, test.

At one stage, the government instituted a novel and admirable "host" function, in which gay peer educators were paid to receive and orient those coming for testing right in the STD clinics. For a time, Chamochumbi worked as a guide in an STD clinic, paid by the Health Ministry itself. He says:

People from the [*gay*] scene have always been marginalized. When you went to a clinic, they would see that you were homosexual and not treat you, saying that you were a *sidoso* [*AIDS-infected*]. . . . So we, the hosts in the different health centers, we would concentrate on that, to change the staff's way of thinking, from the head doctor to the guard at the door. At least in my health center I achieved it.

Brazil has installed similar care monitors and guides in its primary care facilities handling HIV. But unlike the Brazilian case, Peru's "hosts" did not arise out of a consolidated advocacy movement but were dependent on project funding and the entire context of test-promotion; by December 2000, the peer counselors were disappearing from the clinics, and things were back to normal.

Not accidentally, it appears that Lima's in-house STD guides, for all their sympathy with the users, were not mere patient advocates but part of the testing machinery. As one explained:

They can contact guys in the gay scene, they take them to the health centers, and we there talk to them and tell them why they're there, and the majority agree to get the test.

In a few cases those aware of the implications of this pro-testing bias were willing to suggest its dubious ethics in at least some instances. In the words of Carlos Cáceres:

> In reality there was a lot of doubt about the ethical criteria to obtain informed consent, criticisms in relation to what would be done with the people whose test came out positive because there was no support structure for them. They did the test to find out the incidence rate, a big sample with two types of screens, which will show those more recently infected with fewer antibodies. So it's a very interesting test technologically which enables you to determine things that couldn't be determined before.

To meet with the gay/MSM peer educators in Villa Salvador, one of the *pueblos jóvenes* (poor suburbs) that have mushroomed around the capital city in recent decades, my guide and I took a collective taxi from downtown Lima and sped along a freeway for nearly an hour. Once off the main entrance road, the community is entirely self-contained and isolated from Lima, rather than a "suburb." Villa Salvador even has its own internal taxi system, comprised of tiny, three-wheeled enclosed carts built onto motorbikes, costing one sol, or about 30 cents. In these vast shantytowns live many of Lima's millions pulled into the orbit of the capital city during the great rural-urban migrations of recent decades. Poverty and unemployment are endemic; as we drove by, idle men stood in a circle around two others duking it out while unconcerned teenage girls pushed their baby carriages along the dirt alleys.

We found the group of eight fellows meeting in a schoolroom and organizing their activities. All openly gay men, one a gender-bent hairdresser named Fabiola, they described their ongoing, patient outreach work with gays, hustlers and the many straight-identified local men who will engage in homosexual relations. Inevitably, they insisted that going for the test was central to their health promotion activities. Fabiola seemed dignified and strengthened by her role as a recognized peer educator and was undoubtedly very good at it.

In all fairness, the drawbacks of pushing the test must be balanced against the unlikelihood that their peers would receive HIV education in any other way. But once cohorts are built, much of the work involved in this variety of peer education slips into a sort of holding action, of keeping people involved in the cohort, rather than organizing them for political or social action.

Chamochumbi explains:

> We had to work Fridays and Saturdays and Sundays. A lot of times we had
> to work with the cohort, in trips and workshops. Keeping them together is
> pretty hard.

Of course, with priorities placed on maintaining the steady flow of testing
subjects for a research cohort, the vagaries of project-driven funding and
on-again, off-again educational initiatives will leave some participants by the
wayside. Says Lescanso:

> Víctor was a transvestite who didn't talk much in the meetings, she was very
> shy. She confessed that she was a sex worker but was ashamed to say so until
> finally she decided to tell the group. People reacted very well. On her own,
> she made the decision to stop working in commercial sex. She said she
> didn't want to do that anymore, that she felt she could help many
> people and that being a peer educator had changed her life. . . . But when
> [the project] shifted to the ministry, Víctor went back to the sex trade.

The questionable emphasis on testing among peer education projects in Peru has
not escaped the notice of the other NGOs involved. A few activists are willing
to level a direct criticism of the approach promoted both within the ministry
and sometimes through the NGOs themselves. Says psychologist Ana María
Rosasco:

> It's directly related with the university in the United States, the work being
> done there, which is certainly very respectable, but it does respond to those
> interests, and I think the social component of the project was left out, every-
> thing to do with the construction of an organization within the gay com-
> munity or with the people who are drawn into the project, empowerment.

Some critics go so far as to suggest that in Peru, research historically was not
utilized to further prevention; rather, the entire prevention apparatus existed to
further research. But would any prevention have taken place at all without the

impetus of a research agenda? The personification of this ambiguous dynamic is Dr. Jorge Sánchez, the doctor who ran the Peruvian AIDS program for six years under Fujimori. Even his critics agree that Sánchez was instrumental in pushing prevention and services for gay men at a time when other countries could not or would not devote resources to them. At the time of our interview, Sánchez was associated with the University of Washington and the Fred Hutchinson Cancer Research Center in Seattle. With his U.S. colleagues, he has created a joint, Lima-based HIV Prevention and Vaccine Trials Network known as IMPACTA to conduct "both vaccine and behavioral intervention studies" among gay and homosexually active men.

From the offices of his new NGO in Miraflores, Sánchez dismissed his critics with considerable disdain. The government's AIDS budget, he says proudly, was $600,000 a year when he took over; when he left, it was $6 million, the second-highest priority in the health portfolio. Although we only had a few minutes before he was to catch a plane to the United States, I could almost write his defense of the cohort projects before he offered them: that through these activities, thousands of people in Lima, gay and straight, learned about HIV and AIDS. Otherwise they would not have. If useful research emerged as a result, all the better.

A parallel argument no doubt emerged when VIALIBRE established its own clinical service to respond to the HIV epidemic. VIALIBRE's move into the provision of medical services could have been criticized as "substituting" private resources for what should be a public responsibility. But without these substitute services, of course, the beneficiaries would have had little or none at all. Today VIALIBRE has an efficient, multifaceted program that has worked hard to put itself on a solid financial footing and maintain its political independence. The combination of prevention and clinical activities made overwhelming sense from the beginning in Peru. Given the vacuum created by an unpredictable, often weak central government, strategies to fill in the gaps always would face similar dilemmas.

Many people were pushed into HIV testing in Peru while the country could not provide adequate medical services, much less antiretroviral therapy to keep people alive. Access is now improving, but if the organizations had been quicker, stronger, or more united, might not the history of AIDS prevention and care been different? What had weakened the social monitoring role of the NGOs that had pioneered services and invented methodologies?

One rather obvious response is that the NGOs lost their autonomy and were gradually absorbed by the government and molded to its utilitarian ends. Carlos Cáceres, a longtime observer, bluntly says:

> I think the NGO movement has been very, very weak and was totally co-opted by the Health Ministry because it didn't develop any other type of leadership.

Others paint the government takeover as a mixed bag: good for the public responsibility the takeover implied, good for the greater reach of government-based programs, but bad for the way the programs themselves changed as a result. In the words of Pablo Anamaría:

> The problem is that as the NGOs have become employees of the state. It's not that [*the state*] absorbs these ideas as its own and consciously acquires the political will to respond. It contracts the NGOs to keep doing what they have been doing for years. But if you look closely, it's the NGOs working for the state, not that the state has understood or committed itself.

This subsidiarity logically plays out in a certain loss of critical independence, as Jorge Bracamonte explains:

> Here's an example: A couple of years ago the Health Ministry called for bids for a purchase of medicines. However, two weeks later they changed their minds and decided to redirect these funds to other programs . . . so the medicines weren't purchased, the bid was shelved, and the organizations didn't say anything.

But if the organizations are weak or too easily tamed, how did this situation develop? Did they lose their critical edge or never have a chance to develop one? Did they fail to join forces in their dealings with the government? Couldn't the international funds that flowed into Peru in substantial amounts have strengthened them more?

According to Bracamonte, a partial answer is that the social turmoil, the violence and the scythe of AIDS itself broke the continuity between the founding generations and later ones, leaving only the testing-oriented and utilitarian practices described earlier. He implies that the autonomous AIDS movement was unable to resist subtle absorption by the state because the early lessons were not passed on and because too many of the key veterans simply did not survive.

He identifies three waves of activists: the founders of MHOL; his own, buffeted by repression, dictatorship and disillusion; and the current leadership, in a sense reinventing the wheel:

> I think the gay movement in Peru is paying the bill for AIDS. The founding generation has practically disappeared. There is no political reflection or continuity within the movement. The links which existed with peers in the northern hemisphere are gone. It's incredible, but movements like MHOL today are more parochial than they were at the beginning.

Thus, the situation is thus ripe for a pragmatic, task-based approach to AIDS in which the underlying strategic, policy or even ethical considerations are obscure. He continues:

> Everyone gets involved in prevention work and forgets reflection and criticism . . . so what's lost is an affirmative political discourse that defends pleasure and all the rest, related to human rights. The activism does not have a clear, strategic point of reference.

The political dimensions of AIDS, the reduction of stigma, advocacy for people with HIV, everything connected to building communities or strengthening the social fabric would not enter naturally into the logic of the state apparatus. If the social movement was incapable of adding these elements, they were unlikely to be included.

Despite the farsighted and theoretically rich work by many early activists, much of the nongovernmental prevention efforts around HIV in Peru quickly were grafted onto official policy and programs. Although the massive expansion of prevention initiatives is certainly a positive outcome, their pronounced bias as test-recruitment vehicles stirs legitimate doubts about the efficacy of this training. Remarkably few critics lament the extent of the subordination of prevention education among gays, transvestites and sex workers to the vagaries of the state or the role of epidemiological and vaccine-related research. Logically, people testing positive for HIV or the organizations that represent them would be those most likely to question the testing protocols. But these individuals are understandably much more concerned with how to access modern drug therapies than with questioning why they were pushed to get tested in the first place. Meanwhile, testing-oriented prevention efforts may well continue to flourish among vulnerable populations of Lima and other major cities, providing needed education to those lucky enough to escape HIV infection while—until very recently—offering little more than sympathy to those who are not.

Indignation and disgust with the dysfunctional state is nothing new in Peru, and in 2004 President Alejandro Toledo's approval ratings were down to a single digit. Despite the determination of its activists, their skill at preserving their institutions under enormous difficulties and the many lessons learned, only the prospect of a major infusion of cash from the Global Fund enabled the country to aspire to distribute the life-saving therapies beyond the 10 to 20 percent who had obtained them around the time of my initial visit, often by buying the drugs themselves. Poverty would have condemned the rest to poor health and premature death.

Fame

O nce we got a call from one of the big insurance companies. They would send their medical tests to the United States, and one came back with an HIV-positive result. They wanted to know how to say to a person that he had HIV and that the company couldn't insure him. We tried to give them some guidance by telephone, to turn them into counselors in two minutes.

They asked if the individual could come to our offices and then a half hour later called again to say that the client was absolutely out of control and that they had to come right over, that minute. A woman said to me, "I don't know what to do. I'm afraid he's going to kill himself."

The man was thirty-two years old and had an important job. He had a completely glazed expression on his face. His first words were "Ma'am, I don't know who you are, but I want you to know that I am not a *maricón* (faggot)." I said, okay. He went on: "They say they can't insure me, that I have HIV, I have AIDS. But I am not a *maricón!*"

He began to relate his life story and repeat it over and over: I'm married and separated, and I have a girlfriend. I sleep with my ex-wife, with my girlfriend, and with another woman. What do I do? Do I have to tell them all?

I just told him not to make any decisions at that moment, that it didn't mean he was going to die, that he was going to keep on living—all the techniques we've used for years. But he was unreachable. It was impossible to penetrate his despair. The toughest cases in counseling for HIV, normally they calm down in an hour, but this one lasted almost four. And he left pretty much as he had showed up, crying but with no tears. It was very sad and very dramatic. My only satisfaction is that I convinced him not to talk to anyone when he left and not to take any action.

We didn't ever hear from him again, but he is a very public figure here. Sometimes I see him on television, and I have to go into the next room even though I live alone because it makes me enormously sad.

—Elena Droguett
Former Coordinator of Direct Services
for People with HIV

CHAPTER TWO

Mexico: Fatal Advances

MEXICO	
Population	102 million
First reported case of AIDS	1984
Total estimated HIV infections	160,000
Male : female ratio	5.3:1
Estimated number of people needing antiretroviral treatment	40,000
Number receiving drugs	29,000
Adult women using birth control	68%
Gross domestic product (GDP) 2003	$626.1 billion
Per capita income (2003)	$6,230
Annual per-capita spending on health	$221
Official unemployment rate	3.0%
Estimated underemployment	25%
Mexican revolution	1910–1920
PRI rule begins	1929
Tlatelolco Plaza massacre	1968
Homosexual Front for Revolutionary Action stages First gay-rights march in Mexico City	1979
PRI rule ends with election of Vicente Fox	2000

A preexisting movement for gay emancipation did not pave the way for an effective response to AIDS.

Mexico City's main plaza, the Zócalo, is flanked by a huge Catholic cathedral just yards from the Aztec altar excavated in 1978, complete with the ceremonial stone for offering still-beating human hearts to the sun god. Around the corner is another vast church edifice officially belonging to a congregation but long since turned into an ad hoc community center where the usual ideological filters of the church hierarchy clearly do not apply. There a gay and lesbian cultural festival was in full swing one November evening, and a crowd had gathered in preparation for a performance act rumored to include some unusual tableaux vivants with animals. While a panel of lesbian authors, gay writers and assorted activists droned into a bad public address system, their remarks echoing unintelligibly off the massive stone walls, nine-tenths of the public paid only polite attention and pursued their private devotions, quite like the worshippers at the cathedral across the square long familiar with the outlines of the ceremony.

In a city of 20 million inhabitants, it is hardly surprising to find a hip, outré scene reminiscent of New York's East Village functioning amid the amused indifference of a society far too vast to notice it. But the similarities end with the air of audacious modernity. A knowledgeable observer says the new, glossy gay magazine cannot get any advertising; the Mexican breweries that do advertise in European gay periodicals will not touch it for fear of their male brand loyalists. Instead of prosperous and sophisticated gay and lesbian organizations and social services, the local AIDS-related groups are fragile outposts with limited coverage, permanently juggling foundation grants, government contracts and other fundraising schemes to survive. Their beneficiaries often have to be just as creative. The walled border crossings between San Diego and Tijuana or between Juárez and El Paso divide populations of Mexicans who, on one side, can get care and medicines from those on the other side who cannot.

Given the heavy influence of the United States on everything in Mexico, it would have been difficult to brush aside the early news emanating from the U.S. Centers for Disease Control and the major gay colonies to the north about "GRID" (gay-related immune disorder, the first name applied to what eventually became known as AIDS). But the proximity and the particularly sensitive nature of the relationship inevitably colored the way Mexicans absorbed that information. Where those uneasy about GRID in remoter parts of Latin America could dismiss the matter, Mexicans were forced into active forms of denial. Mauricio Ramos is a psychologist who works for Mexico City's main HIV clinic:

> I'm from Sonora, a little town near the border. In 1982 a friend and I went to Texas and Arizona, and we had heard something about the "pink cancer." We had just come out to each other. Then probably we ate something bad and got diarrhea, and we said, "Oh no, we have AIDS!" We were going to die! The next day we were fine.

A Harvard-trained epidemiologist and one of the first figures within the Mexican medical establishment to sound the alarm about HIV, Dr. José Antonio Izazola, says people refused to believe the bad news:

> I remember it perfectly well: [*The gay groups*] said AIDS doesn't exist. It's just an invention by Ronald Reagan to control our sexuality.

People around the world, but especially gay men, were warily noticing the trickle of reports about the mysterious new disease. But Mexicans, influenced or inspired by Stonewall, already had launched a gay-emancipation movement; they were coming together to discuss and debate and eventually merge into groups that were highly politicized and ideological. As a result, they were quick to decide that the phenomenon either was or was not real. Journalist Alejandro Brito, for example, recalls that the idea that AIDS was an invention of the CIA was popular.

Even in the United States many gay men promptly declared that the AIDS panic was a sham or a scam; how much easier for the Mexicans to decide that it was some sort of North American humbug. As Izazola says:

> Here in Mexico in 1985 the organized gay groups rejected the information about AIDS. I stopped working as a volunteer [*treating sexually transmitted diseases*] in LAMBDA, which was a homosexual liberation group, because

they said that AIDS was an invention by the reactionary right-wing. This reaction was very strong, extremely radical.

Reactions like these were heard in the United States as well and persisted well into the early 1980s. But gay America's plethora of organizations, periodicals and other institutions guaranteed that for every group that scoffed at the reports, another half-dozen were taking them seriously. The early skepticism probably increased the catastrophic levels of HIV infection that eventually occurred in San Francisco and other centers of the gay vanguard, but even there calmer heads eventually prevailed.

Curiously enough, many witnesses recollect that this suspicious reaction was less common outside of Mexico City where other gay-rights groups had formed such as in the border city of Tijuana, across from San Diego, and the conservative university town of Guadalajara in central Mexico, places that could only dream of having free, gay-oriented STD services like those in Mexico City. Both these provincial capitals spawned early movements that dealt with AIDS relatively quickly. According to discussions with locals in both cities, the AIDS-skeptic position did not strike any chords. But this ardent, albeit brief, reaction did mark the first reports about HIV/AIDS in Mexico City and seems to have had a considerable, long-term effect.

One explanation offered for the heavy ideological tone of AIDS skepticism in Mexico City is the crushing weight of Mexico's virtual one-party state, which was ruled for seven decades by the Institutional Revolutionary Party (PRI), an ossified system that would not crack until nearly twenty years after HIV infection arrived. Where social movements in Peru or Argentina might be more or less connected with or sympathetic to some mainstream political tendency, the PRI's corporatist domination of nongovernmental expression precluded such links, especially in the years after the 1968 Tlatelolco massacre.[1] In this view the impenetrability of the country's political culture affected the kind of gay movement that emerged and its radical, ultra-left bent. The movement described by

---

[1] On October 2, 1968, troops and plainclothes agents opened fire on a demonstration in Mexico City at Tlatelolco Three Cultures Plaza. Although there are no reliable figures, some three hundred people are supposed to have died, effectively crushing an effervescent student movement.

early participants was fully alienated from virtually everyone: the conservative PRI, of course, but also the traditional Marxist left and most gays themselves. As Brito recalls:

> We felt we were living in a revolutionary moment, part of a change. We are direct descendants of '68, the student movement, Stonewall, new possibilities of social involvement outside the political parties in Mexico.

Brito, the 40ish director of *Letra S*, a monthly supplement on AIDS and sexuality that appears in the newspaper *La Jornada*, explicitly links Mexico's congealed politics to the way the embryonic gay organizations absorbed and reacted to the news of AIDS in the 1980s. Miles from the centers of power and the possibility of influencing policy, the first gay groups, says Brito, reveled in being "marginal within the margins."

> We didn't have any chance of expressing or positioning ourselves, and marginality strongly affects people's psychology, the direction a movement takes, and there is a lot of scrapping. The salient feature is resentment towards society and humanity that displaces rationality, logic and the movement's own interests.

Brito, a measured, somewhat phlegmatic man of slight frame and careful demeanor, is broadly respected in the interlocking gay- and AIDS-activist circuits, itself a minor miracle and testament to his intuitive diplomatic skills. In describing the early period, he does not shrink from self-criticism. From a working-class family, Brito was a beneficiary of the PRI's decision to broaden access to higher education, "to keep the reserve army of unemployed busy longer," he says, echoing his early proximity to the Marxist left. Once in the highly politicized university setting, Brito was attracted to the Trotskyists' analysis of society, which included fully integrated gay sexual politics. He says:

> I was in one of the first groups, LAMBDA, in 1980. They were propagandistic groups more than anything, discussions about gay identity and how to proceed. As it was closely linked to socialism, to the left, they were also discussions about the revolution.

Into this fresh and provocative yet intellectually overheated environment, radical, even outlandish postures sprouted like spring buds. Conspiratorial views of the hostile society could make perfect sense. Brito continues:

> Our enemies were the bourgeois families. They had to be changed and destroyed. I remember a book that was very influential, called *Death of the Family*. It's a logic in which you feel yourself so revolutionary that social reality can be deduced by applying well-worn formulas.

Like, because of imperialism I can't find a boyfriend?

> Right.

Mexico's gay and lesbian movement was drawn to the left, says Brito, in part because it was "the only space open to us." He recognizes that the early ideas effectively guaranteed that the movement would have limited appeal.

> Almost as a requirement to come into the movement, you had to declare yourself a socialist and also a revolutionary, not just any socialist. I remember a discussion in one of the gay marches about whether to let in a group called "GRUPO W," who were middle-class guys with no left-wing connections. People said they were bourgeois conservatives. One of the slogans in the marches was "I'm a Trotskyist, I'm a lesbian, I'm a homosexual of the Fourth International!" (*Alejandro Brito*)

Small wonder that the news of a gay plague emerging in the United States would get short shrift. Izazola blames this phenomenon for what he calls the "Great Defeat" in which the epidemiological data of a homosexually transmitted epidemic were essentially ignored.

> The Great Defeat was not inflicted by the bureaucrats. It wasn't done by my homophobic boss who didn't want to accept this. It was the gay groups which refused to engage in prevention with their peers.

Not everyone goes along with this peremptory diagnosis. Some, like Jorge Huerdo, a leader among people living with HIV who died in 2002, believed that gay politics made no difference and were irrelevant once the epidemic took root. Huerdo said:

> I think that what happened with the gay movement in Mexico was that AIDS grabbed us by surprise. So the agenda of the fight for gay and lesbian rights had to be postponed because there was an emergency, people were dying. The main leaders of the gay movement became infected with HIV/AIDS, and the heads of the movement began to die.

By contrast, others, including some who were among the HIV skeptics, claim that the organizational experience, bizarre as it was on some levels, enabled those slowly waking up to AIDS to consolidate into organizations quickly and efficiently. Juan Jacobo Hernández helped formed one of the first AIDS-related organizations, Colectivo Sol (Sun Collective), and was instrumental in the construction of a Latin America-wide network of AIDS NGOs. He says:

> We were connected, we had an idea of how to mobilize, how to be activists and that sort of thing. I think that here in Mexico without the previous gay movement, the response would have taken five more years, definitely.

By contrast, those closer to the service-oriented, rather than political, aspects of the epidemic tend to dismiss the seeds planted by the gay-Marxist brigades. Rodolfo Ruiz of the Guadalajara AIDS services group CHECCOS (Humanitarian Committee for Joint Efforts against AIDS) says that with or without them, things would have occurred pretty much the same:

> I don't think it had any impact at all. Guadalajara is a very conservative city with a large number of gays in which everything happens underground. So then AIDS came along to show how many gay and bisexual people there are.

Still others contend that the early rejection of AIDS by the gay skeptics could have been more damaging but that the long-term impact was negligible because of the impact of the disease. According to Brito:

> Reality reasserted itself. [*The rejection*] didn't last long and was never
> hegemonic. There were rumors, but no one defended it as a thesis because
> the reality of your friends starting to get sick was much more palpable.

Even so, Brito concurs that the earlier gay-liberation experiences did not really pave the way for an effective response to AIDS, the sort of relatively smooth transition seen elsewhere in the region in which participants would merely shift ground and take up new projects from their already consolidated organizational base. A few individuals were still around who recalled the radical days, says Brito. But:

> Unfortunately, the gay movement went into crisis even before AIDS made
> its first appearance in Mexico in 1983. It officially blew apart in 1984 in one
> of the marches where people almost came to blows.

Despite these varying opinions on the influence of Mexico's minuscule gay liberation efforts on AIDS prevention, drug access advocacy or the other issues of the Mexican epidemic, no interviewee suggested one possibility that is implicit in some of the analyses: that the early gay groups actually made things worse.

Sooner or later throughout Latin America, almost everyone involved in AIDS, even recalcitrant governments, recognized that the two issues of homosexuality and AIDS prevention were linked. Eventually it became clear that "peer educators," gay men themselves, had to carry the ball on the issue, to convince their friends by many subtle and clever means to take precautions and to set aside their own prejudices about people with HIV.

But the fairly broad consensus seen today was not easily or automatically reached and certainly not with the required dispatch. The learning curve, although varying widely from country to country, was painfully slow. Meanwhile, AIDS was not a mere technical puzzle that experts and policy makers finally "got" but rather a life-and-death issue for many thousands of people.

The delays and errors were devastating; a similar situation can be seen today in Asia, where political and community leaders turned a blind eye during the crucial first years.

Political, as distinct from individual, denial plagued the AIDS crisis from its outset, as chronicled in the United States by Randy Shilts's account, *And the Band Played On*. The title itself hints at Shilts's thesis that the lackadaisical reaction to AIDS was a cultural response, a sharp contrast to the panicky efforts to solve Legionnaire's disease, and that it had everything to do with which individuals were being stricken with the disease: not war heroes like with Legionnaire's but marginalized groups such as heroin users and homosexuals, both favored punching bags of the Reaganites eager to please the Republican party's radical Christian base or crime-conscious middle America. In Latin America and the Caribbean, unenlightened macho values predominated, and gays were not organized or strong enough even to complain.

As a result, says Dr. Izazola, statistical data was expertly gathered and then roundly ignored. He says:

> I believe we are incapable of utilizing the information and the data that we collect, to understand the process we are undergoing. What has been lacking is intelligence, in the sense of the English term, to be able to pull together the *facts* and convert them into *information*.

Izazola recalls the disastrous popularizing of the "risk group" categories—gays, Haitians, junkies—a counterproductive borrowing from medical science that further stigmatized the accused groups. Following the contemporary wisdom about AIDS dating from the 1980s, he argues that whole segments of the population cannot and should not be labeled "risky," especially if they are already in danger of segregation or harm.

But, Izazola adds, the reaction to this reaction was, well, reactionary. Risk differentials, after all, are real. Certain people are at more risk for heart attack, accidents, sickle-cell anemia or other health problems than others. By ditching the "risk groups" handle completely, many people lost sight of an important epidemiological fact: that certain groups of human beings were very much more "at risk" for AIDS, more vulnerable, more endangered, more exposed, than others.

And the facile elimination of any distinction among the entire population in the new wave of AIDS slogans such as "Everyone's problem" or "Ignorance is the Worst Risk" simply ignores extremely relevant facts. One need not condemn or stigmatize women in prostitution to recognize that their activities carry special risks not shared by the rest of the population.

Fed by the yellow press, historical prejudice and professional sloppiness, Mexican public opinion—in a process repeated to a greater or lesser degree around the world—quickly transited from the concept of groups "at risk" to the idea of "risky groups," people who were inherently dangerous and perhaps ought to be segregated, if not boarded onto ships and sunk far at sea. Such thinking naturally appealed to uneasy citizens who did not particularly care to alter their own sexual practices but felt safer seeing strip joints and gay nightclubs raided and their supposedly risk-laden patrons dealt with. When this approach proved useless, as well as outrageous and discriminatory, the reaction created a new falsehood. Izazola explains:

> "We're all at risk"—that's a fallacy. Or, "Ignorance is risk behavior." So those who had to get the information first, those who were getting infected, were abandoned. I'm talking about the 1980s, but some things remain true in the 2000s.

Guadalajara, Mexico's second-largest city, is home to six universities and famed for its Catholic traditionalism. Despite this notoriety, the city also produced one of Mexico's most audacious and ultimately successful gay-rights movements, just as its state government fell to the conservative opposition National Action Party (PAN) a few years before the 2000 election of PAN's presidential candidate, Vicente Fox.

But although Guadalajara may be straitlaced and conservative, it also celebrates learning and culture with unusual vigor and panache. One of its downtown plazas is dedicated to its "Illustrious Sons" (esclarecidos, literally "enlightened") and is ringed by an extraordinary row of statues of its favorite intellectuals, including not only the usual generals and politicians, but also a historian, several writers and musicians, even an anthropologist, including Agustín de la Rosa, called a "wise man and benefactor," and José Zumo, "teacher, painter, writer and humanist thinker." There are also a couple of favorite daughters. Any city that could celebrate the liberal arts so enthusiastically should be given a chance to explain itself.

Pedro Preciado is a stocky, tallish man with a goatee and mustache. Although locals said he would be unavailable for interviews, that he didn't talk about the old days, Preciado showed up in sweat pants and an open-necked black shirt for a long, nostalgic talk in the bar of a comfortable, colonial-style, downtown hotel. Indeed, he seemed eager to recall his early activist years and began his answers with a lengthy preamble. He described gay life in hidebound Guadalajara twenty years before when he struggled to emerge from the closet in a traditional, Jesuit-educated family with a lawyer father and a pianist mother. His narrative reflects a fascination with the self-awareness process entirely fitting for a gay-lib pioneer.

> The first information I remember getting about homosexuality was in the library of my house, in an encyclopedia to be exact. I knew it was abominable, I knew it was horrendous, nefarious and of course I developed all the guilt associated with these ideas. I still retain a lot of traits from my years of obscurantism and self-repression, the existential anxieties, some fears, some phobias—anyway, there's a lot to explore there.

Out of this sociocultural hothouse emerged one of the best-known gay emancipation groups in the country, the Grupo Homosexual de Orgullo y Liberación (Homosexual Pride and Liberation Group, GHOL). But despite Preciado's central role, GHOL did not emerge from the educated, prosperous middle class but precisely the contrary. As his narrative makes clear, GHOL's first members were "street queens," scarcely adolescent kids who were living their sexual politics in the city's rough, seedy bars and downtown parks because they had nowhere else to go. Preciado explains:

> We were all adolescents; I was the oldest. The average age was something like sixteen or seventeen. Naturally, we were very excitable and very much chatterboxes and hyperactive, and the feeling that we were young, liberated, or in a process of liberation, that made the group very fun-loving, with lots of sex.

Preciado himself, an anomaly to be sure, had entered into this unusual ambiance through his own intensely personal drama.

> In my first forays I realized that on the street there were certain looks, certain "glances that stir panic." That's how I met someone, Jorge Romero Mendoza, who was my partner, the love of my life, the man I loved. I was twenty, and he was about fourteen, but he looked older. When I met Jorge, I finally was able to have sex normally. He used to hang around downtown and had been in jail several times for being gay, at the age of fourteen.

Preciado, the middle-class schoolteacher, tempting his own future and his social and family situation with his furtive sorties and dangerous glances, suddenly found himself amid an unimagined reality of impoverished, sometimes abandoned gay boys, surviving and on the lookout for pleasure and romance. He was utterly captivated. He says:

> To have met Jorge, coming from a very poor, dysfunctional family, with a mother who washed clothes to support him—well, that world fascinated me. I fell in love with him, with his body, and with his world too, and the two of us eventually went to live together. From the standpoint of living a gay life, of living homosexuality fully, to cruise, to break your own taboos, to break your own chains, they were beautiful years.

In Preciado's narrative emerges an unmistakable association between the simultaneous crossing of two social barriers, the break with two taboos: sex and social class. His family, getting wind of his activities, promptly suggested that he change his name. But the problems he and his group faced had nothing to do with whether the American Central Intelligence Agency might be engaged in a germ warfare plot against homosexuals, as their peers in the capital were debating, but rather how to turn a frolicsome and uproarious assemblage of marginalized homosexual teenagers into a political organization. What is remarkable is that they managed to do precisely that.

One of their first public events, a rally in defense of gays and lesbians, stunned some Guadalajara residents into a grudging realization that they might just have a point. Preciado says:

> There was music, speeches, a lot of information. I think that for the first time some reporters with a more humanitarian sensibility and many officials were enormously surprised. . . . Some of the coverage began to change its tone.

Once the door had been forced open, the terms of debate and discussion would never quite be the same. When work related to HIV/AIDS became an urgent necessity, homosexually active men could be considered not only citizen-subjects with rights to their sexual autonomy and privacy, but even protagonists of the work itself. But as is so often the case in these AIDS memories, the results came at a cost. Except for Preciado himself, not one of the original founders of GHOL remains alive.

Despite being PAN country and therefore theoretically closer to official Catholic rigidity on matters of sexual health and AIDS prevention, Jalisco, the state of which Guadalajara is the capital, has one of the best AIDS programs in the country. On this point, opinion is virtually unanimous. Since 1995 Dr. Patricia Campos has headed the program, which is housed in a modern white building in a ministry compound in the Zapopán suburb. Her civil service staff is more cordial and relaxed than their counterparts in the hectic megalopolis. Inside a glass booth sits the ISAVEC Voice and Data Intelligence System, an automated database for epidemiological tracking. Boxes in the hallway are marked "Street Brigade," a name used for the outreach workers who deal with women from the commercial sex business.

The mild-mannered doctor in her late thirties wore a sundress with a deep décolletage, a gold cross on a chain and tiny, gold, sunburst earrings. Unlike many AIDS officials, who are assigned the post during their public service careers, Campos was drawn to the personal dramas of her patients and the need for a coherent policy response as a medical student. She recalls:

> My first contact with a person with HIV was in the emergency room. I was very fearful because I didn't know what to do. I had all the myths, just like

everyone else. However, it was clear even then, in 1987, that all the emergency room personnel rejected him.

Later Campos wrote her thesis on HIV seroprevalence among sex workers and as a result ended up educating these clandestine women. Struck by her own lack of training or familiarity with HIV in medical school, Campos pursued a master's degree in public health. "Even with the epidemic picking up steam," she recalls, "we never heard the word AIDS mentioned once the whole time."

> I graduated in 1987, it wasn't so new by then. In all those years we didn't hear it mentioned at the University of Guadalajara, which graduates three hundred students every six months. The doctors of my generation didn't have a clue.

In the early 1990s Campos became interested in the budget and methods being employed by the state AIDS program and how they compared to the work of the nongovernmental sector. The official work followed traditional ideas of public health education, such as talks by staff to schoolchildren. "A waste of time," Campos says categorically. By contrast, community groups were more innovative, she explains:

> The NGOs already were more advanced in terms of prevention, developing specific materials for the gay community or women or parents. The NGOs were more efficient in their work with fewer resources.

Campos sent her study and its results to the new provincial government, where the opposition PAN had just broken the PRI monolith. She outlined four main recommendations: restructure the AIDS council that set policy; decentralize activities to reach the entire state of Jalisco; incorporate non-health-related sectors in the work; and put more resources into prevention.

To Campos's astonishment, the incoming authorities took her report seriously.

> Two months after taking office, the new governor and the health secretary got in touch with us and told us that they thought the proposal was excellent,

that AIDS was a major challenge and that the new government wanted to work on it and that with all this information available, it seemed to them that we were the best people to put it into practice.

In the succeeding years the state's AIDS budget rose by 1,300 percent; the government AIDS council expanded from fourteen to forty-two permanent members, including officials from outside the health sector and, for the first time, nongovernmental representatives. Today the council revises all aspects of government policy on AIDS in Jalisco, including spending decisions, and 20 percent of its funds are reserved for NGO use.

Although not all clinicians are moved by their patients in the same way, Campos's experience in treating people for HIV/AIDS clearly affected her.

I still see [patients] as their physician. I think it's something I will never stop doing because it enables you to keep your feet on the ground, it's a permanent education. It's so important to learn how to live the here and now, to know that this may be our last day and that death can arrive for some before others.

In all my discussions and interviews about AIDS in Latin America, I found no other cases in which an incoming government called on representatives of the organized NGO sector and told them to take over. In Mexico's Jalisco state, deep in the traditional heartland of militant Catholicism, a right-of-center political party did just that.

In Mexico City, meanwhile, the spread of HIV infection had quickly neutralized the doubters and propelled some of them into AIDS work. Organizations began to consolidate to address the epidemic, and Mexico gained early points with international donors when its government set up a national AIDS program and began to articulate an official response. Only Brazil moved more quickly, and there the first government programs were regional, based in São Paulo, rather than nationwide.

José Antonio Izazola, contracted by the health ministry in 1985, labored to convince top decision makers to pay attention to the new epidemic, starting with small research projects and eventually pushing for a more permanent program. "In Mexico the international money began to flow early on," he recalled. "You wrote three pages and got $50,000."

The World Health Organization and its regional counterpart, the Pan American Health Organization, as well as other major donors were eager to find governments taking AIDS seriously enough to form part of a multisectoral strategy to slow its spread. Citizen activism, although very welcome, was not enough: to generate a broad impact, governments had to drive the national response. The presence of the Mexican government, said Izazola, "completed the circle."

Nonetheless, convincing the government to take AIDS seriously was no easy task, especially because of the identity of the main sufferers and authorities' disinclination to dedicate time and money to gays. Izazola says:

> It's a rigid, macho structure, but that's the challenge. The basic problem is
> how to make sure the [*epidemiological*] data aren't thrown out the window.

For international funders, another important element was the formation of alliances among the diverse nonprofit groups and social movements that were starting to recognize the need for action. In some countries this coalescence began to occur naturally; in Mexico the donor agencies got ahead of the process and pushed for a broad-based coalition, which eventually became Mexicans against AIDS, headed by gay activist Arturo Díaz.

Díaz, a portly, jovial figure who was elected as an openly gay alternate deputy to the Mexico City provincial legislature (the titular deputy is an open lesbian), was not available for an interview, but he clearly has had a controversial history in Mexico's gay and AIDS politics. Although he did not really have an organizational base when Mexicans against AIDS was formed, Díaz soon came to lead the coalition and wielded considerable authority over the funds to be distributed among its members. As his former secretary, Anuar Luna, recalls, "There was a whole entity, a council, but most of the decisions were made by Arturo."

The formula was ready-made for catastrophe. Without clear guidelines for awarding the all-important resources, conflict and suspicion were guaranteed.

Ninel Díaz (no relation to Arturo) works for Ave de México, a prevention and service-oriented group to which she was drawn through her gay friends, some of whom became infected and fell ill. An energetic, frank activist popular among her peers, Ninel Díaz said her organization entered Mexicans against AIDS optimistic about the possibilities of joint efforts and coordination.

> We sent several projects to be financed, and who knows if Ave's were misplaced or got lost or what, but they didn't get in. Yes, that's exactly it, they weren't presented. So there was a big fight because people think it's some sort of scam. In fact, there are still papers floating around out there about it all.

Luna, who had reached Mexicans against AIDS after being fired from his secretarial job with the state oil monopoly, Pemex, for being HIV-positive, concluded that the groups were far too immature for the ambitious role the network was supposed to play. He says:

> I think that an NGO which is starting out, which doesn't have much experience, cannot be giving out money to other organizations and less so if there isn't a favorable atmosphere for assigning funds.

Meanwhile, from Izazola's perspective, Mexicans against AIDS suffered from a knee-jerk, critical posture in which anything emerging from the Mexican government was completely useless almost by definition. He recalls:

> They used all their resources with the aim of outshining the government, to show that the government "does nothing about AIDS." It was black and white. The truth is that there were gaps, but it wasn't true that nothing was done. So the second part was: the only ones who know how to do things right are we NGOs. That destroyed any chance of communication. It was a divorce.

Such comments echo the sorts of facile automarginalization that would be natural to many Mexicans after seven decades of bureaucratic rule by an unresponsive, PRI-dominated state, which Peruvian writer Mario Vargas Llosa once famously called "the perfect dictatorship." Luna, who witnessed the entire period from inside Mexicans against AIDS, agrees that the activists' attitudes were one-sided:

> There was political debate, yes, directed externally, a bit like Mexican politics, a good level of criticism of what is wrong, but inwardly it was very blind. Maybe [the government] wasn't so nefarious as we perceived it, but anyway, we didn't like their policies.

As a political bloc to denounce government inaction, Mexicans against AIDS worked fairly well with Arturo Díaz leading the charge. But its internal divisions and the resentment of Díaz's skillful use of the coalition as his power base finally led to its collapse. Díaz was forced out, and a year later the network fizzled.

The damage left by the aftermath of Mexicans against AIDS suggests the dangers of forcing unions among disparate groups. Mexico, once the poster child of the international agencies, suddenly was almost blacklisted. According to Ninel Díaz:

> There was a recommendation not to finance anything in Mexico because of the problems among the organizations. With the power struggles and all that, no one wants to get near it—a lot of tension in the atmosphere, distrust.

Years later, she adds, another attempt to form an AIDS network was met with stony silence. "No one went."

> All this was a disaster, everyone working on their own and any talk about joining forces was frankly nuts. One or two groups would be your allies, but the rest would be more or less your enemies. There was a huge amount of trashing of other people's work.

In terms of horizontal coordination, the scorched earth left by the demise of Mexicans against AIDS would take nearly a decade to reseed.

A turning point in reopening the communications channels came with the discovery of the efficacy of the combination drug treatments for HIV infection around the time of the 1996 Vancouver International AIDS Conference. As occurred pretty much everywhere, including the wealthier countries, AIDS activism was boosted by the specific need to obtain these expensive medicines for people who would die without them. Public opinion, somewhat uncomfortable with demands for sex education or about interventions among homosexuals or drug users, could more easily identify with the pleas of AIDS patients for access to life-saving drug therapies. Luna explains:

> In Mexico everyone was divided. Nothing changed until 1996, just as in a lot of places, with the triple therapy. Vancouver created new hopes, right? And we had to be prepared to make sure that this hope got to everyone. (*Anuar Luna*)

During an international congress of infectologists in Mexico City in April 1997, groups of HIV-positive people staged a dramatic, rush-hour protest and blocked the downtown streets leading to the meeting hall. The country's top public health authorities were prevented from reaching the event, and the routine technical seminar was quickly overshadowed in the news media by the far more interesting guerrilla tactics of people with HIV. Jorge Huerdo, who claimed leadership of this seminal event, pointed out that despite Mexico City residents' fatigue over street protests, the public's reaction to the "march of the AIDS patients" was remarkably supportive:

> First the drivers began to insult us, but when they realized that we were demanding medicines, that we were fighting for our lives, a lot of them got out of their cars, turned off their motors, took our signs and joined us. It was marvelous.

This march, mentioned by several veteran activists, seems to have marked not only the beginning of effective drug-access advocacy but also a certain revitalization of other aspects of the AIDS movement and a more cooperative spirit. After years of helplessly watching patients sicken and die, clinicians now had real options. Care-oriented projects, advocacy and prevention could begin to rediscover their specialized niches, and old rivalries could be reexamined. In addition, with the growing numbers of people living with HIV and AIDS everywhere in Mexico, there was no shortage of work to be done nor people more and more inclined to do it. The need for new levels of sophistication and skills also became more urgent. As Huerdo said:

> I think having won with these blockades, to sit down and negotiate with this type of officials who are real wolves with sharpened fangs—you think you have an agreement signed in blood, and the next thing you know, months later nothing has happened. Maybe it doesn't sound very nice, but the educational level in this country is very low.

Meanwhile, in the new or invigorated groups of HIV-positive people, the same conflicts that had plagued the previous attempts at horizontal cooperation resurfaced in slightly different form. According to Luna:

> There was a big fight within FRENPAVIH [the PWA network]: Is this an organization of people living with HIV, or is it an organization of people affected, or of organizations? And that started a new division.

But as Luna himself admits with a laugh, the apparently all-important theoretical issue was not as substantial as it seemed; personal relations were:

> We had a big fight at the [Lima AIDS] conference, and we slugged it out in front of everybody.

Over what?

> I don't even remember!

Why would a nonissue block people's attempts at organizing in the face of such an urgent need? Although similar conflicts emerged all over the continent, it is curious that Mexico City reports continuous struggles over concepts, as if on some level the sectarian ghosts of ultra-radicalism still cannot be entirely left at the door. Eventually, however, the many actors and groups that had broken off contact were either able to operate independently or reexamine their relations. Alejandro Brito believes:

> We're now in a more mature stage of the process. There's also less confrontation with the authorities because the government has taken over a lot of the demands of civil society.

Curiously, the language used to describe the improved relations among the once bitterly hostile groups echoes, sometimes explicitly, the evolution of Mexican society toward greater appreciation of individual rights and diversity, as well as the underlying long-standing inequality and injustice of the society. Brito continues:

> We're all drinking from the same spring. We all start from something that unites us, which are human rights, the discourse of human rights.

Preciado echoes this perspective:

> This country very slowly is becoming less intolerant, more democratic because there is a fundamental problem in Mexico, which is the awful distribution of wealth. I think that as long as this problem continues, it'll be hard to talk about democracy in Mexico.

If ultra-left politics was the logical result of seventy years of quasi-dictatorship under the PRI, perhaps a more nuanced style of civic activism is a natural development to emerge along with the demise of the PRI stranglehold.

In 2000 the Mexico City municipal government moved to establish the AIDS-specific Clínica Condesa, and the percentages of HIV patients with access to the new medicines within the public health system crept slowly higher. However, Mexico faced a special problem: The North American Free Trade Agreement (NAFTA) meant that the Brazilian solution of producing cheap, generic anti-retroviral drugs to compete with those from the big laboratories was out of the question. In addition, the prevention camp, in its attempts to raise alarms about the gravity of the epidemic, exaggerated the numbers of people needing the expensive treatments. This worked against attempts to convince policy makers to open the checkbook for HIV drugs.

Dr. Jorge Saavedra, a soft-spoken man in his forties, was the first director of the Clínica Condesa and now manages a World Bank-funded program for the Mexican government. He says:

> The authorities were nervous because they said, Well, everyone tells us that we don't know the size of the epidemic, and some even talk about millions of infections. So the money won't cover treatments.

But popular pressure was to prove irresistible. As late as 1994, Mexico's health minister vowed "zero funding" for AIDS treatments; now the government is committed to providing full antiretroviral treatment to all those who need it. As the epidemic grew, the groups of people living with HIV mushroomed along with it. Izazola explains:

> The government sees NGOs all over the place asking for comprehensive treatment. Now it's irrelevant if they're united or not. They're all asking for the same thing even if they're enemies.

At the same time, the relative progress in getting Mexico to provide an adequate clinical response to HIV has generated two new phenomena: one that seems not to bother the authorities particularly and another that is more worrisome for the future of all work around HIV/AIDS: the black market in HIV medicines and signs of a drug-induced demobilization.

> It's a fact that a lot of people sell their drugs, and a lot of people have to buy them.

So says Eugenio Pazarín, a slightly built fellow of no more than thirty. Pazarín works for the Mexican Network of Persons Living with HIV/AIDS, a small organization that tries its best to keep up the pressure for good services and regular drug supplies and to provide solutions for some of the many Mexicans who still slip between the system's cracks. During a visit to the Gabriel Mancero Hospital in a modest, middle-class part of the capital, we watched as over a hundred HIV patients gathered in a second-floor landing overlooking the central atrium. They are part of the twelve hundred regular hospital patients who come roughly once a month to get their antiretroviral drug supplies. The scene was not unusual or particularly disturbing for anyone familiar with public health systems in Latin America: in fact, the physical conditions are above average. None of the clients seemed to be in much of a hurry, and the clinical files, identification cards and other papers were passed back and forth to the nurses with relative dispatch, cordiality and admirable organizational efficiency.

But confidentiality obviously went out the window long ago at Gabriel Mancero: every person there was fully aware of the HIV-positive status of every other. Names were shouted down the hallway for each person to come forward and receive their prescription. No doubt this normalization of HIV disease is a boon for those facing it; nonetheless, the entire scene illustrates the enormous force of personal and perhaps collective inertia in the face of an unpleasant reality. Among those awaiting their drugs, there was an air of resigned consent and making the best of a bad business—after all, despite the indignities, not everyone with HIV in Mexico was lucky enough to be crowding around the magic pharmacy door.

Pazarín finds the system imperfect, lamentable and probably permanent. Most important, the great majority of those subject to it do not dissent. He explains:

When they started to give out medicine in this hospital, the patients were putting on the pressure. Now, because the dynamic has changed, the vision has changed. At least in this hospital the patients aren't [mobilized]; they don't care. Even if you ask them to sign a petition because of a shortage of some medicines, they'll read the letter and say, Ah, it's for Abacavir and Zerit, but I don't take either one. I'm not signing.

The atmosphere during the monthly drug handout session was quietly social, almost festive. Many of the mostly male patients seemed to be acquaintances catching up with each other's news. There were no obvious complaints or suggestions of resentment. Because most of the drug distribution was handled by the employment-based sector of the Mexican health system, those currently or once employed were more likely to be receiving coverage—a bias favoring men. After the fight for access had achieved a measure of success, the sharp edge of the earlier militance naturally was dulled.

In fact, according to the late Jorge Huerdo, the brilliantly effective demand for life-saving drugs that had pushed governments into a corner throughout the hemisphere had a simple solution: provide them. Huerdo said:

> The thing is that now some groups defend the health system tooth and nail.
> [*They say things*] are functioning marvelously well, that the infrastructure and
> technical and psychological services are sufficient for dealing with everyone
> living with HIV.

According to some early activists, during the crest of the wave of self-help organizing and advocacy by people with HIV or AIDS, having the virus was a sort of seal of credibility. Mauricio Ramos says:

> [*I remember*] a meeting in an AIDS congress, there were two doctors, and the rest
> were seropositive people. So the banner was "I'm so-and-so, and I'm seroposi-
> tive," as if the problem of being seropositive gave them a degree in organizing,
> and the rest just happened automatically. I've always objected to that.

By elevating the figure of the HIV-positive individual, by humanizing the story of the epidemic and making the public aware of the multiple human dramas occurring within the statistics, the AIDS movement found itself with a powerful tool for advocating humane, nondiscriminatory treatment and, eventually, a broad social commitment to providing the new drug therapies. At the same time, turning the tables on stigma came at a cost. As the AIDS epidemic became a collection of moving, human narratives and shifted from disease and death to medicines and recovery, all other issues associated with HIV—along with the voices expressing them—were muffled.

One issue that got left behind in Mexico and elsewhere was prevention. Anuar Luna's case is typical of the gay adolescents and young adults who did not get the services they needed to avoid HIV infection. Luna says:

> I had a pretty strong conflict around my sexual orientation, so along comes this disease related to homosexuality—it was like a premonition. I had a sort of religious conflict, a complaint with God. I come from a very religious family of evangelical Protestants, which is worse than Catholicism. Evangelicals don't have forgiveness.

Even years after the arrival of AIDS and several rounds of attempts to articulate a response, the existing gay organizations were not providing individuals like Luna appropriate help. In addition to the hyper-ideological tendencies that put some people off, the orientation services Luna encountered lacked the subtlety he required. He explains:

> What I wanted in a gay organization was to find psychologists who wouldn't want to persuade me to be homosexual but would help me to understand what it is to be homosexual and how to recover or put together all those elements which you know aren't functioning right.

Although Luna eventually found what he was looking for, it was too late to avoid HIV. Even today, counseling and mentoring services that could help newcomers stay HIV-free have far from the coverage they need, he believes:

> If you go to bars in Mexico City, you see no information about AIDS, nothing. It's very, very serious in a country like this one where such a high percentage of the cases are men, gay men. We have a homosexual epidemic.

While the movement of HIV-positive people was scoring historic victories, the prevention side remained divided and immature. The early gay radicalism could find its descendants among a host of gay and lesbian movements and expressions, including a slick gay magazine and the risqué performance art staged in a former convent. But although the gay-prevention gap is on many minds and is included in the latest government programs and project proposals to the Global Fund, current efforts still reflect the early disunity and fragmentation.

Gay-focused attention to the HIV epidemic remains occasional and far from systematic. Alejandro Brito explains:

> There is a very clear divorce in the AIDS fight where a lot of people got into the care part, the diagnosis, the blood test, counseling, all that, and the drug banks, which was a top priority at first. But it all got detached from the prevention side. There's very little among the gay population. New groups appear every day to work in prevention among gay people, but they're like isolated workshops, not systematic work based on a strategy. It's very disconnected.

As late as 2002 a World Bank AIDS project had to be redesigned to include more attention to the ongoing gay AIDS epidemic. Some gay groups still shy away from the homosexual epidemic, eager to delink homosexuality from associations with the "pink plague." Izazola is particularly scathing on the subject:

> Here we have gay men who want to do prevention work with housewives or train doctors, sex workers who want to work in high schools, and not one gay organization interested in prevention among gay men. I call it "internalized organizational homophobia."

The once over-the-top, supermilitant Mexican gay scene of the 1970s mutated into an oddly defensive posture unusual in Latin America. According to Brito, many members of the new generation of overwhelmingly gay health activists remain uneasy about the double stigma of AIDS and homosexuality:

> I think the gay community was ignored in favor of the general population. Groups began to form, movements against AIDS more than a gay movement, and began to replace it. There weren't any strategies. I don't see continuity, not even in the original groups.

The Mexican public health system had to stage regular mass-distribution scenes like the one at Gabriel Mancero Hospital because of another aspect of the Mexican response to AIDS: the burgeoning black market in antiretroviral drugs.

An unintended but predictable by-product of the partially successful fight to gain access to life-saving medicines was the appearance of beneficiaries ready to cash out: people who would opt for short-term income at the risk of their long-term health by selling their medicines to those to whom free access was denied. The Mexican parallel drug market became famous throughout the region, and entrepreneurs—some but not all of them HIV-positive themselves—traveled regularly to Mexico City to stock up on contraband medicines. Some simply made enough to pay for their frequent trips; others exploited the lack of drug access in their home countries to create a lucrative business by buying drugs in Mexico and reselling them elsewhere. Although in Chile the parallel market remained clandestine and even persecuted—medicines changed hands in scenes reminiscent of a cocaine buy—the Mexican authorities know about and tolerate the reselling of HIV drugs. In fact, AIDS service organizations themselves often do the reselling, ostensibly for the benefit of their other projects.

A 2002 visit to an AIDS NGO on a quiet, residential street of Mexico City confirmed the ease with which a total stranger could negotiate prescription drug buys. Despite some initial unease on the part of the person in charge, a visitor without an introduction could receive price quotes for a range of HIV drugs, all of which would be resold from the stock provided by the Mexican government free of charge to its beneficiaries. The drugs are considered the property of the recipient as soon as he or she receives them; thus, beneficiaries are free to turn their donated products into a business opportunity at the cost of the Mexican taxpayer.

The consolidation of AIDS groups engaged in this quasi-legal trade with government-funded free drugs produced certain anomalies for those public health services denting the parallel market by providing universal drug coverage. As Condesa Clinic staff psychologist Mauricio Ramos commented after a tense meeting with NGOs, "No wonder they're pissed off. We're putting them out of business."

As of this writing, the Mexican AIDS groups and the lively gay and lesbian scene in Mexico City no doubt are filling the broadly recognized gaps in prevention and services. Treatment access will expand steadily, and price relief should make the burden on the Mexican state manageable, if not exactly light. New infections remain worrisome, given the government's commitment to providing costly treatments, and the black market is unlikely to disappear as long as other countries in the region do not provide similar levels of drug access. But in Mexico HIV infection is no longer an obstacle to living a normal life in many circles. The frequency with which many interviewees concluded their remarks with the information that they themselves were HIV-positive, had nearly died, but now were putting their lives and their jobs in government ministries back together—was striking. Jorge Saavedra, the World Bank project manager, explains that he found his professional and personal lives intersecting:

> I got infected in 1985, but I simply refused to accept it and didn't want to hear about it. But when the authorities said that the drugs didn't work and all that, well, I had to go public with my status in order to say, Yes they do! Because I got sick in 1995, I had zero CD4 cells, was hospitalized, they had to bathe me and feed me, and I began to take the medicines and got better, and now I'm working perfectly normally. . . . [So] it's a myth that the drugs don't work in a person at very advanced stages of the disease.

Another witness who wished to remain anonymous shared his feeling that being HIV-positive was not an obstacle for romance.

> The best moment was with a friend with whom there was some erotic empathy. I was honest and told him about my [HIV-positive] status, and he said it wasn't important if we took care. I think those moments are meaningful because in the end you have a moral and ethical responsibility, and I think that way you function sexually more fully. I thought he would reject me, but he didn't. It's something that only I can perceive and understand. Nothing can compare with the smile of a man who says, "So what?"

Gay Mexico has come full circle from its days of lavender insurrection. Alejandro Brito is perhaps an apt representative of the veterans of the retreat and near disappearance of gay politics in the 1980s. Nevertheless, in 2000, the first year of the conservative PAN government, his gay-oriented supplement on sexuality won Mexico's national journalism prize. "That's quite something," he says, "if you consider it talks about oral sex, anal sex, orgasm, pleasure, and what-have-you." Brito calls his current posture "radical humanism" and suggests that his own and the gay movement's middle age has made them both more tolerant:

> I view things from a more inclusive perspective and—why not say it?—more attuned to beauty. Because to see how people construct these networks and connections and mutual support, despite all the base emotions we all have, it's fascinating.

Pedro Preciado recalls the first gay marches in Guadalajara with three hundred people; now thousands attend, including many sympathizers who are not comfortable joining in directly but who line the streets. Twenty gay bars have sprung up in the city. Preciado's story, however, recalls the losing side:

> I'm tired. I have to restructure my finances because no one is going to support me when I'm old, no one. There's a group of very close friends with whom I hang out every day, we work together, share ideas, talk, we still talk about gay issues, and they have AIDS. So that's my family.

Despite the city's praiseworthy efforts on the epidemic, all the founders of GHOL except Preciado himself are now part of history. He continues:

> I also feel the need to hide away, Tim. Having lost Jorge was something that I still don't want—I don't know if I accept it. I'm talking about my unconscious. He was my political comrade, my lover, my sex partner, my idea partner; we were in jail together, him fifteen times and me twelve. We were hungry together; we got beaten up by the cops. We shared everything, you know? And now he doesn't exist. Even now, that hasn't really sunk in.

Peñalolén

T he telephone rang one day in 1994 from a woman in Peñalolén saying that her son was about to die and she needed help. I set out very early to see him with Miguel, a charming, funny and light-hearted young fellow who worked with us who was HIV-positive.

We found the house, where everything was closed up and dark. There were a number of chairs set up around a sofa, and in each one a neighbor was sitting looking down at her fingernails while the mother served juice. There was a bundle turned toward the wall on the sofa. Miguel went to talk to the mother, and I turned to the women and said, "Excuse me, ladies, what are you doing here? Why is everything so dark? Can we open the windows?" And I realized that the lump on the sofa had moved.

Although the fellow apparently couldn't talk, I insisted that he turn around so I could face him. His mother was appalled at all this, so Miguel kept her back, saying "Make me some juice, we're thirsty!" The mourners from the neighborhood all left. Finally the guy opened his eyes and sat up even though his mother was having a fit—the dead had arisen! So I said to him, "What would you like to do right now? Shall we go outside?" He said yes, and we went and sat on the front porch and started to talk.

He said, "I'm sick." Yes, I said, you're sick. Would you like to go for a ride? His mother really was having a heart attack at that idea, so we put it off until the next day. But we were talking, and the windows were open, his mother had started to do her usual housework. He was no longer a corpse.

The next day he was all dressed and ready, speaking perfectly well, although he had trouble walking. All the neighbors came out to greet him as we got into the car. We went to the office, and I had prepared beefsteak, toma- toes, onions, and we had a big lunch right in the office. I almost killed the poor guy because it gave him diarrhea, but anyway he just got a little sicker. But he was having a grand time.

He started to talk about death. "I'm probably going to die," he said. Yes, that's probably true, I told him, but then again we're all heading in the same direction, some earlier, some later. "But you know," he said, "my mother wants me to have a child, so I would like to get married and have a child." And I said, "Excuse me, but you're gay. Why do you want to make a woman unhappy and be unhappy yourself, just to be married and have a child? Why do you have to do what your mother wants? Forget her, tell her to go adopt one. Tell her that you're gay, and you don't have any desire to have children." That was the tenor of our conversation, and two days later he came back relieved and said, "You know, I talked to my mother, and it's all clear now."

I saw him two or three more times before he fell really sick, semiconscious. We put him in a church hospital in San Bernardo, on death's door for real this time. He was in a corner, curled up in the fetal position facing the wall. Suddenly he began to make the rattling sound that precedes death, and I said to his mother, "Take him in your arms. Didn't you have him in your arms when he was born? Now he needs you to be with him, put your arms around him."

Then a nun appeared praying out loud from a distance, "Holy Mary, Mother of God!" and ordering everyone out of the area. I shut her up immediately and said, "Ma'am, would you please be so kind as to stop praying out loud and stay away from here?" The mother was emboldened by this and agreed, so the nun had to make herself scarce. The fellow died in the arms of his mother. It was very good to have made contact that day for that reason and to insist that there is happiness, even in the moment of death.

—Elena Droguett

CHAPTER THREE

Costa Rica:
The Velvet Glove

COSTA RICA	
Population	4.1 million
First reported case of AIDS	1984
Total estimated HIV infections	12,000
Male : female ratio	7:1
Estimated number of people needing antiretroviral treatment	3,000
Number receiving drugs	2,000
First AIDS prevention NGO established	1990
Adult women using birth control	80%
Gross domestic product (GDP) 2003	$17.5 billion
Per capita income (2003)	$4,280
Annual per-capita spending on health	$285
Unemployment rate	6.7%
40-day Costa Rican civil war	1948
President Oscar Arías wins Nobel Peace Prize for Central American peace plan	1987

How a vibrant sexual health movement can turn into a spent force and disappear without a trace.

In the mid-1990s Costa Rica was the headquarters of an enormous, nongovernmental AIDS-prevention and advocacy enterprise known as ILPES, the Instituto Latinoamericano de Prevención y Educación en Salud (Latin American Health Prevention and Education Institute). Years before the man who would become its director, historian Jacobo Shifter, had fought a historic and ultimately successful battle with his own university over discrimination for sexual orientation. As a result, he was a natural and credible leader to deal with the arrival of HIV. He soon became a respected, almost feared figure in Costa Rica and throughout the region, where ILPES trainers, researchers and advisors fanned out to advise and train grassroots groups taking up AIDS work, reaching as far afield as Ecuador, Bolivia and the Caribbean.

When I visited Costa Rica in 1994, ILPES was running twenty-two programs: clinical services; training for peer educators; jail workshops with inmates on sexuality and addiction; counseling; sessions on death and dying; safe-sex training and holistic gay-consciousness workshops; and many more. ILPES's telephone hotline had a separate office downtown, as did its drop-in center for women in the sex trade. Shifter was a prolific publisher; over the following years, he brought out a series of attractive volumes on jailhouse sex, prostitution and other hot topics related to the AIDS universe.

The ILPES offices, in a quiet, residential neighborhood of San José, bustled with activity as the gay peer educators designed and printed their weekly bulletins and flyers inviting bar patrons to use the telephone counseling and other services, then made way for the evening workshops and other activities. Doctors saw their patients in another building to protect their privacy. Antonio Bustamante, a Cuban-born resident, ran ILPES's jail program begun by Shifter himself. At one dramatic session I attended, drug-dependent convicts clamored for him not to miss the next week's appointment, explaining that without it, they would quickly return to consuming the *bazucos* (cigarettes laced with coca paste) readily available in every prison. I later invited Bustamante to Chile, where his deep grasp of prison dynamics and practical suggestions for educational activities caused a sensation among correctional officials.

The entire operation hummed with efficiency and institutional solidity. The Dutch embassy in San José enthusiastically funded Shifter's operation with substantial sums, causing other groups to grumble over ILPES's privileged position. Shifter and I briefly discussed the possibilities of collaborating on a research project in Chile, a plan that never bore fruit, I was later told, because the Dutch were unwilling to extend ILPES's reach that far south. But at one point the hand of ILPES seemed to be nearly everywhere in Latin America where AIDS-related work was taking place.

When I returned to San José to research the situation seven years later, ILPES had virtually disappeared. The single remaining telephone number was connected to an answering machine, but the woman who eventually returned my call said Mr. Shifter was out of the country. Others insisted he was not. Wherever he was, Costa Rica's AIDS prevention and care innovator was keeping an extremely low profile.

Costa Ricans are quick to point out that the country is an island of relative prosperity in Central America; they are proud of the contrast between themselves and the destitute, war-torn countries on all sides. Fully a quarter of the country's current residents are economic refugees from Nicaragua. Unemployment is relatively low, and Central America's violent upheavals of the 1980s and 1990s largely passed Costa Rica by. It was logical to suppose that Costa Rica would be the first on the isthmus to generate a modern, competent response to the AIDS epidemic, and ILPES's appearance was entirely consistent with these expectations, a professional operation on the cutting edge of prevention and care, churning out publications and fully engaged in all the theoretical and conceptual debates as they emerged. But by 2002 something had happened.

Today Costa Rica provides most modern AIDS medicines to all registered patients, the first and so far the only country in Central America to do so. Its official discourse on HIV/AIDS prevention and care is consistent with the recommendations emanating from the UN agencies that put together "best practices" guidelines.

And yet my brief visit left me with the distinct sensation that today, very little is being done about preventing new cases of HIV in the country. There is dynamic, although unfunded, AIDS treatment activism, as well as worthy shelter-type projects to help people with advanced AIDS to cope. But the AIDS billboards had disappeared, and the outreach programs, the storefront drop-in centers, the gay-consciousness groups and other creatives responses to dealing with people's day-to-day vulnerabilities, all those initiatives that the existence of ILPES once suggested always would be available in Costa Rica, seemed to have vanished. Costa Rica is a revealing example of how a hale, innovative and professional service organization—along with a good chunk of the social movement to which it was once linked—can simply vanish.

Giselle Herrera, the longtime director of Costa Rica's AIDS program, is rumored to guard her post jealously. She is personable and charming, readily available and easily amused, while at the same time very much a medical doctor—she called herself a "specialist" four times in response to my first question. Some local activists said that the government's AIDS program had been on hold for years due to rivalries within the ministry, but Herrera suggested only that political support was lacking at the top. She said AIDS was not currently a priority and so could not compete for scarce government resources, especially given the considerable sums spent on medicines. She was unusually frank about the errors that the program had committed in its early years, saying:

> We started out doing contact tracing, just as we always had with syphilis and chancroid. But when we started contacting gay men who were living a double life, most of them reacted violently. We even got death threats.

In addition, Herrera's staff quickly realized that the numbers of sexual contacts involved in the epidemic were far beyond the program's capacity to track down and that public education was the only sensible alternative since no treatments could be offered in any case. Herrera describes her team's early visits to the gay clubs as "useful because of the thirst for information, but also a bit ridiculous" and echoes what is now common wisdom, that peer education among marginalized groups is probably the only effective long-term strategy. And she nods appropriately in the direction of nongovernmental organizations as best equipped to carry it out:

> We realized that what we thought was marvelous work in fact was all wrong. We had to change to peers, people who would organize themselves, form their own NGOs, while our program was more focused on training these people as agents, and we would concentrate on doctors and health workers in a different area.

This exemplary spirit of self-criticism and foresight is consistent with Costa Ricans' characteristic sophistication and quick grasp of the principles that should govern social policy. But one element was lacking: Who would support the NGOs that were to carry out this admirable labor?

Herrera recognized that the Costa Rican government has dedicated few resources to prevention but resisted any suggestion that it bears a responsibility for what may or may not be happening in the private sector. She says:

> The NGOs have to exist and have to raise funds. What happens is that N-G-O means that they do NOT depend on the government, right?

She agreed that the ministry could theoretically contract certain services to the NGO sector but added that this was unlikely. Eventually she fell back on technical-administrative arguments:

> Right now from the legal standpoint, the Caja [*the state social service agency*] cannot do it. From my point of view, I mean, from my authority, I have no role in this aspect. I can't—it's not within my responsibility or duties. The ministry has no budget to support the NGOs, it hasn't any. I don't see it as very likely.

Although Herrera did mention one NGO, the Foundation to Fight AIDS, or FUNDESIDA, which had obtained funding and "supports" the government center, she mostly criticized Costa Rican NGOs for not having put down adequate roots and achieved self-sufficiency. Referring obliquely to the ILPES story, she blamed the current situation on the NGOs' "breech birth," on the fact that they did not emerge organically but rather were created by the funders themselves, then became too reliant on cash injections from the outside. Herrera says:

> Today they are not firmly established in the society. Right now I think an NGO working in AIDS should be completely connected with the society and have its own resources.

The analysis also could fairly be applied to her own favorite, FUNDESIDA. What Costa Rica's long-term AIDS chief did not mention is that FUNDESIDA is not really an NGO at all, but the government in civilian clothes.

Guillermo Murillo is an excitable, voluble activist who came to AIDS work from the treatment and care side. It could have been different, as Murillo himself recognizes, as he and his then partner were aware enough of the dangers to seek an HIV test as early as 1984. His narrative graphically illustrates the dangers of a negative test result and of excessive faith in medical science:

> I recall that immediately after breaking up with [his partner], I continued to have sex with other people with all the risk involved and used condoms only when the other person suggested it. One of the things the doctors said was, Well, AIDS appeared in 1981 and already by 1984 the infectious agent had been identified. So that meant a tremendous medical and scientific advance in the speed with which the virus had been discovered. That automatically made them certain that very soon they would have the vaccine against the disease as well, something that you still hear about a lot, the idea of the vaccine.

After learning of the death of a former partner, Murillo suddenly realized that his sexual practices were putting him at risk. But he acknowledges that the realization came too late.

> It's not a justification, and I'm not trying to blame them, but it could have been one of my justifications, to calculate that the virus can last five or ten years before developing, but the vaccine will arrive in two or three. So what's the problem? I didn't internalize it.

In those years, medical care for HIV was hit-and-miss, both technically and in terms of quality of care, and Murillo was alienated by his first trips to the local hospitals.

> I saw how the secretaries treated people, so that scared me, and I just avoided all medical care for several years . . . until I started to feel that the HIV was beginning to affect my body so that then I began to reconsider and start looking.

Nervous about sharing his HIV status, Murillo found information and help through a relatives' group, without acknowledging publicly that he was really attending for himself. As was true for many people in those years, the peer atmosphere was both comforting and scary.

> I loved just the fact that I wasn't alone, but on the other hand it was frightening. It was the period in which one or two people would die every week in a group of fifteen coming and going. We would ask, Jeez, did so-and-so not come this week because he didn't feel like it or because he's dead?

Nonetheless, the meeting also produced a stimulus to act. With the direct experience of inadequate treatment fresh in his memory, Murillo soon was ready to go public with his complaints. The occasion was a public forum on treatment access. Until that time, only non-HIV-positive people dared discuss the epidemic publicly. After telling his close friends and family that he was gay and HIV-positive—to the complete surprise of a schoolmate who had known him for twenty years—Murillo took his struggle to the arena of public opinion.

Government officials defended with considerable pride Costa Rica's record in providing full antiretroviral treatments for its citizens covered by the public health system—one of the first in Latin America to do so. But Richard Stern, a U.S. citizen and longtime resident, has a more skeptical view. Stern, an affable fifty-ish psychologist, sticks out even in gringo-heavy Costa Rica. With his calm, loping stride, worn sneakers and unassuming dress, Stern seems vigorously unconcerned about making an impression. Although not heavyset, he struggles with his waistline; at a friendly lunch he insisted that guests take the leftover rice along with them to spare him further temptation.

Meeting the soft-spoken, avuncular Stern is a bit of a surprise for anyone who has followed his activism and read the blistering articles and communiqués emanating from his computer in recent years. Stern has electronically tongue-lashed UNAIDS, the World Health Organization (WHO) and its Pan American counterpart (PAHO), local governments and the nongovernmental world as well for what he considers their lethargy and incompetence in not getting modern AIDS treatments to the people who need them in the seven countries of Central America and around the Caribbean. Once an internal UNAIDS memo characterizing him as "hysterical" slipped past a member of the Geneva staff and ended up in Stern's e-mail; they did not hear the end of it and had to issue profuse public apologies. But he remains matter-of-fact about the controversies, saying:

> People are dying as we speak; that seems urgent to me, and if other people don't see it that way, well, then we disagree, don't we?

He is also a regional pioneer in using the Internet to increase activist impact. From his home office and starting with nothing more than his $20-a-month Internet connection and knowledge of the region's AIDS treatment politics, Stern fired off articles, reportage and unvarnished challenges to those in charge about the continuing delays and obstacles to treatment access. He is especially withering about the UN agencies and "the millions they spend sending people around the world and staying in $180-a-night hotels."

Stern became involved in AIDS work through a counseling job at ILPES, which began providing psychological services for gay men and lesbians before the epidemic had taken root in the country. People with HIV began to seek help at ILPES, but in those days, says Stern, there was little to offer them. Therapy was frequently interrupted by death:

> People would come in for a session one month and then not come back the next month, and it was very, very traumatic.

Almost as an afterthought, he accompanied a group to push the government to provide the first AIDS drug, AZT, and saw for himself how officials dragged their feet on the issue. Stern explains:

> It didn't really ever get off the ground. The woman there said she was going
> to follow through on it, but it was just lip service: "I'm going to study it and
> get back to you in three months." We complained a few months later, and it
> was the same run-around. I was very green, but actually what we did was
> very interesting. I started a petition about the AZT, and for some reason a
> professor in one of the universities distributed it, and all of a sudden we had
> eight hundred signatures, which we delivered to the government.

By lucky chance, this all occurred in the spring of 1996, just months before
the historic Vancouver International AIDS Conference, which showcased
the revolutionary triple-drug therapy and broke open the treatment-access
debate. Although obtaining AZT would not have made much of a difference to
patients, getting the triple therapy would. The far higher stakes were a powerful
motive not to let the bureaucrats off the hook.

Of all Central American countries, Costa Rica offered people with HIV
their best opportunity of convincing a government to respond, given the country's relative economic and political stability and credible social services. Stern
urged his HIV-positive friends to hold officials to their rhetoric.

> I already had a group of people with AIDS who were coming to see me, who
> were my friends, who were concerned about the issue. I told them, This is
> something that means something, and your government—everybody says
> this is a great democracy here in Costa Rica, with universal health care.
> Yeah, it [the triple combination therapy] is expensive, but it's something that
> they're getting in other countries. I wrote an article for La Nación, and the
> group began to consolidate around this issue.

But Stern was already a veteran of unpleasant NGO conflicts, having
criticized Shifter's management at ILPES and demanded fiscal transparency
from colleagues at another gay-oriented group after a regional conference. It is
not hard to see the uncompromising Stern refusing to countenance any corner-
cutting and slowly alienating himself from the ambitious NGO managers trying

to make their way in an environment of scarcity, competition and old-boy networking. Now he prefers simpler structures and, failing that, to go it alone, to avoid the "typical NGO bureaucracy that holds you back."

Stern's ad hoc committee began to negotiate with the government, which responded with a foreign consultant's report claiming that triple antiretroviral therapy was impossible in Costa Rica. Stern explains:

> The consultant from the States come down and wrote this phony report to show how it would bankrupt the health care system. So the government printed it up in color and distributed it all over the place.

With typical disdain, Stern characterizes the report as "completely false, of course," and he points to the fact that today, with universal coverage, the health care system continues to function, "even if they have had to cut back on the number of chauffeur-driven cars."

On hearing official sources describe with pride the full coverage of anti-retroviral drugs for people with HIV in Costa Rica, one would never guess that the government consistently had dragged its feet on treatment access and was forced into its current position through a lawsuit. Stern says:

> The government [had an] intermediary whose job was to placate the group and stall things as long as possible . . . with vague promises, but nothing in writing.

Costa Rica not only prides itself on being a sort of Swiss island amid the backward, it is also home to the Inter American Human Rights Court, which hears complaints on human rights violations from all over Latin America. In addition, its political system allows citizens to bring petitions straight to the highest level, without exhausting lengthy lower-court procedures first.

Shortly after the unsatisfactory mid-1997 interview mentioned by Stern, three people living with HIV sued the government, arguing that they were being denied the right to life. Although technically in danger, none of them actually was sick at the time, which weakened their legal argument based on an imminent danger of irreversible harm. That changed when in August Stern got a call from an old friend named William García—from the hospital.

> In all the years I had known him, he never told me he had AIDS. So I went there and said, The only thing I can think that can help you at this point— he weighed about a hundred pounds—is if you're willing to sign something and go public. The next day he signed it.

Stern's group phoned the judge's assistant every day to say that García was going to die. "That doesn't seem to mean much in Honduras or Guatemala," says Stern, "but in Costa Rica it did." Finally the court ordered the government to provide García's medications and followed up with similar rulings in favor of the other three petitioners. They were quickly followed by a dozen more and then a third group. When the judges tired of the steady stream of lawsuits, they ordered the government to include everyone. By December, barely four months after the first legal complaint, Costa Rica had universal coverage for antiretroviral drugs.

For William García, however, the breakthrough came too late. The treatment did not reverse his condition, and he died in October.

Compared to the bureaucratic resistance in other Central American countries, the Costa Rican experience is still remarkable, especially for the successful use of its republican institutions. Of course, the country does not recognize pharmaceutical patents and has long produced its own generic copies of drugs, bringing the cost of universal antiretroviral access down to just several hundred dollars a year per patient. But the successful legal strategy and especially the appeal to the human right to life was a significant lesson for the region.

Nevertheless, this happy ending is not really an ending at all, given that the milestone drug therapies for HIV are a far cry from a cure, as anyone burdened with taking them will quickly confirm. In some ways, the relatively quick resolution of the drug access issue has pushed the more complex questions of sexuality and prevention farther into the background, and not just in Costa Rica. Says Carlos Valerio of the Defensoría de los Habitantes, a sort of human rights ombudsman within the government: "The state feels that it is doing its duty on the AIDS issue by paying for medicines."

With the NGO world in a rebuilding stage after the sudden implosion of the granddaddy ILPES, casework and support for people with HIV/AIDS is led by the Fundación Vida (Life Foundation), one of the few early groups that has survived. Its director, psychologist Cristina Garita, agrees that people with HIV/AIDS in Costa Rica enjoy better conditions today than before, but adds that they still depend on the vigor of private activism, which remains very fragile.

> The conquests that have been achieved, the things that the government has done, it hasn't been out of the goodness of its heart. It wasn't humanism, it was activism and a lot of things. Just like developing leaders, they don't just appear; the organizations produced them.

The disappearance of ILPES, the drying up of foreign aid and the lack of willingness by the government to consider direct support has left nongovernmental organization work in Costa Rica weak. Garita says the latest attempt at an NGO coordinating committee responds to the recognition that the NGO sector is "sinking."

Meanwhile, a new actor in the AIDS field in Costa Rica appeared: the local office of Rotary International in charge of AIDS-related initiatives with support from its world Rotary headquarters, which has a history of work in this area. Rotary is currently carrying out a $500,000 AIDS project in four countries of the region, but as its director, José Zamora, told me, their work is:

> a prevention and education campaign at the level of the general population. Especially with a heterosexual message, in order to reach all secondary and university students.

Zamora explained that of course Rotary recognized the existence of homosexuals, as well as "lesbians, prostitutes and alcoholics, whatever you want." But he acknowledged that local Rotarians had opted to avoid political hot potatoes like homosexuality:

> The Ministry of Education does not accept that there are homosexuals and does not accept that there are sadomasochistic relations. It does not accept

many situations that are a reality. So for us to sign any sort of agreement with them, we have to remove all these things.

So homosexuality, along with kinky sex practices, had to go. In addition, Rotary operates on the common belief that the gay population has already received enough attention. Zamora explains it this way:

> The homosexuals went to ILPES, and ILPES had a ton of money, right? The heterosexual never thought that he could acquire AIDS. So a lot of money was used up—I'm not saying it was spent badly or well. What I mean is that a lot went for that, and the general population didn't receive a thing. So the infections began among the housewives, and I imagine you are aware of the statistics in Nicaragua. In Nicaragua, in Panama, in El Salvador it's a problem of heterosexuals. The only country that we could say it is fully homosexual is in Costa Rica, where it's evenly divided.

Zamora sounds like as the typical latecomer to AIDS education who makes peace too quickly with official prejudices and shelters his conservative approach under a dubious our-hands-are-tied posture. His epidemiological argument about an even male/female split in infections in Costa Rica is wrong too. But in the midst of this strange colloquy, Zamora revealed that he was not talking out of his hat:

> We have a case in our family, and the family is split over it. I have a relative with AIDS, a sixteen-year-old. Of the eight of us, only four are dealing with the situation—not including our mother. If you have lived the experience, it makes you a different sort of person. And that is what has happened to us.

A Nicaraguan immigrant whom I met on the busy main street of San José showed me to a weekday meeting of a Christian-oriented gay group that meets once a week above an Internet café. Years after the vanguard gay-consciousness workshops generated by ILPES, this expression of gay esprit de corps—fairly common around the region as Latin American gays and lesbians seek ways to resolve their sense of spiritual orphanhood—struck me as harmlessly cordial, a good outlet for religious gays. But it was a sad substitute for consciousness-raising about sexual emancipation and rights. The session inevitably sank into a sort of lightly salted preaching, and the final benedictions leaned heavily toward dialogues with a kinder-gentler deity who was petitioned more to overlook homosexuality than to embrace it. Several of those in attendance said they enjoyed the atmosphere because it was "healthier" than the commercial bar scene, by which they meant it was less focused on casual sex.

On the official side, Carlos Valerio, who pushes the AIDS issue from within the government, calls the second half of the 1990s a "black hole" for AIDS, a time in which prevention work essentially came to a halt. A very recent national AIDS plan was finally drawn up sometime in 2000, but the admirably complete document may not be taken very seriously by those who count: one government official lent me the office's only copy and asked me to be sure to bring it back later.

AIDS consciousness is probably quite high in gay San José, no doubt due in part to the lingering effects of the efforts of ILPES. Richard Stern recalls that four to five hundred people a year, mostly gay men, once passed through the peer-educator program, a lot for a small country. On the other hand, if an advertising message needs to be repeated to sustain its impact, AIDS prevention must inevitably be losing its punch as the silence around safe sex deepens.

For this situation to change any time soon, the Costa Rican government probably is going to have to modify its hands-off stance. As with Chile and Mexico, Costa Rica suffers from the disadvantage of being not quite rich and not quite poor. Its per-capita income and other macroeconomic statistics are enviable by Central American standards; therefore, foreign development aid is much easier to justify in Honduras or Guatemala. Agencies think that local sources, both public and private, should be tapped more effectively. Says Stern:

> I don't completely disagree with that. There are hundreds if not thousands
> of gay people who think nothing of spending $20 at a disco, having drinks,
> taking a taxi, but to get them to contribute to a service organization, it's not
> easy. The gay community here is affluent, you can easily get six hundred
> people in a bar spending their money. I think that at some point through

a process of evolution like in the States, the community has to decide what its priorities are.

But if their priorities do not include community groups, then what? At the UN meeting on AIDS in June 2001, Costa Rica finally agreed to provide $50,000 to the main NGOs in the field; later the money was reported to be "trickling in."

FUNDESIDA came up frequently in my discussions with activists and with Dr. Herrera herself. But surprisingly, no one pointed out that the office of this "NGO" is located in an unusual place: the same clinic building that houses the national AIDS program of Costa Rica. Miriam Fernández, its director and to all appearances its sole employee, readily acknowledged that the group's main purpose was to support the government's efforts, given that its mainly European donors were loath to provide funds to governments—apparently, they never realized that that was exactly what they were doing in FUNDESIDA's case. Its office stocked materials from previous campaigns and could easily have been mistaken for a health ministry storage room. But this dubiously cozy relationship between the state and a supposedly non-governmental entity was entirely unremarkable to anyone in Costa Rica.

Cristina Garita at Fundación VIDA has managed to navigate the somewhat treacherous waters of Costa Rican NGOs, including surviving in the shadow of ILPES. Garita observed that Giselle Herrera "wanted to work on certain projects that the government was not going to support." So the essentially phony NGO could siphon funds into the projects without needing to win political support to develop them. The collaboration was so organic that even veteran observers such as Garita were scarcely aware of where the state ended and this unique "NGO" began. She explains:

I never could learn if the things that were being done there were FUN-DESIDA or the government. That's a very internal matter. All the NGOs identified these actions with the government.

Of course, as Garita points out, many public entities such as hospitals utilize independent foundations to channel resources. However, given the particular nature of AIDS work and the worldwide consensus that an independent civil society should play a key role, it is certainly questionable to see what cynics would call a GONGO (government-organized NGO) scooping up scarce international aid money for official programs that the state itself is unwilling to pay for—especially if by doing so it squeezes out resources for truly independent groups.

Herrera's comment that the NGO sector had grown overly dependent on external funding and had not paid enough attention to achieving self-sufficiency rings decidedly hollow in this context. The Costa Rican government may have had other priorities besides AIDS prevention, and ILPES clearly had little trouble attracting large sums for its burgeoning operations while they lasted. But the eminently reasonable Costa Rican state did not back up its rhetoric with money, did little to support independent initiatives, and certainly showed no inclination to share resources during the heyday of interest in AIDS from international funders.

My last day in San José was brightened by running into an old acquaintance whom I had been unable to track down. He was heading to a private clinic where a friend was registered to receive his antiretroviral therapy and where the doctors had "miraculously" pulled him back from the verge of death. We headed for the institution, located across the street from one of the city's main hospitals. Expensive paintings by Costa Rica's best-known artist adorned the walls, and the clinic appeared to be in tiptop shape.

When I asked an administrator for details about the operations, he seemed to panic, and his lower lip trembled. Yes, the clinic had treatment and study protocols with pharmaceutical firms and worked closely with the national AIDS program. One of its board members was none other than—once again—Dr. Giselle Herrera. Patient care and services, my old friend assured me, were excellent. To him, the interlocking of state/NGO/drug company spheres under Herrera seemed perfectly normal.

Unsurprising in the overlapping concentric circles of Costa Rican society, this acquaintance had also once worked for ILPES. He had tried to find someone for me to interview to get an idea of what had happened to the one-time octopus of AIDS activism in Central America. But no one was talking.

Apparently, ILPES's near-total dependence on a single source of support had been its Achilles' heel; when the funder changed its mind for whatever reason, ILPES was gone.

Despite the limitations of its response to the AIDS epidemic, Costa Rica still stands out as an island of relatively enlightened AIDS policies, and its reputation as the gay mecca of Central America is certainly intact. But the impetus which the AIDS epidemic once represented for joining disparate social and community forces and stimulating a long-term process of sexual emancipation seems to be largely spent. What survives are independent social welfare services linked to the epidemic and focused on casework, services that can act as watchdogs over public health and other agencies, filling in the gaps here, demanding a better governmental response there. Additionally, there still exists the landmark activism and advocacy around access to essential drugs and, by extension, other available medical treatments, both including and beyond the AIDS phenomenon, even when costs appear to be prohibitive.

But Costa Ricans dissemble when they downplay the considerable resistance to the government's current policies or try to suggest that it welcomed potential rivals in the AIDS field with open arms. More likely the government opted for a passive acceptance of these groups and their activities as a sort of rival businesses. The non-confrontational approach is quite consistent with what the locals describe as the tolerant but highly private and individualistic "Tico" character. As Guillermo Murillo puts it:

> The historians say that it's because of the way of life during the colonial period and the first years of independence, where there was a little house every hundred meters or kilometer, and so each family got used to living in its own little circle and nothing more. Also we haven't had the political conflicts as in most Latin American countries that would unite people in a struggle. So more than pacific, Costa Ricans are passive.

An atmosphere of nonaggression and formal nods to modern, enlightened social policies may be ideal for the possibilities of doing business, for which Costa Rica is also quite renowned. ILPES arose and thrived for a time because of strong personal links among key individuals, but without these, other local groups might have wandered for years before figuring out how to attract the available foreign resources that the government was capturing for its own worthwhile projects. Stern has developed a characteristically peremptory view of all this:

> I have no illusions about democracy in Latin America or that people who run governments really care about their citizens. I think money is the name of the game among 90 percent of public officials throughout Latin America, figuring out a way to—I won't necessarily say to do illegal things, but to keep from spending it.

But true to form, Stern does not let the NGOs off the hook either.

> A very big issue that people don't talk much about—but it happens everywhere—is a cultural factor: in Latin America there is a more authoritarian concept of the director and his right to sign the checks, to get his cousin to do the repairs and his sister to bake the cake or whatever, and people consider it okay. I didn't. The funding sources make a big mistake when they don't either—because they do close the organization when the money is misspent.

Curiously, ILPES was not at the forefront of treatment-access activism when it suddenly broke out. The organization's Dutch funding agencies, like most, were fuzzy at first about the difference between treatment access and treatment-access *advocacy*—funders thought that groups were asking help to buy drugs rather than to push for policy changes. They may well have missed the importance and significance of this battle and shifted their posture only gradually in the course of the next few years. Nonetheless, it seems odd that such a juggernaut of AIDS activism as ILPES could have missed out on what quickly turned into the key issue of the late 1990s in Costa Rica and everywhere else.

By contrast, Stern, first through the gay organization Pink Triangle and then independently, flooded the Internet with news, demands, reportage and calls to arms over the situation in Central America. He notes that the groups, despite their previous conflicts, were fairly united at the time of the initiation of the legal strategy:

> Some didn't want to sign, and some other groups who sometimes came to the meetings were kind of scared. But nobody sabotaged it.

Elsewhere, as will be seen in the next chapter, sabotage did indeed occur. But the Costa Rican committee shepherding the initiative could afford to operate as a loose, ad hoc assembly. Although the risks of public exposure were considerable, the potential rewards were enormous. Luckily, everything happened too quickly for the institutional rivalries to interfere. Nor did the government aggressively seek to undermine the groups: That would not be the Costa Rican approach.

Today treatment access is in a number of ways the victim of its own success. Universal coverage has removed the issue from the agenda: the local activists cannot compete internationally for support with their peers in Nicaragua or Honduras in far worse straits. Meanwhile, the drama of the issue displaced both prevention concerns and the public debate about sexuality that characterized the early period of the epidemic. Without people dying left and right, the sense of crisis and urgency is much reduced.

In 2001 Murillo and others successfully sued the government again over the long absence of prevention campaigns in Costa Rica. But there bureaucratic stonewalling by the government agencies responsible for prevention education is far more effective. Francisco Madrigal of the Central American Center for the Investigation and Promotion of Human Rights (CIPAC), a surviving gay-rights group, says the Education Ministry ignored two formal requests for an explanation: "The deadline passed a long time ago, and nobody says anything."

Despite the country's reputation as an island of tolerance for gays, sexual politics is in a slump in Costa Rica, although the surviving groups did manage to draw out the main presidential candidates during a recent campaign to discuss same-sex marriage. But a gay health movement built around HIV/AIDS is a thing of the past, and gone with it is the steady drumbeat of messages reinforcing safe practices. With treatment assured and the activist scene somewhat demoralized, middle-class gays are not panicking or as worried as they once were. For their part, the foreign funders are unlikely to resuscitate the patient with so many facing far worse conditions elsewhere.

Meanwhile, without a new crisis, things probably will muddle along pretty much as they are with outfits like the Rotary club, with its cautiously limited approach, moving in to fill the obvious gaps in ongoing AIDS education. As Madrigal suggests, Costa Rica is tolerant about what happens privately but almost as slow as anywhere else in dealing with the ongoing gay epidemic.

Despite their complaints, Costa Ricans are almost sanctimonious in admitting that their trials are minor compared to what happens in nearby Honduras or Nicaragua. "At least no one gets killed here," said one with a laugh. In Central America, that counts for a lot.

The Gospel

We got a call one day from a family asking if we could provide help for their relative who was bedridden with late-stage AIDS. We hadn't really developed a system for that sort of thing, so I asked if we could come out and visit them to see what the situation was. The caller was an elder sister of the patient, and it turned out that they were a large family of evangelical Christians. The house was way out in Cerrillos near the Santiago airport. When we got there, a lot of people were coming and going, little kids, babies, siblings, neighbors, you name it. Elena and I were ushered into the bedroom with his mother, two aunts, cousins, nursing moms and their babies, a whole scene. We discussed the service that we could provide, how many hours a week, whether they needed someone overnight. Everything was going along fine, and we were on the verge of leaving when I realized it didn't add up. Why were they asking for bedside care with all these people milling around? Since I had learned that the person involved sometimes doesn't really want the service that the family is asking for, I said I needed to talk to him in private. So everyone left.

I pulled my chair up to the bedside and asked him if he agreed with the idea that our volunteers would come and look after him certain days. The guy was in bad shape, really skin and bones. I don't think he would have survived a ride in the ambulance at that point. It was the first time I had dealt with someone in that advanced state of emaciation in which the face is so deathlike that it disconcerts you. He said he didn't really want a stranger to be changing his soiled clothes, and I said that was understandable. But then he changed the subject. He started to talk about his life and the partners he had had. He said he was bisexual and that it was a sin. My first reaction was to say, No it isn't! But the guy was adamant and started to discuss theology with me. I really didn't know what to say.

Finally, he asked me what I thought of what he had done, and I said that from my point of view, since I didn't go to his church, that the most important thing was how he had acted with his boyfriends, how he had been as a human being. Had he been decent toward them, or was he a jerk? He said he thought he had infected one with HIV. Intentionally? No, of course not. Well then. We went back and forth like that. We talked about how people relate to each other in their sexual and intimate lives, how you have strong feelings and sometimes do things you regret, but that's all part of it. He wasn't convinced, but he loosened up about it. As for the service, he said that he would like to talk to a psychologist first. So we arranged that.

After the psychologist he asked for a doctor visit, and we managed to get that too. Every time Elena would drive the person to the house in Cerrillos and shoo everyone else out so that the two of them could talk. I asked the psychologist and the doctor whether he wanted home visiting services after all or just to talk about his life, and they pretty much indicated that it was the same subject over and over. The request to help out with care really was a vehicle for something else he needed.

After the three visits we didn't hear from them again until about a week later. The sister called back to thank us and said that her brother had gathered the whole family around him one night. He said that he was going to die now and that he would see them all in heaven. They started to sing their church hymns, and he just slipped away very peacefully.

I realized that he didn't need us to change his sheets or to fluff his pillows but to talk about his double life since everyone else around him condemned it, at least officially. He did too, and I think that was what prevented him from letting go. It seemed as though he had to cling to that belief in the afterlife, but at the same time he was afraid that he'd lost his chance to reach heaven. He talked to the whole lot of us and got the same answer, so I guess he decided it would all be okay. I always thought it was ironic that three agnostics had managed to convince a Christian fundamentalist that he was saved.

—Anonymous

CHAPTER FOUR

Guatemala: The Iron Fist

GUATEMALA	
Population	11.6 million
First reported case of AIDS	1984
Total estimated HIV infections (2003)	74,000
Male : female ratio	2.1:1
Estimated number of people needing antiretroviral treatment	13,500
Number receiving drugs	3,500
First AIDS prevention NGO established	1988
Adult women using birth control	38%
Gross domestic product (GDP) 2003	$24.7 billion
Per capita income (2003)	$1,190
Annual per-capita spending on health	$91
Unemployment rate	7.5%
Military rule	1954–1982
Estimated deaths during civil war	200,000
War ends with peace treaty	1996
Bishop Girardi murdered after issuing human rights report	1998

Human rights are a hot potato, but Catholics and sex educators get along fine.

Politics in Guatemala is a continuation of warfare by other means. What would be recriminations elsewhere may quickly turn into threats in Guatemala City, the City of Eternal Spring. As in Colombia, when Guatemalans receive death threats, they leave. Even at the more mundane level of personal squabbles, violence is often the preferred method of conflict resolution. The daily papers are full of matter-of-fact items such as the ambush shooting of an entire family in a passing automobile because one rider had refused to pay a debt. The legacy of Guatemala's four decades of genocidal civil war, suspended but hardly resolved with a 1996 peace treaty after producing some 200,000 deaths, remains scarcely buried below the surface.

In the AIDS field, the well-founded fear of entering into anything smacking of politics, even health politics, had a peculiar manifestation. Says Giovanni Meléndez, a psychologist involved in AIDS projects:

> The issue of the NGOs has been pretty controversial because in a sense they were always associated with a political tendency, and for a while it wasn't advisable to work in an NGO or be mixed up with them because that meant being against the government, to take an openly left-wing position.

This was particularly true of any nongovernmental organization involved with indigenous populations or raising the flag of "human rights," an essential element of AIDS-related work, given the enormous social discrimination and stigma associated with HIV infection. On the other hand, continued Meléndez, health programs might not immediately produce this associative hot potato because they "suggested well-meaning, less conflictive people."

Where "human rights" is promptly interpreted as support for the armed rebellion, the temptation to stick strictly to care-oriented charity projects such as AIDS hospices or Christian volunteer home care must have been enormous. When I visited in 2002, the Guatemalan government felt no threat from this particular type of nongovernmental initiative; in fact, it managed to find an extraordinary $500,000 for one such project, as Dory Lucas, the head of the national AIDS program, explained proudly:

> The full budget request was granted so we could work with civil society organizations that take care of people with AIDS to carry out their humanitarian work.

Nonetheless—and here the parallel with Colombia weakens—reproductive health politics seems not to have generated the virulent repression common to other social initiatives. The AIDS NGOs go about their business relatively unmolested, and during the Second Central American Conference on AIDS (November 13–16, 2001), at which I served as media liaison, HIV-positive people and their supporters paraded through the city and held a brief rally in the plaza of a traffic circle. This event took place near the conference site, the Camino Real Hotel in the tony uptown part of Guatemala City. Joining the march was a small contingent of the city's huge population of street children, some no more than four years old, who interrupted their usual activities of begging and dodging the police to dance merrily alongside the marchers.

At the Health Ministry, however, the knives were drawn when Kathleen Cravero, the number two person at the central secretariat of the United Nations Programme on AIDS in Geneva, visited. The meeting took place hours before Cravero opened the conference with a call to regional governments not to squander the two- to three-year "window of opportunity" available to them to put a brake on the epidemic before infection rates among sexually active adults rose above the 2 percent mark, considered by some to be the point of no return for AIDS. In front of other UNAIDS officials and me, Mario Bolaños, the health minister, wasted no time in trashing a local doctor as a cynical exploiter of people with AIDS. The Guatemalan government, he insisted, would have nothing to do with such players and their "perverse interests."

Despite singling out a private doctor for his fury, Bolaños suggested that if the Global Fund for AIDS, Tuberculosis and Malaria were to provide money for Guatemala, it should be channeled through an independent third party. By no means, said the minister, should the resources be sent straight to his government.

The implication was patently clear: If you send the money to the state treasury, it will be grabbed.

Gloria Castro is a mild-mannered woman in her forties who works for the Catholic Archbishopric's social pastorate from an office near the presidential palace in Guatemala City. Widowed by the political violence, she nods toward the corner of the pastorate's meeting hall, occupied by a memorial to Bishop Juan José Girardi who was beaten to death with a paving stone in his garage in 1998, days after releasing a report on human rights violations during the civil war. In the 1970s and 1980s the military dictatorships in power often perceived Catholic church hierarchies throughout Latin America as unreliable at best and riddled with sympathizers for "Marxist" opponents of the ruling juntas. The dictatorships took as proof of the church's disloyalty and penchant for harboring communists its support of human rights organizations where relatives of the victims of torture, disappearance and assassination sought redress.

In most countries of the region, the end of military rule enabled the more conservative forces within Catholicism, aided by the late Pope, to reassert themselves and impose a cozier relationship with business and political elites, as well as to shift its institutional attention to public morality and especially sexuality. Not in Guatemala. There the heirs of the death squads continue to operate with relative impunity, and Catholicism remains highly suspect to the temporal powers. Not surprisingly, the church in Guatemala seems far less concerned with policing sexual politics.

Castro recognizes that AIDS organizations generally view the Catholic church as a rival, if not an adversary, for its well-known official positions on condom use and sexual autonomy. Almost anywhere else, Catholic-sponsored approaches to HIV prevention would tend to focus narrowly on appeals to abstinence and partner fidelity. Castro's description of the Guatemalan pastorate's AIDS initiatives is superficially consistent with this general posture:

> The family is very important for the church. We provide sex education, and we consistently insert the human values that the church promotes: abstinence, chastity for youth and mutual fidelity.

But this is not the whole story. Castro concentrates her efforts on the Catholic flock who have little awareness of their personal risk, due to the now-historic association of AIDS with gays and commercial sex. She is one of the many church-related activists who are personally open-minded and tolerant while being ideologically convinced that sexual dissidents are on the wrong path. As a result, she is simultaneously capable of welcoming and forging genuinely close relations with the mostly gay HIV-positive group that meets weekly at the pastorate and casually commenting that their prevention workshops emphasize how "normal" heterosexuals also can acquire HIV.

But the apparently seamless conformity to official dogma does not fully describe Castro's approach and, by extension, the potential of Guatemalan Catholicism in the AIDS field. For starters, the pastorate has an active and enthusiastic program addressing the issue, a program that consciously attempts to break out of the church's traditional care-provision role in the health sphere to include discussions of prevention and at least some sexuality. Its workshops have been expanded to eleven provinces, and the approach borrows heavily from popular education methodology that the country's reactionaries violently hate and what in another context would be called "empowerment." Castro explains:

> We don't offer people beans or a place to sleep but the chance to gain consciousness, to critically analyze their reality and the reality of the country and on that basis carry out their commitments as [Catholic] laypeople.

During the civil wars in El Salvador, Guatemala and Nicaragua, such educational approaches by Catholic activists to social issues such as land reform or political domination eventually stirred political movements that alarmed elites and motivated them to launch their genocidal campaigns. Although recollections of those terrible years are still quite fresh, sexuality workshops using these same techniques continue nonetheless.

Indeed, the monolithic stance on AIDS in Catholic circles is both real and illusory. Although the hierarchy toes the official line, individuals provide the local nuances that Catholic institutions reflect in dealing with the AIDS issue. In some countries Catholic charities provide useful services and discourage discrimination; in others the archbishop indulges in stigmatizing and condemnatory rhetoric. Opposition to condom use is almost universal, but some church figures simply avoid the subject so as not to feed the polemics around prevention campaigns; other clergy will fight sex education and tolerance for pluralism tooth and nail.

The workshop approach Castro describes, while safely within the strictures of dogma, inevitably opens up possibilities rather than dictating behavior. She says:

> We have an ethical obligation to speak about condoms, to explain them, to tell people what the situation is, everything about that. However, we also give them the opportunity to see that there are not just advantages. We as the church speak about what we promote, and we tell them of the importance of their own reflection and their reality. So everyone has the chance to decide for themselves.

This flexibility is a far cry from the ideological warfare seen in other Catholic enclaves that often exists with high-level support; rather, it is a Catholic church not entirely reincorporated into the arms of the conservative financial and ideological elites, encouraged by the current papacy's systematical reversal of the "preferential option for the poor" announced at the historic 1968 Medellín (Colombia) conference by Latin America's bishops.

In Guatemala's case, the perpetrators of the massive violence are still protected and actively operating in the country, with religious figures and believers ready targets. Not surprisingly, the church hierarchy distances itself from the alliances with temporal powers common elsewhere in Latin America to block initiatives on contraception or sex education. Although the pastorate's focus remains traditional, its AIDS initiatives suggest concerned prevention education rather than ideological combat. In fact, Castro attends the AIDS NGO coordinating meetings and is well regarded by her secular colleagues. In addition, she remains open to unexpected influences, saying:

> Contact with people living with HIV/AIDS is very important in this issue because through that conversation, by getting close to them and generating trust, they make you see life in a different way. They also make you see and recognize things that, otherwise, probably you wouldn't.

Despite the Catholic church's historic preference for charitable works, the country's ruling elite must view it as unreliable and permeated by enemies in the ongoing class- and race-based war. Without the natural outlet of a hospice or "dignified death" clinic like those favored by other Catholic charities, the pastorate's role is likely to be distinguishable from but increasingly compatible with secular AIDS campaigns. Indeed, given the country's social and sexual conservatism, church-led AIDS programs may well open wedges that other programs could not. Castro explains:

> Now in these provincial parishes, we had a little trouble at first. It scares a lot of people. They say, But why do we need to know about this? We're not going to get infected. Within the church, many people operate on the idea that we're all this or that, but that's not true either because we're just like anyone else. We show them that at a given moment, given the number of people infected in Guatemala, it's going to be knocking on their door. Maybe it will be a friend, a relative, someone in the community or they themselves.

Models such as that developed by Gloria Castro's colleagues may have an even larger role to play in the future in Latin America if the much-heralded heterosexual epidemic really takes hold in the region. (This situation appears to be occurring slowly but steadily in most Latin American countries, although it is still a far cry from what is happening in Africa or even Asia). The entire issue of women's position in the epidemic—as an especially vulnerable group, as actors and as people with HIV—is complex and full of contradictions. Although feminist critics are correct to point out that many women's issues have been ignored in the handling of AIDS, women—at least in their reproductive function—were always a far more compelling cause for official and media concern about HIV infection than homosexual men. The earliest reports may have trumpeted the "gay plague," but very soon thereafter newspaper and television audiences were moved by dramatic tales of the truncated lives of "innocent victims"— HIV-positive newborns—suggesting that everyone else with AIDS was guilty. Infantile innocence fit neatly into traditional Catholic concepts of original sin with AIDS the symbolic ejection from the Garden of Eden for the sin of carnal knowledge. Even today for many people it is intuitively "unfair" for babies to get AIDS, unlike adults who somehow "earn" it through sexual pleasures. Although these early subtexts were exposed and roundly criticized, children suffering from HIV disease still attract more solidarity and concern than their adult counterparts. When I took calls on our hotline through the 1990s, people often phoned to offer material or moral support for projects for HIV babies or toddlers, but were far less eager to donate to services for grown-ups.

Prevention of HIV infection among newborns worldwide has been accomplished most successfully by screening pregnant women and using prophylactic drugs to suppress the virus during childbirth. But even there subtle discrimination often prevailed: In many countries perinatal (mother-to-child) transmission was treated early on, but far less effort went into providing the HIV-positive mothers with life-saving drugs because the same sympathy did not extend to them. Many of the earliest women who acquired HIV infection faced enormous stigma if their situation did not result from an errant husband—and often even if it did. Women were quickly blamed for their HIV-positive status, but as feminist and other authors have noted, it is difficult for many women to protect themselves because they do not exercise real control or autonomy over their sexual lives. Aside from the physiological vulnerabilities women face due to their greater areas of genital mucosa and the ease of infection when HIV-laden sperm remains in the vagina, women also suffer from social and economic disadvantages that restrict their ability to refuse sexual relations or to determine the conditions under which they will occur. Women more often face sexual violence or abuse, depend economically on male partners and are culturally indoctrinated to serve others and think of themselves last. Social norms place lower value on women and girls; some societies prefer women to be ignorant of sex and associate sophistication in this realm with promiscuity. In short, a sort of "gender fault line," to use a memorable UNAIDS phrase, traces the progress of heterosexual HIV epidemics around the world.

For all these reasons, preventing those mothers and other women from acquiring HIV has been far less successful because structural elements are harder to address than mere gaps in knowledge or shortcomings in the provision of specific services. Even more problematic from a methodological point of view, women as a population group are hard to reach for HIV education purposes, even harder than the so-called hard-to-reach groups such as gay men, injecting drug users and sex workers. Although these latter groups tend to have geographic meeting points, intragroup codes and some degree of self-identification as part of a persecuted minority—all elements that peer educators can use—women may not. Only a tiny minority of women will participate in social or political activities as women (although they may do many things as parents, members of a religious community or the like), and in any case, these active women are not likely to be the most vulnerable. One important exception is the area of reproductive health services, where women are very likely to gather, but many practitioners realize that women are least in control of their lives precisely in that area.

The United Nations agencies that deal specifically with the issue of women and AIDS, such as the UN Population Fund (UNFPA) and the UN Development Fund for Women (UNIFEM), acknowledge this situation indirectly in the kinds of prevention activities they promote. Some involve gathering women or girls into training sessions or workshops, but most are targeted much more broadly at youths or the entire population, at changing social attitudes about gender roles, keeping girls in school longer and/or encouraging women to achieve economic independence. Not only are interventions exclusively for women hard to shape for practical reasons—how do you reach women without simultaneously including men?—but if male behavior is so often at the root of the risks women face, women-only projects only will address one side of the problem.

Governments have an ambiguous and often exasperatingly comfortable attitude toward the problem of heterosexual transmission and women with HIV. On one hand, they are inclined to use transmission between heterosexual partners to downplay the inconvenient aspects of the epidemic, such as homosexuality and prostitution, while at the same time they resist the truly historic task of reducing women's vulnerability by treating women more fairly in all areas of social and economic life, and providing competent sexuality education and reproductive health services. In addition, governments have a pervasive tendency to ignore the high rates of homosexual transmission because the lives of the men involved simply are not a priority concern of the average government official.

In the Guatemalan case, the early militance from gay-oriented activists led the state to celebrate less troublesome projects and to reinforce its intention to see what it chose to see in its statistics. According to official statistics, Guatemala's AIDS epidemic is among the most heterosexual in the region and perhaps in all of Latin America. Only 15 percent of all HIV infections are attributed to homosexual contact, far below the 40 to 80 percent common elsewhere around the continent. This might reasonably be grounds for directing most prevention energies toward the massive indigenous and rural populations. But as often occurs, Guatemala's epidemiological data may be less of a guide for action than a result of the actions already taken.

Dory Lucas, the AIDS coordinator for the Guatemalan government, occupied a small office behind the main Health Ministry building in Guatemala City, which was in the midst of a major housecleaning operation at the time of our visit. Wearing a black suit and a gold bracelet and watch, she expressed pride at her government's role in the AIDS issue and noted that her own appointment "broke the paradigm" because she is not a medical doctor but a specialist in communications from the NGO world.

Without prompting, she defended the government's role from its detractors. Criticism is appropriate when nothing is happening, she said, but "if the government is responding to the country's demands, you have to give it credit." NGO leaders, she instructed, simply fail to understand the role of the state:

> Look, for a lot of people it's hard to understand that the ministry has a guiding role, that the Ministry of Health is the manager in Guatemala. The laws say so. Decree 272000 says so.

Like a patient schoolteacher setting out basic lessons, Lucas explained the slow progress in putting the technically excellent but inoperative AIDS law into force:

> A lot of people think a regulation is like a law. A regulation is not a law. It is a procedure accompanying the law, and this has delayed the process greatly while the ministry consults lawyers and juridical specialists.

As for the pattern of AIDS in Guatemala, Lucas confidently stated that it was "primarily heterosexual":

There are more heterosexual cases, more notifications of men. Then [*come*] women and afterward of course, children who are born with the HIV virus.

Unfortunately, her explanation is internally contradictory. If the epidemic is fundamentally heterosexual, why are more men infected than women? Given women's greater physiological vulnerability, a heterosexual epidemic should produce at least an even ratio of HIV infections, if not a slight majority of HIV-positive women, as seen in some African countries. Due to Guatemala's social conservatism and the natural reticence of men to mention homosexual relations when seeking medical care, the built-in desire for a heterosexual epidemic is a self-fulfilling statistical prophecy while the reality of people's sexual practices may be quite different.

Ruben Mayorga, a medical doctor and head of the gay-oriented group Organización de Atención Social Integral Sostenible (Organization for Comprehensive and Sustainable Care), or OASIS, in Guatemala City, estimates the real figure for homosexual transmission at 40 percent of all cases. Mayorga explains:

Unless he's a total queen, a man will always be [*counted as*] heterosexual. Plus, people don't want to be recognized [*as homosexual*]. There, women have done us a lot of damage, and they're partly right. Because when they find out about a bisexual man, they accuse him of everything. A bisexual man cannot exist.

Given its disinclination to recognize homosexual transmission, the central government unsurprisingly is more disposed to discuss its AIDS prevention work far from the capital and its gay-consciousness or gender-sensitive prevention and care groups. Lucas says:

Look, AIDS was very centralized at the level of the capital. Here there was excellent work, but no one wanted to go to the interior of the country where there are no means of communication, where you have to ride a bus for eight hours. So sure, here there is work. Civil society is well regarded here. But in the interior of the country, no.

Another factor is that the more astute, experienced and critical NGOs are nowhere to be seen in the countryside. In fact, Lucas is so disliked by the main groups that her appearance at the regional AIDS conference would have provoked a walkout, if not a public shouting match. She is accused of single-handedly sabotaging the previous coordinating work of the NGO council. According to Mayorga:

> You know what we did that was very simple and easy? Trainings for the organizations. We got trainings in evaluation, prevention project design, statistical analysis. We had a whole training program for the organizations, and it all died. Because of her.

Thus, it is hardly surprising that Lucas prefers her work in the provinces, focusing on indigenous and presumably heterosexual audiences. Her doors, she insists, are always open. Of course, she adds, "Those who don't ask, we don't respond." But Lucas said the government did have its NGO allies. One of the high points of the government's performance, she said, is its work with a group of HIV-positive people called Gente Nueva (New People) Fully "on message" like her superior at the Health Ministry, Lucas volunteered another attack on the government's bête noire, Dr. Eduardo Arathoon, the same man who had attracted the minister's unprovoked ire. "We are providing medication to twenty-seven people after an NGO stopped serving them," she said, adding that the Guatemalan government even put the beneficiaries to work in the national program. The government also employs them as consultants, she added. "This strengthens them as they then have a means of survival." Whether the average Guatemalan can get decent services or avoid discrimination or not, the government could showcase this organization as proof that it is doing its best.

Although many more people in Guatemala receive their AIDS drugs through the social security system that covers all employed people—which Minister

Bolaños warned was teetering on bankruptcy for that very reason—the famous twenty-seven drug therapies provided to Gente Nueva attracted far more attention as an emblematic case. The interpretations available are not just different—they describe parallel universes.

Dr. Eduardo Arathoon is a gray-haired medical doctor of about forty-five, with a florid countenance and a mild demeanor that nonetheless suggests a fairly wicked temper beneath. His acquaintances say he does not shy away from controversy, which was evident from reading the newspaper. His narrative about the famous twenty-seven drug therapies now being provided directly by the Guatemalan state begins with a clinical trial in 1997. When the pharmaceutical company agreed to keep supplying the most expensive of the three drugs (Crixivan) for five additional years, Arathoon's outfit, the Association for Comprehensive Health (ASI) obtained and began to administer an agreement with two ministries to provide the remaining two drugs. When the arrangement ended with a change of government, Arathoon encouraged his beneficiaries to follow the Costa Rican strategy and sue the government. But Guatemala is not Costa Rica. Arathoon explained in an e-mail:

> When they found out about the lawsuit pending in the courts, the Health Ministry audited us to try to prove that ASI was misusing the funds. We passed with flying colors . . . and [*the auditors*] were called on the carpet for not having found any "smoking guns." They were furious.

The government had lost a battle, but it was not in the habit of losing wars.

Arathoon's patients' lawsuit was technically successful; the petition was granted in January 2001, then appealed by the government. But the medicines did not appear. Much was at stake in the legal battle because, just as in Costa Rica, a victory could easily force the government's hand. In fact, there was no reason to think that only HIV patients would be the eventual beneficiaries of a victory. Arathoon's e-mail continued:

> If they give the medicines to these thirty-one patients, the others from the clinic could follow with a suit for their medicines as well because they can't discriminate. If this occurs in the AIDS field, all the other patients—heart,

diabetes, kidneys, cancer—would ask for their medicines too. The ministry
would find itself forced to work for the health of the Guatemalan people.

Arathoon clearly does not believe that the ministry is in the habit of doing this.
His version of the endgame that followed was that the government offered to
guarantee drug supplies for the entire group of patients if they would withdraw
from the lawsuit.

> So they stabbed the other AIDS patients in the back. On the other hand,
> I understand that they were very afraid because the drugs were running out
> and the courts weren't resolving anything.

As I witnessed firsthand, Arathoon was then vilified systematically.
"It's pretty frustrating to have to put up with so much crap all at once," he says.

Rather than being the ophidian villain top government officials describe
whether anyone asks or not, Arathoon apparently tried to break legal ground for
people with HIV as was done in Costa Rica. He continues to pay a heavy price
for provoking the ferocious ire of the Guatemalan state.

Ismar Ramírez was the person selected by the congress organizers to represent
people living with HIV/AIDS in the opening ceremony. While the health minister's advisor, Julio Argueta, ostentatiously used his cell phone at the front table,
Ramírez chastised the government for limiting its political role to the reopening
of an AIDS hospice dedicated to "death with dignity."

During the remainder of the congress, HIV-positive delegates from all seven
Central American countries spoke about the situations they faced, some
haltingly, others more systematically with ubiquitous PowerPoint graphics. In an
informal meeting one local delegate avoided requests for an interview, not from
privacy issues but because he said he felt incapable of addressing the questions.
On another occasion Cravero from the UNAIDS office met with the HIV-
positive representatives before heading back to Geneva. Governments would
be encouraged and rewarded if they placed the involvement of People Living
with HIV/AIDS (or PLWA) high up on their priority lists, she promised, and
more funds would be available to those who do it sooner. Despite the obstacles,

officials from the region's health ministries were clearly feeling the pressure to deal with demands for drug access. Regimes impervious to the policy implications of the HIV epidemic during the long infection phase and uncooperative on sexual health issues were being pulled kicking and screaming into dealing with their HIV-positive citizens.

Nevertheless, three years after this regional conclave, PWLA representatives complained that the agreements reached there still have not produced the anticipated and promised results. Writing from Costa Rica in mid-2004, Guillermo Murillo challenged the Pan American Health Organization to explain why the technical entity it promised to create to evaluate and approve cheaper generic HIV drugs still is not up and running. Despite ample funding and technical assistance now available, half the governments of Central America are still unable to put HIV medicines into the hands of those who need them.

While driving through Guatemala City late one night to the hotel in a downtown area, an NGO leader pointed out the Club Guatemala, where teenage debutantes of the local elite hold their coming-out parties. A few days before, a journalist colleague had shown me the notorious police headquarters located on the same block that had housed a dungeon for torturing prisoners during the civil war that had lasted four decades and only had ended five years before. Given the sad state of human rights in Guatemala and its recent genocidal history, appealing to respect for the human rights of people with HIV/AIDS is a very tough sell. In such a hostile environment, it is no wonder that those working on the issue managed to find common cause and to overlook their ideological and personal differences.

Although I had gone to Guatemala to talk to people about their work in HIV/AIDS prevention and care, the main activists were busy preparing for the regional conference that took place during my visit. I was recruited to act as press officer and saw an efficient, collaborative event that reminded me of the best periods of NGO unity elsewhere. While Guatemalan officialdom reveled in its crude unfriendliness, the main civilian actors there seemed to be getting along famously. In countries where governments were more permeable and enlightened, such horizontal goodwill was extremely rare.

Rapid Intervention

One day the phone rang around noon, and it was a woman calling from the psychiatric hospital. She was weeping bitterly. Her twenty-four-year-old son had just been hospitalized after a suicide attempt. She came from a long way away, and her son had called her to say that he wanted to talk to her. He was a university student and had been diagnosed with HIV. He had a boyfriend, but apparently they didn't really get along all that well anymore even though they still lived together. This fellow had decided not to live with HIV, and that's what he told his mother when she came to Santiago.

The suicide attempt had occurred in the following way: He was talking with his partner in their apartment and suddenly ran to the sixth-floor window and tried to jump out. The boyfriend managed to get hold of him and calm him down, and then he called the guy's mother. She arrived three days later with an uncle, and in the middle of the conversation the guy did it again, went to the window and tried to throw himself out of it. They could only hold onto him by his trousers and shoes, shouting from the sixth floor and with the boy hanging out the window. They were holding him by the ankles, and the boy was yelling, "Let go of me, let go!" Some people heard them down in the street and called the cops, who came and knocked on the door, but no one could go open it because both the uncle and the mother were still holding onto the guy. The cops finally knocked the door down because the woman was screaming, "Come in!"

So the police took the man to the psychiatric hospital, and that's where his mother was calling from. He'd been there two days and kept saying that he knew exactly what he was doing. In fact, in the hospital he tried to do it again, this time cutting his wrist right through an artery. They caught him and bound up that wound, but there was nothing they could do about the wound he had in his mind and heart.

When I got this call, I started to think rapidly and asked her to stay where she was and that I would find a social worker and a place for him to stay that night. But her idea was that once her son was released, he would head right back for the sixth-floor apartment and try to jump out again. She was distraught, so I said, Okay, let me think. I'm going to find someone who can help you and someone who can help him. So come over to our offices—take a taxi, and we'll pay for it—and tell him that you'll come back in forty minutes.

So that's what she did. She arrived in a taxi to our offices, and I had found a social worker. The uncle came later, and we were all four in the office trying to figure out what to do next. We got a place for the fellow to stay and the relatives on the first floor to stay with him, and I called back the psychiatric hospital to say that we were coming over when the doorman told me that he had signed himself out and was gone. That his arms were okay, and since he was an adult, he had just asked for the ambulance half an hour before and left.

At that moment I tried not to let my face show what I was hearing. But I had to ask where he had gone, and they understood that he had gone back home. We called over to the apartment, and all we could hear were shouts and cries, a voice screaming "Where's his mother? Tell her to come over right away!" It was exactly as we thought; he walked into the apartment, opened the window, and jumped out. At that moment the body was lying on the street covered with newspapers.

With all this shouting over the telephone, it was impossible to hide what had happened. They understood everything, and the woman started to wail and say to the uncle that the boy was dead. The uncle said that he was determined to kill himself in any case.

I felt so guilty over that situation: If I hadn't told the woman to come over, perhaps the boy would still be alive. I had to ask for psychological counseling for myself, and they told me that there was nothing I could have done to avoid it. I don't know if they said that to console me, or if it was really was the truth. Who knows?

—Elena Droguett

CHAPTER FIVE

Trinidad and Tobago: Living with People Living with HIV/AIDS

TRINIDAD AND TOBAGO	
Population	1.3 million
First reported case of AIDS	1983
Total estimated HIV infections	29,000
Male : female ratio	1.9:1
Estimated number of people needing antiretroviral treatment	4,700
Number receiving drugs	1,000
Adult women using birth control	53%
Gross domestic product (GDP) 2003	$10.2 billion
Per capita income (2003)	$7,260
Annual per-capita spending on health	$214
Unemployment rate	10.9%
Independence from Great Britain	1962

A world conference for people living with HIV fails to notice those doing so just down the street.

The tenth International Conference for People Living with HIV/AIDS took place in Port-of-Spain, Trinidad, in October 2001, sponsored by the worldwide body that attempts to speak in the name of this now 40-million-strong population, the Global Network of People Living with HIV/AIDS, or GNP+. Although Caribbean countries together have a high per-capita HIV infection rate, with their tiny populations the entire region has fewer total HIV infections than Uganda. As a result, the Caribbean can slip by unnoticed in the AIDS debate. When the world is divided up into regions, the Caribbean usually is grouped with Latin America due to geographic proximity, but its epidemiological patterns are quite dissimilar from those on the Latin American continent. In addition, the language barrier often makes joint action or alliances impractical.

Even within the Caribbean, coordinated action is problematic. Nearly every group of islands is an independent country with its own health authority and political dynamic. The islands' dependence on tourism has made many Caribbean leaders aware both of the risks of an expanding AIDS epidemic and of the dangers of letting the news leak out. Coherent and effective responses have been rare. To further complicate matters, several of the biggest islands with the most serious epidemics are isolated by additional factors: The Dominican Republic is Spanish-speaking, but in practical terms light-years from its cousins in Puerto Rico, which is part of the United States, and the politically anomalous Cuba. Haitians, the worst off of all in HIV prevalence, speak Creole.

The Latin American regional branch of the world alliance of AIDS NGOs also includes the Caribbean in its portfolio. One consequence is that many of those engaged in AIDS work in Latin America met the first generation of activists from places like Trinidad and Tobago, Barbados and Jamaica at the earliest continental gatherings. But aside from the difficulties of simple communication, it was never clear that their region really had much in common with Latin America when it came to AIDS.

Therefore, my observer visit to the GNP+ confab taking place on the region's largest island was motivated by questions about two issues: the current shape of the movements around the world of people living with HIV and AIDS and the realities of AIDS in these tiny, insular Caribbean states known to outsiders only as picture-postcard resorts.

Trinidad and Tobago, with a population of 1.3 million, is the largest and southernmost island group of the Antilles chain and is perhaps a bit more connected to Latin America than many of the other islands. Students from the nearby Venezuelan mainland travel there looking for cheap English courses. In addition, the country produced one of the first openly HIV-positive activists in a developing country, playwright Godfrey Sealy, who courageously broke both the AIDS and the homosexual taboos in the early 1990s. Sealy says:

> I wrote a drama in 1989 on AIDS, the social circumstances surrounding the virus, and also with homosexuality as well because the lead character is a bisexual man. I've always been of the firm belief that early in the epidemic we needed to deal with men who have sex with both men and women because intuitively I know what this society in the Caribbean is like. I know Trinidad, and even though it appeared to be a gay disease in the beginning, I know from our cultural experience here in this country that a lot of men sleep around with women, so obviously the virus would have started to spread out of the gay community or whatever—I don't know about any gay "community" per se in Trinidad.

The slightly built Sealy is a personable and amusing figure whose illness has affected his ability to walk. He reached the conference site in the Hilton atop a small rise off the city's vast central park, the Savannah, after a slow climb with help from escorts. Sealy made light of the cultural narrowness of his native island and expressed pessimism about his compatriots' ability to imitate strategies applied successfully elsewhere, saying:

> If the Brazilians hadn't done what they did, or the Costa Ricans, a small place like that, they wouldn't have got their medicines. You need to have that kind of open, in-your-face movement.

Although the Caribbean may look to visitors as tropical and free-wheeling, sexual mores in Trinidad are surprisingly straitlaced, as any reader of the

Trinidad-born Nobel novelist V. S. Naipul quickly will recognize. The main streets of Port-of-Spain are dotted with storefront evangelical churches such as the Tabernacle of Prayer, giving the capital the feel of an inner-city Baltimore or Washington, D.C., dominated by Baptist preachers and their conservative flocks. Dr. Courtenay Bartholomew is the director of Trinidad's Medical Research Foundation and considered honest and well intentioned by others involved in HIV/AIDS in the country. He opened the island's Alcohol and Drug Awareness Week, which coincided with the GNP+ conference, with his own version of the AIDS acronym:

A—Alcohol
I—Incest
D—Drugs
S—Sex

He warned that the country would soon be divided into "the chaste and the dead" if Trinidadians did not alter their bedroom habits. This doomsayer discourse has long passed into disrepute elsewhere, but its confident adoption by a leading activist clinician suggests the retrograde local atmosphere.

Muriel Douglas, the head of Trinidad and Tobago's government AIDS program, said sex education still remains virtually taboo. "We have to say 'promotion of a healthy lifestyle' to get around the resistance," she said with a laugh. On the other hand, apocalyptic, evangelical interpretations of the AIDS phenomenon abound, such as the free, four-color newsprint weekly *UPSTREAM* featuring articles on why Carnival should be banned for five years and counseling young people on how to face "sexual addictions." Although the morality campaigns often include calls to avoid prejudice and discrimination, the overall tone on the islands, says Dennis McComie, of Artists against AIDS, who has a decade of experience, is of fear and ignorance.

People will still ask you ridiculous questions like whether you can be infected from a mosquito or from touching "them." All the classic ones— they should be weeded out and put on an island somehow, for their promiscuity, they brought it on themselves, God is punishing gay people, the works. You still have to deal with that.

With a large ethnic Indian population adding its particular form of clannish orthodoxy, one can appreciate the enormous obstacles Sealy confronted with his matter-of-fact honesty. He says:

> My escalation with the play, people assuming that I'm both homosexual [*and HIV-positive*], and besides going about in rural communities and talking to reporters and the media, that sort of thing—I came out on the front page of a weekly. I didn't make any hoo-hah about denying it. I just went with it. I went with my gut feeling, this was going to be my struggle from then on.

More than a decade later Sealy is still pretty much on his own as a publicly HIV-positive Trinidadian. Despite the attendance of dozens of others at the world conference, not one dared to join him as the public face of AIDS in Trinidad, except for a conference organizer and longtime activist who spent several years in Canada working for AIDS organizations. Nor did the GNP+ conference, which took place in quiet obscurity on the wooded Hilton hilltop, seem likely to add anyone new.

In statistical terms, homosexual transmission of HIV is not demonstrably the principal factor in the Caribbean—the largest group, 20 to 30 percent, is "unde-termined." Many observers think this phenomenon indicates a hidden homosexual epidemic. According to AIDS program director Douglas, male-male sex accounts for only 7 percent of the Trinidadian cases. But, she added, the first female HIV diagnosis occurred in the third year of the epidemic, which makes immediate hash of the official statistics.

In Trinidad as elsewhere, gay men tended to be especially alert to the appearance of AIDS among their peers. But the claustrophobic insularity of the island and the enormous cultural intolerance of homosexuality made the usual sorts of peer-group educational techniques, based on frank conversations about sexual matters, highly problematic.

Nigel Celestine is an artistic producer who sidelines as a costumer for Trinidad's famous Carnival celebration. Although sympathetic, he has kept his distance from the tentative steps to organize what everyone on the island skeptically termed the gay "community," with broad quotation marks and raised eyebrows. He participated for a while in the Wednesday night "Chatroom" meetings where a dozen guys would hear a speaker or talk about their experiences. But these discussions presumed a degree of confidentiality. Celestine explains:

> Personally from what I have seen, I don't have a lot of faith in a lot of these groups because when you speak about your experiences, the very next day somebody can call and say, Oh, I heard this and I heard that.

As for a gay community, "It has never existed, and I don't think it ever will," he says, and notes that homosexuality is still punishable by law in Trinidad.

> You can't show any affection on the street. There are some drag queens who walk the street and get a lot of abuse from the police. But they have clients. The fact that they are out there on the street every night, that's another thing that we don't discuss. It means somebody is paying them, the men with the cars and the money who have the families and kids and everything at home.

According to Sealy, Trinidad's very repressiveness makes this particular form of forbidden fruit particularly tempting.

> I don't know about women, but men in this country, all you have to do is get a guy in this country drunk, and that is it. I'm not making up stories here. It's so taboo that it makes it more interesting. And it will be interesting, it will be VERY interesting [laughs]. Come around Carnival, oh my God, it is outrageous and so blatant.

Hand in hand with the somewhat morbid fascination with homosexuality goes a high level of homophobic violence. Says Celestine:

> I know friends who have been raped walking home, four or five men have attacked him. I mean, four men holding him down. We had to rush him to the hospital, he had to get stitches, it was not a very nice sight. Emotionally he was a wreck. It's not reached the papers because, again, the whole shame, they don't want family to know, so there are a lot of unreported cases.

I mean, I myself don't walk the streets at night. I do not because there are a lot of sick people out there.

In fact, gender violence seems to be considered fairly normal, judging from the news reports in the Port-of-Spain tabloids. An item that appeared during the GNP+ conference described the conviction of one Hubert Carrington for smashing his estranged wife's skull three times with a block of concrete because she went to church instead of visiting him. However, the jury reduced the charge to manslaughter after deciding that he had been provoked—an argument not even put forward by the defense.

Given this heady mix, it is hardly surprising to learn that heterosexual transmission quickly has caught up to the early homosexual epidemic. Women currently constitute nearly 40 percent of the 29,000 estimated AIDS cases in Trinidad and Tobago—some 3 percent of the entire adult population. Two-thirds of those diagnosed are under twenty-five years of age.

Arranged along Trinidad's huge central roundabout, the Savannah, are the impressive "Seven Sisters," ornate Victorian-era mansions once occupied by colonial administrators when the islands were possessions of the redoubtable queen. Old-fashioned British names remain popular among locals as well—my interviewees included, aside from Godfrey and Nigel, Bartholomew, Oswald and Cyrus. Likewise, the tightly drawn sexual mores of the Victorian period, long ago transformed or buried in England itself, live on in this erstwhile fringe of empire.

Cyrus Sylvester, a burly six-footer close to forty years old, runs the group household where the gay Chatroom once met. Despite the heat, he wore a knit skullcap and a black shirt and sported earrings in the shape of pencils through his lobes. He spoke wearily of the difficulties of keeping the gay-consciousness organization moving forward. All the backward attitudes are rife, he said, with men pretending not to take the "passive" sex role because of in-group prejudices against "bottoms." He says:

Gay men here can talk about the physical act of sex but not about sexual health. Sex with gay men involves a lot of psychology, a lot of mind games.

Sex, strictly, exclusively sex, remains the center of clandestine gay life in Trinidad, he insisted; anything else does not stir much interest. Although a continuation of the weekly sessions might be useful, Sylvester felt that the entire exercise had pretty much run its course. Condoms had been introduced, people had gotten the basic facts, but anything beyond that simply would not gel—or so far, hadn't.

McComie, who has tried to educate youthful Trinidadians about HIV, extended this habit of denial to the entire society:

> It's a very strange phenomenon, this kind of neutral area of confusion or if they actually don't care. It's frightening. They are stymied and plagued by huge religious domination.

Such an environment is hardly welcoming for gays facing HIV infection as well. One activist received his diagnosis in the middle 1980s. "I went straight to the Savannah and sat down to contemplate my fate. I dealt with it totally on my own." He couldn't confide in friends: "I mentioned it once to someone in 1992; the next day your business is on the street." The denial and lack of privacy, he said, make it hard for sexually active HIV-positive adults to inform their partners about their status.

Jeffrey Stanford, another of the group's principal figures, died of AIDS-related causes during the week of the GNP+ conference. By chance, I had arranged for an interview with one of his close friends, what locals call a "Syrian" or "Trinidad white" for his light complexion, for the same night as Stanford's funeral. When I arrived with my guide, he was dead drunk. Sitting on the screened-in porch in the cool evening breeze, we suggested that perhaps it would be better to come back another time. But despite his incoherence, this well-known local figure insisted on trying to carry on an interview and rambled sadly for half an hour about the difficulties of homosexual life in Trinidad; when I tried to interrupt him and leave, he became violent.

Plenty of people within and beyond gay circles in Trinidad recognize that the repressive environment, including the current illegality of homosexual acts, is blocking prevention efforts. Over the last two decades, many authors have outlined how individuals' vulnerability to AIDS infection is affected by social context, by factors quite independent of their levels of knowledge and even their conscious intentions to protect themselves, and Trinidad is an excellent example. "Cultural self-oppression," says Sealy, makes gay organization impossible.

> It would be a dream come true, but it will not happen. It is not even happening in the politics. The people in the country are very much aware that the government that we have now is so corrupt. The ministers get into fistfights, they can't even speak English properly. But everybody sits back and complains. That's what they do.

The strategy of influencing peer norms among a given group, the theory which guides many community-based AIDS education models, will be undermined if the group itself scarcely exists, if its members are unable to generate a sense of membership or horizontal identification. Sealy continues:

> They don't even recognize how low their self-esteem is. They think they are all evil, an abomination, because the religion thing is very, very strong. And even as progressive as some of us are, we even have embedded in our brain that we are critical of ourselves. God does not like us because—even I myself sometimes have been going through these things, so much that I have been to a spiritual advisor, a Catholic priest, to talk about it. You feel better as a mass murderer in this country than as a gay man.

McComie concurs:

> Everyone walks around in the closet. It's a country with only 1.3 million people, you want to be able to keep your friends and be loved by your mother and father and brothers and sisters.

At the conference's opening plenary, Denzil Douglas, the prime minister of St. Kitts and Nevis and, according to organizers, one of the "better" Caribbean heads of state on the AIDS issue, noted that the gender gap in new HIV infections was closing and that some countries already had nearly a one-to-one male/female ratio. The Caribbean was home to a thousand HIV-positive children, he added, and on some islands over 1 percent of pregnant women were already HIV-infected. "This is not a homosexual disease!" thundered the prime minister in the first and only mention of homosexuality during the entire ceremony. The crowd, composed of at least two-thirds gay men, erupted in stormy applause. While the prime minister is certainly correct in technical terms, the reality of HIV in the Caribbean is that homosexual transmission is playing a very significant role, and the eagerness to downplay that fact can only impede attempts to address the epidemic. Recognizing the very real problem of heterosexual transmission in the Caribbean does not have to make the gay islander invisible.

Given the obstacles to determined HIV prevention education, an obvious alternative approach to raise consciousness about the epidemic is advocacy for adequate services, respect for the social rights of people with HIV, treatment access and the like. In fact, the staff at Trinidad's main HIV testing and care clinic, the Queen's Park Counselling Centre, took advantage of the international visitors' presence and went on strike during the week of the GNP+ conference to protest shortages, poor working conditions and the theft of their operating budget by corrupt politicians. But although the site is located just a few hundred yards from the hotel where the world event was being held, no one at the conference learned about the strike. It was covered in the local newspapers, but the mostly Spanish-speaking delegates did not see them.

A Trinidadian reporter from *The Express* newspaper was delighted to show me this slice of local reality, an illustration of the endemic incompetence and high-level venality that permeate public services. As we left her newsroom, she pointed to an elderly colleague getting onto the elevator, a fellow reporter who had beaten a murder rap, she said, through his courthouse contacts.

Located in a rambling old residence set back from the ring road that forms the hub of Port-of-Spain, the clinic was full every morning with people packed shoulder-to-shoulder on benches awaiting their test results or doctor's appointments. According to union steward Ian Francis, a clinic nurse, sixty to seventy people come there each day, a quarter of them for HIV-related causes or testing. Confidentiality, Francis quickly acknowledged, was zero; I saw the patient files crammed into a hallway cabinet, accessible to any passerby. Results of the HIV test, which is administered in only three sites throughout the country, take a month.

Reporters descended on the clinic each morning during the strike, and indignant staff awaited a visit from a ministry representative. They showed reporters the "work-in-progress" in the next-door facility, which was to have become their new clinic headquarters. Building renovation had begun there only to be abandoned halfway; the place was torn apart and left unusable, with half-installed insulation hanging down from the ceilings in strips. "It's been that way for a year," said one nurse, shaking her head. When asked what had happened to the construction, Francis explained that they could never find out and that everyone assumed the funds for the project had been siphoned off somewhere along the line.

During one morning picket, a ministry official in Indian-style dress tried to reassure the strikers that they would be heard. "Things have broken down in the system," he granted, but he was not prepared to discuss the matter further. "I have come to see, no more." Nurses and doctors listened sullenly. "People pay 60 TT dollars (about U.S. $10) for their HIV test result," whispered one. "Where does that money go? We never see it."

Nurse-midwife Muriel Douglas, who has headed the national AIDS program for the last nine years, has an office tucked away in a downtown office building far from the Health Ministry but next door to the government-funded Rapport AIDS education program for youth. Wearing a black cotton jacket over a pink satin blouse and sporting a UNAIDS pin, Douglas was very optimistic about recent progress in the country and summarized the planning meetings that the government had just completed, the sorts of exercises that UNAIDS encourages in countries where things barely have gotten off the ground. Her recital included all the right elements and the familiar UN jargon about mobilizing "stakeholders," such as businesses, youth, midwives, unions, churches, doctors and dentists, even insurance companies, all to be guided through their "strategic planning" processes in partnership with the government. Interrupted with a question, Douglas was slightly petulant. "I'm giving you the whole process, and I'm getting to that," she said, returning to her litany of "interim plans" and "national strategic initiatives."

McComie is not convinced by the official optimism. An elegantly dressed, shaven-headed "Trinidad white," McComie is an executive with the Trinidad-Tobago Electric Company and organized Artists against AIDS, a private educational initiative. He and his friends consider Muriel Douglas well meaning but without solid political backing or adequate funding. In McComie's opinion the country is a "classic example of AIDS denial":

> It was only with the GNP+ conference really that even the minister has been able to say something about it [AIDS]. . . . We've been lobbying for a decade and a half. The national AIDS program is completely paralyzed by bureaucracy and indecision.

McComie explained that if someone gets HIV in Trinidad:

> You get extremely depressed, particularly ill and you die. Unless of course you have enough money to fly to Miami and try to organize a [treatment] cocktail, for 5,000 TT dollars [U.S. $850].

McComie says he got involved when working as a journalist and seeing for himself the disaster in the making.

> You talk about fear and ignorance now!? There was just this absolutely terrified populace. They didn't want to talk about it at all. That got me involved. I thought the only way to face this fear was to try to find out everything I could about it because Trinidad has suffered from a decade of misinformation.

Artists against AIDS decided to use the islanders' proclivity for art and music to transmit the messages and sensitize the population. "Trinidad is very conservative and also full of extremely talented and creative individuals," McComie said. Indeed, calypso songs on taxi radios address every social issue of interest, from the explosive racial politics on the island pitting blacks against Indo-Trinidadians to a fairly reactionary AIDS tune sung for the delegates that had GNP+ conference delegates cringing.

McComie had made some very slow progress with his own bosses at the utility, who accepted the idea of putting AIDS information into the monthly bills. But, he adds dryly, "We are considered leaders in this because nobody else is doing anything." Denial, secrecy and shame still prevail:

> There is no appreciation or understanding of all the trauma and personal angst and the repression that obtains in this country.

When I told him that Mrs. Douglas had been very optimistic, McComie laughed:

> We are very optimistic people, and we meet a lot and talk a lot about lots of things. [*But*] I've been in this since 1983, and I really can't say except by blood, sweat and tears of anything else that's happened apart from our own efforts.

Although these complaints sound familiar to anyone who has been involved in the issue in Latin America, the high prevalence of HIV infection in Trinidad and Tobago make the situation there particularly worrisome. Says McComie:

> The pressure to get government and the corporate sector moving is now having some small impact, not huge, but they are realizing now from the results that their own human resources are being affected, that people are off work on almost a daily or a weekly basis because they have to bury a member of the family or they're late for work or can't come in because they have to take care of someone. This is now a window of opportunity this year for us to get things going. It's almost too late.

Tourism, a key element of the local economy, is also threatened. As Nigel Celestine explains:

> Within the last few years, because of the high rates [*of HIV infection*] the government has had to acknowledge publicly that we have a problem,

particularly in Tobago, because there you have the people who will ply their
[sex work] trade, the very street-tough-looking boys who don't identify
themselves as gay. And of course a lot of these guys have their girlfriends.

Trinidad and Tobago exemplifies the Caribbean's cultural and political
obstacles to an effective response to AIDS. Indeed, one UNAIDS official frankly
said that "nothing" was happening in the area on HIV/AIDS—no doubt this is
an exaggeration, but it is symptomatic of the frustration international agency
staff feel in dealing with intractable governments. The formal links with Latin
America have left little trace; people from the AIDS groups around the Spanish-
speaking region barely know their Caribbean counterparts, and the Port-of-
Spain meeting added little to the mutual familiarity. Possible go-between
countries, such as the Dominican Republic, Cuba or Puerto Rico, were either
absent or invisible at the GNP+ conference.

Oswald Warwick of the UNAIDS office in Port-of-Spain, himself a native
of Trinidad, saw "some movement" both in Trinidad and elsewhere in the
Caribbean. "We're beginning to get there," he said hopefully, if for no other reason than the increasing visibility of large numbers of sick people. Governments
are beginning to put AIDS on their agendas and are looking for allies, he
insisted, even though only family planning oriented NGOs are really "strong
and mature." The region tends to act as a bloc, and now that the multilateral
bodies are concerned about the issue, said Warwick, we are "on our way."

Indeed, in 2003 the World Bank loaned $20 million to Trinidad and
Tobago for AIDS prevention, care and treatment as part of a seven-country loan
package for the Caribbean. The bank duly noted in its announcement that the
growing epidemic could eventually knock 5 percent off the islands' gross
domestic product, reason enough to take corrective action. Although the GNP+
conference did not focus on the human dramas occurring down the street, the
gathering undoubtedly played a role in pushing the HIV/AIDS issue along
during the key policy discussions in Geneva, Washington and throughout the
region. The courageous individuals, small groups and beleaguered health workers trying to confront a galloping epidemic in the face of enormous cultural
resistance may finally have resources adequate to the task. If the World Bank
funds reach them, the workers at the Queen's Park Counseling Centre clinic

trying to serve dozens of people with HIV per day may finally get their roof repaired.

At the conference site, delegates from around the world—including a Cambodian fellow who had spent a traumatic eight hours under guard at the Los Angeles airport for lack of a U.S. transit visa—tried to absorb workshops and plenary sessions on matters such as the workings of the new Global Fund, treatment access, and an HIV-positives-only workshop on the barebacking (unprotected sex) craze, which drew an excited crowd. But the struggle of the clinic staff taking place just down the street was not on the agenda, and the Trinidadian union representatives were shy about forcing their way into the conference hall or seizing the microphone, a tactic that the crowd, accustomed to the confrontational tactics often employed by AIDS groups, would surely have recognized and appreciated.

My Trinidadian reporter friend lent me her office to make up a leaflet calling on the delegates to come to support the strike on the last day of the conference. Out of the three hundred present, six walked down the hill to see what was happening with Trinidadians living with HIV/AIDS and the fight over the services they mostly do not receive: a German, a British fellow, two African women from London, an elderly Canadian anthropologist and his wife. Not one delegate from "the South," any of the Latin American, Asian or African countries represented at the GNP+ conference, showed up. Except, I suppose, me.

However, during the closing ceremony of the GNP+ event a few hours later, the African delegates stood front and center in a bloc to complain formally that their region had not received enough scholarships to attend. GNP+'s president solemnly apologized from the podium, to a burst of applause from the entire plenary session.

Peter Piot, the executive director of UNAIDS, attended the GNP+ conference in Port-of-Spain, sending a powerful signal of the importance the international AIDS organization places on the HIV-positive groups. (A few weeks later, Piot would bypass the Central American AIDS Congress in Guatemala City, organized by prevention-oriented groups from the seven countries.) Piot reiterated the potent and mutually reinforcing mix of pressure for access to medicines, along with continued interest in innovative prevention measures. For a while in the 1990s, he admitted, the idea of massive expansion of treatment was dismissed by the big donors, who assumed that costs would never permit the luxury drugs available in the developed world to trickle down to Africans and Asians.

But activism and moral argument, including North-South alliances, said Piot, had shifted that debate definitively, a highly significant advance for future AIDS and public health policy. For all its shortcomings, the GNP+ meeting was part of that process. Recent positive developments in international trade law have forced the pharmaceutical multinationals to consider public, not just commercial, interests in emergencies such as AIDS. The Brazilian model of guaranteed, free antiretroviral treatment proved that drug delivery and clinical management were possible, even with poorly educated patients and minimum infrastructure; the World Bank finally bowed to pressures and accepted drug provision as part of strategic AIDS plans for the Caribbean and other regions. Since the bank is a major donor, said Piot, this is big news, a "breakthrough."

Nonetheless, Piot added, only an estimated 5 percent of the millions of people with AIDS around the world were getting the life-saving medicines. It was not a time, he cautioned, for too much self-congratulation to distract us from the fate of those left behind.

In the very earliest years of the AIDS epidemic in Chile, a minor incident occurred that, in retrospect, seems emblematic of the inherent conflicts of any social movement fighting to end abuses and to lobby for the resolution of the urgent needs of a given group. The incipient HIV-positive self-help group there, which had boldly gone public to demand respect and policy changes, one day received a donation of vitamin supplements, cases of a nutritional tonic for people facing immunological weakness. The leaders of the group promptly divided them up among themselves, arguing that the organization was for "people with HIV/AIDS," that they themselves fit this category, *ergo*, they would enjoy the benefit. There was no discussion or expression of uneasiness about the nonexistent boundaries between their political role and their personal situations, and in fact any attempt to debate the action was abruptly overruled. When Piot warns those lucky enough to be sitting in a world conference about the fate of their peers back home or even down the street in a deteriorating and bankrupt facility, he is gingerly touching on a sensitive, unresolved point.

In fact, leadership of the HIV/AIDS movement by those directly affected is both potent and full of pitfalls. The juxtaposition of a conference of the official, global representatives of 40 million people with HIV/AIDS and the stark reality of people with AIDS in the host country of Trinidad and Tobago highlighted the gap between rhetoric and grassroots practice on the issue. In any political struggle, properly warmed phrases must fill the public debate for a certain period like a faucet dripping into a vast bathtub before these sentiments finally spill over into some sort of public policy. However, the fact that "people living with HIV/AIDS" have now constituted themselves so effectively as key players has created a disturbing ambience of untouchability around those who have surged into public or semipublic view. How could delegates and GNP+ staff remain so unmoved and so placidly ignorant of the realities facing their supposed brethren in the host country itself even as local advocates explicitly used the presence of the conference to publicize their desperate situation?

Eventually, when and if HIV really becomes a chronic and manageable condition for most people in the world and the grim old days are just an unpleasant recollection, organizations of people living with AIDS will no longer be above criticism. In Brazil, the period of exclusively HIV-positive groups already is seen as somewhat old hat, with the logic that seropositivity really does not mean all that much in the complexities of everyday activism.

The enormous success of the policy of pushing the essential role of people with HIV in every forum, committee or AIDS-related body has strengthened a permanent sense of entitlement and—despite their protests to the contrary—an aura of victimhood among HIV-positive representatives, especially in the internal workings of the AIDS bureaucracies, networks and movements. People living with HIV/AIDS do not face the same standards as others within the AIDS universe; the permanent subtext of individual drama and the undeniable courage required to share an intimate, personal story tends to obscure political responsibilities.

This response originates in the early stigma and discrimination that AIDS brought with it, and it is a credit to all the social engagement it generated that we have come this far in the other direction. Nonetheless, while people with

HIV/AIDS undoubtedly have a special sensitivity to many of the issues involved in the epidemic, as a group they are no more or less concerned with the welfare of their fellows than any other set of human beings. And given the urgency of their personal needs, they may in some cases be less objective than outsiders about the implications of their actions. After all, HIV-positive activists usually become involved with the issue when it affects them directly, when they see what poor services and discrimination are doing to themselves and to others in the same boat. This is a laudable reaction and a key perspective, but it is not the only possible or legitimate one. Others joined the efforts without acquiring the infection but from equally valid motivations. People living with HIV have much to say about the epidemic, but they are not automatically right. For now, however, such a statement is heresy.

Air Travel

In all the courses I have taken on counseling and orientation for HIV, they always say not to get involved with people. In my case, I'm an old woman, so there's no risk of love affairs or anything like that, and I'm aware that you have to maintain a certain distance. But sometimes it's absolutely impossible.

Once a young fellow came to see us, very pleasant and formal. He was a flight steward for an airline and very worried about his HIV diagnosis. "I'm afraid of getting sick. Plus, I'm not sure what is going on with me." He rolled up his sleeves and showed me a Kaposi's sarcoma lesion. "Is this the beginning of the end?" he asked.

I said that I wasn't a nurse or a doctor or anything like that, but that I knew this was a disease that could be benign or very serious. But seeing him sitting there so healthy-looking, it seemed he was all right, just with the problem of thinking to himself, When am I going to get sick? When am I going to die? I don't want anyone to see me like this—all that.

I told him a lot of things I had learned about HIV, that people sometimes got sick but that you had to recover as quickly as possible so as to not slip into something more serious. What was making him lose weight wasn't the Kaposi's sarcoma but his nerves. He was very worried about the future. We stayed in contact and dealt with medical issues. I told him to call me any time, literally.

One week he did and said, "Please come over right now, I'm very sick, and I think my time has come." I left immediately and took someone from the office who is very gentle and capable of calming anyone down.

His partner opened the door of a very nice apartment. The fellow was in bed with a high fever but dressed in a turtleneck sweater, three more shirts and all the blankets up to his neck. So we had him take all that off and put ice on him, and of course in a half hour his temperature dropped, and he was sitting up in bed showing us photographs.

That was the beginning of a sort of friendship, something very special. He would call me and invite me to tea. I told him not to say anything to his family or his boss, but he did anyway. Then he asked me if I could talk to his boss, who called me at home and said, "I think he is homosexual, and I don't like that very much. But he's a good worker, and I want to help him."

He finally found a place to get treatment in the United States since he could travel as often as he wanted and got his medicines there, long before most people in the country. Everything turned out well, and even the company, which historically discriminated in these cases, was perfectly decent with him. So the whole story ended on a completely optimistic note. I think he even broke up with his boyfriend and got a new one.

—Elena Droguett

CHAPTER SIX

Argentina:
Split Perspicacity

ARGENTINA	
Population	38 million
First reported case of AIDS	1983
Estimated HIV infections	130,000
Male : female ratio	2.9:1
Estimated number of people needing antiretroviral treatment in 2004	35,000
Number receiving drugs	30,000
First AIDS prevention campaign	1987
Adult women using birth control	75%
Gross domestic product (GDP) 2003	$129.7 billion
Per capita income (2003)	$3,650
Annual per-capita spending on health	$697
Unemployment rate 2003	16.3%
Military dictatorship	1976–1983
Estimated number of deaths during dictatorship	15,000–30,000
First mention of condom use in government campaign	2001
End of peso convertability, bank collapse	2001

AIDS drugs remained available in public hospitals even when the banks closed and the government went bankrupt. Medicine is business, but prevention lags in the wilderness.

> Here in Argentina two months is long term.
>   —*Pablo Rosales*

Argentina's AIDS epidemic was almost unique in Latin America in that intravenous drug use provoked an early and rapid dissemination outside of populations of gay or bisexual men. Like the later epidemics that hit the Ukraine, Russia and former Soviet states in central Asia, the first wave of HIV infection was concentrated among injecting drug users, with homosexually active men a close second.

Although in the former Soviet zone injecting drugs is associated with the despair and hopelessness of youth facing a dismantled social system, poverty, unemployment and bleak prospects for the future, for some Argentines drug use had a different meaning during the euphoria that greeted the end of one of the continent's most vicious military regimes (1976–1983). Says Alejandra Trossero:

> Around 1986 there was a tremendous fascination, especially among intel-
> lectual circles, with intravenous drugs. People wanted to try everything, and
> I think it was in some way a result, a legacy, of the military dictatorship
> because during the dictatorship you couldn't do anything. Then when [*the
> military*] left, it was like, okay, everything's allowed, so let's do it all.

Drugs flowed into Argentina, and news media quickly picked up on the sensational phenomenon and described it with morbid glee, indifferent to whether they might be encouraging consumption rather than warning against it. Television reports showed the injection process in detail but rarely suggested that there were any dangers involved aside from the addiction itself. Alejandra Trossero, who came of age at this time in Rosario, a northern port city on the Paraná River, speculates:

> [*Drug experimentation*] was also influenced by the people who had left
> Argentina for Europe during the 1970s, some of them without much of a

project for their lives, just to escape [*from the dictatorship*]. They ended up so badly addicted that they came back to Argentina to escape from the heroin.

However, heroin as well as cocaine followed them back home. Rosario was once the last stop for ships bringing foreign goods into the northern Argentine interior all the way to Bolivia and Paraguay. It became a center of drug trafficking and an early focal point of HIV infection. Asian sailors would dock and unload their supplies for access to quick cash, finding a ready market in local bohemian circles. Trossero recalls:

> Every time a ship came in from Asia, we knew there would be heroin on it. I lived just three blocks from the port, and there was a little bar right on the corner that had a book with photos of all the sex workers in the area, an enormous album with all kinds of women, men, transsexuals—you name it. So when the sailors would come ashore, the first thing they had to do was get some quick cash, and there we were, ready to buy . . . at good prices, of course.

Even though HIV in Argentina was in fact at least as much a sexually transmitted epidemic as an intravenous drug phenomenon, the average Argentine often assumed that anyone with HIV had been a drug user. Elsewhere, men with HIV were assumed to be gay and the assumption still exists today. But at the policy level, a new disease affecting drug users was even less likely to engender public sympathy or a grassroots reaction than the "gay plague" touted elsewhere. Although heroin was common in Rosario, in most of the country injected cocaine was the drug of choice. But although drug use is common throughout Latin America, no one has ever been able to explain to me—after I have asked the question for nearly twenty years—why the practice of injecting drugs flourished in Argentina and in parts of Brazil while it has not in Chile and most of the Andean countries.

Meanwhile, the first postdictatorship government of president Raúl Alfonsin (1983–1989) was struggling to deal with the legacy of mass disappearances during the dictatorship and with Argentina's chronic economic instability. A public health problem barely hitting the radar screen was unlikely to attract much official attention. Graciela Touzé of Intercambios (Exchanges), a social service agency dealing with drug use, recalls that the Argentine government avoided recognizing the injecting drug user/AIDS link, despite the obvious statistics. Touzé explains:

> If you admit the size of a problem, you have to take responsibility for doing something about it. And the kind of interventions that were going to be even minimally effective in this case simply were not acceptable in political circles until very recently.

Needle exchanges for drug users and the whole concept later to become known as harm reduction was still a long way off. The harm reduction approach supposes that while discouraging drug use may be a legitimate goal for some projects, many users will continue to consume drugs and will need help to minimize the damage their choices may cause them and others. A couple of foreign donors tried to support work around drug injecting and HIV in the early 1990s, but in general, efforts were not aimed directly at users themselves. For example, Touzé's group offered training for other drug-rehab projects, including church-related therapeutic communities and public and private entities of all sorts.

> It was grotesque in some cases. I mean, you had institutions, therapeutic communities with long-term care, for example, where people would be housed and isolated and only gradually brought back to a more integrated social life, including their sexual activity, which had been suspended. And no one was talking about condom use in these places! Nothing, not even the most elemental information about HIV.

The fact that prevention seemed not to have occurred to policy makers, despite the increasingly obvious links between drug injection and HIV, is typical of Argentina's historical AIDS blind spot. Cures based on total abstinence, with all the complex institutional and professional accoutrements they require, were easier to imagine and pursue; they were also easier to finance, run and support politically, unlike harm-reduction approaches that recognize continued drug use as a reality. Prevention required not only grappling with issues of sexuality but also displacing the focus from the more comfortable realm of medical and clinical experts to less tangible aspects around which a constituency had not yet crystallized.

Of course, Argentina's early nonresponse was not limited to HIV transmission; the country reacted just as placidly to the exploding availability of injectable drugs themselves. Lisandro Orlov is a Lutheran pastor whose church sponsors a refuge for people with HIV. He says:

> During the ten years of the [*Carlos*] Menem government [*1989–1999*], Argentina became a refuge for the laundering of drug money, and wherever the money flows, drug use is close behind.

Menem's decision to establish "convertibility"—a one-to-one equivalency between the dollar and the Argentine peso—as an anti-inflationary strategy made doing business—any kind of business—in the country very lucrative. Drugs were very cheap because of the artificially inflated local currency.

Official passivity in the face of the dual public health emergency—addiction and AIDS—marked the first phase of Argentina's epidemic. Well into the new century, 40 percent of HIV cases in Argentina are still due to injecting drug use. Although drug users joined the list of stigmatized and vulnerable groups along with homosexual men and commercial sex workers, they were far less likely to form organizations or lead peer educational initiatives. Dr. Mabel Bianco, a feminist author, was director of the national AIDS program for a brief period around the turn of the century. She says:

> [*Intravenous drug users*] are very poor people without previous organizational experience for engaging in this kind of work. So the organizations that took on AIDS, those leaders emerge from other experiences, from the homosexual or feminist worlds or human rights work, and that leads to tensions among them because each one has its issues. But the real infected people aren't there because the HIV-positives don't belong to those worlds.

Although AIDS-related groups sprang up in Argentina in the early years, many of them with clinical services of some kind, strong associations of people

with HIV did not emerge until quite late, when the pressure for access to the powerful new drugs spurred more direct advocacy. Meanwhile, the task of organizing
grassroots prevention initiatives once again fell to gays. In the late 1980s the
Argentine Homosexual Community (CHA) put together a campaign known as
"Stop SIDA" (combining SIDA, the AIDS acronym in Spanish, with the familiar
English word "stop") that was unusually sex-friendly and audacious, including a
comic that graphically recommended oral sex as a safer alternative to penetrative
practices. César Cigliutti, who in 2003 was CHA's president and famous in
Buenos Aires for celebrating the city's first gay marriage with his partner that year,
said he had to fight within his own organization to publish the hilariously raunchy
drawings, despite Argentines' typical bravado and reputation for self-confidence.

> The first government campaign was a poster with the face of a guy, but it
> said nothing. "Be aware of AIDS," I don't know, something ridiculous
> like that. We had a meeting and said to each other, If we wait for the
> government to do something, we'll all be dead. So let's do it ourselves.

The CHA also financed and organized improvements at Francisco Javier
Muñiz Hospital, the city's main infectious diseases facility, where most HIV
patients ended up. It took a decade for other groups to imitate this early example
of integrating care, prevention and antidiscrimination work. But despite their
multifaceted approach, the first Argentine activists quickly came to recognize
the gay-specific nature of their initiative. Cigliutti says:

> We were clear that it was for our community, not a discourse aimed at every-
> one. It was strictly for us, and whoever gets it, gets it.

He adds that during this period the Pan American Health Organization, one of
the CHA's few allies, was promoting the single-partner strategy and a traditional
focus discouraging "promiscuity." But gay organizations like the CHA, closer to
the epidemic affecting their friends than an expert body, influenced the entire
medical establishment: Today the Pan American Health Organization's discourse
on HIV recognizes that monogamy is a highly problematic strategy for AIDS
prevention, especially for women who exercise little control over their sexual and

reproductive functions. Gay men sensed from the beginning the dubious protection offered by oversimplified appeals to sexual fidelity.

Nevertheless, despite pioneering efforts in the late 1980s by the CHA and some women's and church groups, a coherent, systematic prevention strategy for HIV in Argentina did not materialize until well into the new century, if in fact it exists today. Unlike the relatively rapid mobilization that occurred to obtain antiretroviral drugs after they appeared in the mid-1990s, HIV prevention had no real constituency, and efforts were notoriously lackluster or inconsistent. Not only was official support for prevention absent during the crucial first decade of the epidemic, when the government finally did act, it often made things worse. Lawyer Pablo Rosales has a practice focusing mainly on HIV-related discrimination cases. He recalls:

> There was one government campaign a couple of years ago that was abominable with famous actors saying, You have to talk to the person, you have to inform them, to talk about it. It was awful because the idea was that if someone has HIV, they should tell you. Which means if they don't say anything, you don't have to protect yourself.

Orlov is equally critical:

> During the entire Perónist government of Menem, there was really no money for prevention. There were very sporadic messages that would last for two or three weeks, always based on fear: Take care, Let them know. There was a campaign that said, Warn [*your partner*] that you have AIDS, was the idea—an absurdity.

In the prevention realm, the Argentine response to HIV looks remarkably backward for a sophisticated albeit troubled country. The CHA's early innovations in the AIDS field did not last; its first president joined the Peronist government under Menem, and the organization suffered years of debilitating internal strife. Although other groups formed, mounted campaigns and established services, their messages found no echo at the top as the government avoided the ideological and political distress of dealing with sexuality—condoms were shown for the first time in an official campaign in Argentina under Mabel Bianco's tenure in 2001.

Governments are responsible for doing something to prevent HIV transmission as an issue of public health, but for all too many of them around the world, the job has been a booby prize of the first order. It requires them to contend with sexuality and face the hidden reality of sexual behavior that violates standards of social propriety. Governments that want to prevent AIDS have to admit that adolescents experiment with sex behind their parents' backs and that adults are sometimes unfaithful to their spouses or engage in homosexual practices. Most governments would rather not start, and as soon as they do so they are quickly punished by religious authorities and social conservatives who argue—with some justification—that nonjudgmental campaigns about these matters undermine traditional sexual mores.

In Latin America it frequently has taken a patient and insistent combination of public pressure, media spotlighting, professional commitment among officials, harassment by doctors and outside intervention to get a country's political leadership to shoulder this unwelcome burden. Argentina simply avoided it. But in another area related to AIDS, even the impervious Casa Rosada could not resist forever.

> The Supreme Court unanimously ordered the government to provide all HIV medicines [in 1997], and this opened a huge door. Even today with all the problems we have, the drugs are still reaching people because there is a strong public lobby on the AIDS issue here in Argentina.
>
> —Pablo Rosales

Argentines won many legal demands on the government in the AIDS field. Lawyer Rosales, himself HIV-positive, has handled dozens of cases involving HIV and AIDS and says that once the initial reluctance to go public was overcome, Argentines quickly applied the Evita Perón approach: speak up loudly and demand that the state respond. He explains:

> There was huge coverage in the media, and that made it very hard for the state to refuse. This is a country that expresses itself very easily, and it's hard for the government to deal with that.

Universal access is now approved and accepted by Argentine public opinion. Even during the financial collapse of 2001 when banks closed and the government went broke, the AIDS lobby held off cuts and kept drug provision relatively steady.

Now that access to antiretroviral drugs is far and away the main AIDS issue in Latin America, Argentina enjoys a fairly benign reputation. But the history of how this happy situation came to pass contains some surprises. This sanguine combination of legal backing and popular agitation did not happen overnight. The floodgates were opened when eight Argentine NGOs tested the judicial waters by suing the government over treatment access, arguing that people with HIV had a right to the new, life-saving HIV drug therapies.

One key group pushing this strategy was Pastor Orlov's Ecumenical Movement for Human Rights (MEDH), which linked AIDS with other, pressing issues of human dignity. Orlov was intrigued about the radical possibilities of the AIDS epidemic in challenging Argentine society over its habits of discrimination and social exclusion. He quickly grasped that a proper response to the epidemic implied changing deeply ingrained popular attitudes toward stigmatized groups. In the late 1980s Orlov wrote about the subtle subtexts of the newly emerging AIDS messages. He parsed the use of medical or religious concepts and their capacity to sustain oppressive structures and frustrate an effective response to the epidemic. Orlov proposed a radical alternative outlook based on the rights and complex realities of the individuals affected, be they gays, prostitutes, addicts—whom he called *persons with homosexual orientation, sex workers* and *drug users*—or the housewife next door. As one of the first voices in the Southern Cone to deconstruct traditional approaches to health education and epidemiological surveillance, the white-haired, soft-spoken pastor knew exactly how to exploit his priestly image to challenge and disorient both church audiences and government functionaries. "The church's task is not to wag its finger at people, but to accompany them," he says. "When I'm asked how many converts I've achieved this month, I always say, 'Just one: me.' "

Orlov confesses almost guiltily that the early years of AIDS activism felt like a "festival of human rights." The stigmatized, the excluded, the socially despised: these were Orlov's favorites, "people who had been ignored, nonexistent, invisible." The focus of his group's AIDS halfway house was never simply charitable but rather political—or, in church terms, "prophetic." Orlov explains:

> This center has to be a living denunciation of all those places where people
> with HIV cannot enter because there are no antiretrovirals for prejudice and
> exclusion and expulsion.

In 1997 MEDH and seven other NGOs brought the famous lawsuit to
force the government to provide everyone with the new drugs. The Argentine
government, which still had not organized a respectable prevention campaign,
looked unlikely to respond to petitions for the costly medicines, despite formal
guarantees. According to Orlov:

> We had the law on our side luckily, but like so many laws in Argentina, the
> theory is perfect, but in the end Congress proposes a law and passes it
> because they know it's irrelevant.

Nonetheless, the suit was successful. Argentina's Supreme Court ordered the
government to ensure that the drugs reached patients, despite the country's
decentralized, federal system. But curiously, many of the better-known groups
providing services for people living with HIV/AIDS did not back the lawsuit.
Plaintiffs ran the risk of being hit with court costs if their suit was unsuccessful.
But even so, the reluctance from potential beneficiaries was surprising. Mabel
Bianco, whose group also joined the case, recalls:

> They didn't want to join in, even when we organized the march to the ministry,
> few of them came along, just one or two leaders and that was it. All those
> organizations big and small which provide clinical services, they didn't join us.

This recollection is surprising for anyone observing the Argentine AIDS
scene today where HIV-positive leaders are particularly outspoken about their
demands and fully integrated in the international networks.

When we spoke in his Buenos Aires apartment, Orlov had just been interviewed
by evaluators from the Geneva-based UNAIDS program at its downtown office.

One member of the evaluation team was a longtime adversary, the former direc-tor of Argentina's national AIDS program during the Menem presidency. Our conversation took place in early 2002 just after Argentina's financial meltdown and the massive "pots-and-pans" protests (*cacerolazos*) that led to the overthrow of Menem's successor as president, Fernando de la Rua. Orlov relates:

> I took out a lid and a spoon and told the foreigners what a *cacerolazo* was, try-ing to explain in English that it was the symbol of the Argentine people recovering their dignity and saying No! No to the inefficient, corrupted officials who have created this desperate situation. I told them, I am going to perform a *cacerolazo* for you so that the doctor leaves this meeting: No more impunity, out you go. Of course, she translated into English that she was going to withdraw, and I said, No, Doctor, you're not withdrawing. I want you to leave, which is different. And she did.

The doctor across the table whom Orlov sent packing was the official named in the 1997 drug-access lawsuit who had had to lead the futile govern-ment resistance to providing the costly treatments. After the dam burst on drugs, Argentine jurisprudence swiftly lined up in favor of those with HIV. Pablo Rosales explains:

> The [*judicial*] view on AIDS shifted, including in labor law because there were a lot of conflicts over firings, and the courts accepted the concept of moral damages in those situations. The issue is well positioned juridically, socially and mediawise, so there are benefits that other illnesses don't have.

All in all, Argentina's record in the drug-access and legal spheres rivals Brazil's. But court rulings and TV interviews alone do not make a social move-ment. It is curious if not mysterious why a sophisticated country with a notori-ously fault-finding civil society was unable to press its leaders into doing something coherent to stop the spread of HIV but could force it to spend con-siderable sums on treatment. Aside from the challenge to conservative social habits, some observers suggest that the resistance to one and rapid assimilation of the other is related to how things are done in Argentina when politics, cash and the state are involved.

In Argentina gnocchis are not just a pasta dish favored by its many citizens of Italian descent; they also are the nickname for a particularly Argentine political custom. Tradition dictates that gnocchis be served on the twenty-ninth day of every month, government payday. But the political machines have so institutionalized civil service featherbedding that the term *gnocchi*s now also refers to no-show employees who collect a salary—or even several—without doing a lick of work. AIDS was not immune to this venerable habit. Argentina's political parties are notorious for rewarding their top ranks and replenishing their coffers by shamelessly milking the state, and the practice did not stop even in the midst of the total financial meltdown that followed the 2001 foreign debt moratorium and fiscal bankruptcy as I witnessed while covering the events personally from the press rooms of the country's Finance Ministry.

When Mabel Bianco took over the reins of the national AIDS program in the middle of a multimillion-dollar AIDS project funded by a World Bank loan, she axed personnel and threatened internal investigations. The AIDS hotline, for example, quickly had become a gnocchi heaven. She says:

> They had rented extra offices outside the ministry, and there was a coordinator who earned $5,000 a month, three or four co-coordinators in charge of something very dubious earning between $4,000 and $4,800 a month. Some of them had two or three contracts for similar amounts in different ministries.

Even international agencies were susceptible to the Argentine way of doing business. Bianco says her predecessors wasted enormous sums on "administrative agreements":

> We had a contract with [agency A] and paid them 3 percent overhead for managing the funds. Then a new one was signed with [agency B] in record time. It was presented on October 15, signed around the twentieth, and elections were held on the thirtieth. The government lost, but the agreement

went forward anyway, and $1 million ends up at [*agency B*] in a very slippery, serpentine way.

If prevention projects were juicy plums to tempt the unscrupulous, even larger and steadier flows were to be found in the realm of triple-combination therapy. Once the floodgates were opened, the government that had resisted the pressure to spend—and the nonprofit service organizations—quickly could adjust to the new business environment.

Alejandro Freyre is the saucy, extroverted director of the Buenos Aires AIDS Foundation and one of the first Argentines to go public with his HIV-positive status. Shortly after he was hospitalized for HIV-related complications at age twenty, Freyre felt compelled to take action. He explains:

> In the hospital I realized that some things didn't matter anymore, some limitations had just died for me. And plus, there was this idea in my family of supporting me in anything I wanted. The kid didn't die! We're so happy! So if I had said, I want to be a transvestite! Great, whatever! They would have said yes to anything.

Freyre broke the ice on a television program accompanied by his doctor and gave out his home telephone number for other HIV-positive people to get in touch. As often happens in the AIDS service world, however, those doing the concrete work of addressing people's immediate needs often find it hard to attract formal support or to translate their efforts into coherent projects that fit the right agency or NGO formula. Freyre recalls with some bitterness:

> My telephone didn't stop ringing twenty-four hours a day. I spent months answering all the calls I would get, months. I had all this visibility on television, but not one organization or foundation called me to say, Hey, we'd like for you to meet us, to work with us. Nothing. In fact, I was left alone, very alone, and no organization took advantage of what I could do.

Freyre could counsel others well because he had plenty of experience with drug labs after trying to find such basic services as the Western Blot HIV confirmation exam and later the viral load test to measure how far the virus had advanced in his system. He recalls:

> I talked to something like twenty laboratories to see who could give me an estimate [*for Western Blot*], and each time I had to speak to a woman behind a desk and a computer and explain to her that I was a homosexual, that I had a positive HIV test result, that I thought I had AIDS but had to reconfirm it, and that my insurance was asking me for this estimate. And the answer was always the same: we don't do it.

But that was in the old days, when AIDS was rare and a bother. Once it became clear that the government would be buying AIDS-related tests and antiretroviral drugs permanently for thousands of potential clients, there was ample motivation to make sure that the public funds flowed toward one's own company. Rosales says the big labs wasted no time in encouraging demand for their products:

> [*Laboratory A*] is doing experiments with patients where they give drugs for three months to a year, and then you have to go find them in the market. So people go pressure the government or social security or even the HMOs that are obliged to provide the drugs. It's really stimulating, inducing demand, and then the state pays.

As head of the government AIDS program, Mabel Bianco found that government procedures for drug purchases were making it too easy for the companies to take advantage of the Argentine state:

> [*The laboratories*] established quotas: we had to buy a million tablets, so it was: You offer $1.10, you offer $1.15, and the other one $1.20, and then in the next round we rotate. So we canceled some auctions when the prices were too high and extended the contracts to six months. They were interested in winning the whole package, so that put an end to the deals.

Argentina was spending roughly $50 million a year on HIV drug therapies when dollar convertibility ended in 2001. But the epidemic continues to add hundreds of new patients in need of treatment per year at a time when drug prices in the developed world are not going down, given the constant demand and the steady addition of new formulas. This enormous flow of state spending provided an opportunity for nongovernmental clinical service organizations to finance their operations. The doctor-led NGOs knew how the system could buttress their quasi-clinical institutions. Freyre explains:

> We have a lot to learn about sustainability from the medical foundations without having to imitate their model. Many NGOs were born to provide a service, but that doesn't pay. So we have to find some way to stay alive. We don't have training in sustainability, and the doctors do because they're businessmen.

Freyre acknowledges that informational, advocacy and prevention work accompanies all the NGOs with clinical services. But he thinks that in some cases it is mere window-dressing:

> [One foundation] is actually two entities with the same name: one is the foundation, and the other is a for-profit company. People think they are going to the foundation, and they are actually visiting a business that charges for the doctor, sells drugs, sells tests and has very few free services.

Even the "nongovernmental" label could be subject to certain dispute in some cases as independent clinics rely on government-subsidized medicines and services to facilitate their operations. Bianco explains the contradictions:

> The system is quite perverse because we in the ministry provided the medicines to the NGOs because they were supposedly nonprofits. But many of them are medical services, so you never know what is being charged by the foundation or the doctor. So in some hospitals the drugs and the viral load tests are covered by the hospitals, but the doctor's visit is done in the foundation, and the patient pays for that.

Furthermore, in most countries of Latin America, a percentage of people living with HIV remain outside the public health system, and the costs are considerable even for comfortably middle-class patients. Because individuals usually cannot buy directly from the pharmaceutical producers, bulk purchases by the independent clinics provide another source of income for the nonprofits, along with the free samples the companies often toss in. Paid or subsidized medicine is no crime, but the arrangement is a far cry from the informal circles of friends that slowly crystallized into the early self-help groups. As with every service in class-stratified societies like these, the tendency toward capturing those able to pay is always a big temptation. Says Freyre:

> There's one group that is aimed at the middle class that can pay, from the
> tonier neighborhoods, people who may go to the public hospital but also
> have enough money to say, Okay, the infectious disease doctor at the hos-
> pital can see me in fifteen days, but why don't I go to the NGO and see him
> tomorrow? It's the same doctor, so why not pay for a visit there?

Getting beneficiaries to pay something ("cost-sharing") long has been recognized as an appropriate way to get people to value services and not feel like charity cases, as well to strengthen a nonprofit's always shaky finances. For example, over the years many groups learned to ask for donations for condoms rather than giving them away in discotheques, realizing that in modern consumer society, people who will pay for a condom are more likely to use one. NGOs also are being exhorted constantly to find ways to earn money and not depend forever on development agencies or the project straitjacket. But the line between sustainability and old-fashioned commerce is particularly hard to tease out in the ambiguous world of clinical services for people with HIV.

Bianco suggests that legitimate demands by users sometimes dovetail a little too neatly with the commercial interests of drug producers:

> You have a whole scene in which the doctors and the drug companies begin
> to work with people with HIV/AIDS, they begin to give them more power,
> but underneath it all is the power to buy medicines. It's a sweet deal.

Orlov, who was adamant about forcing the government to provide universal drug access, dismisses some of the subsequent criticism from HIV-positive groups as tendentious. He says:

> A drug would be unavailable one day, and they'd be writing a press release.
> I told them I would join a lawsuit but that we would have to take proof to
> the judges of what drugs were missing. I was always asking for proof. But
> they were just denunciations without any foundation.

Coherent militance and advocacy will always be necessary in Argentina, given the growing cost burden of the AIDS drugs and the steadily increasing patient pool. But the mixed role of the entities, public and private, now administering AIDS medical services may not make them the best candidates to provide this principled leadership.

An example of AIDS-related clinical services that emerged directly from gay politics rather than from medicine is the group Nexo. *NX* magazine was a glossy gay monthly published in Buenos Aires that cost $7 a copy, a hefty sum even in the heyday of peso convertibility. But behind the so-called Nexo project were concerned medical professionals who were also gay. Says a cofounder, Sergio Maulén:

> We used the office of one of the doctors, then somebody's house until we
> could get our own place. We started doing workshops on sexuality, starting
> from the idea that in the gay community there was still a lot of internalized
> homophobia, people still feeling a lot of guilt.

Nexo, which combined clinical services with its gay-support labors, almost collapsed in the 2001 crisis, and the magazine was discontinued. But its other activities trudge on in a sort of gray area between the political movements and the quasi-private clinical outfits. Its services are not always free but seem not to have morphed into just another medical business either. The shortcomings of the public health services, even improved as they are after two decades, still provide plenty of room for independent groups inspired by the cause of gay consciousness to play a meaningful role.

In fact, Maulén downplays the significance of the curative role in its HIV-related work:

> I think it's not so much AIDS work but the issue of working with people on identity and acceptance, that really goes beyond putting on a condom. To be able to say, This is what I am, I'm happy with it—that seems important to me. That justifies being there, and in principle you yourself are helped by it. The first one to be cured is yourself when you perform a community service.

Argentina is perhaps the most extreme example of political schizophrenia in relation to AIDS: a country that was capable of producing a clinical response to HIV, albeit kicking and screaming, including access to medicines often in the midst of economic collapse. At the same time, it was consistently dysfunctional on public education to prevent further infections.

The Global Fund to Combat AIDS, Tuberculosis and Malaria has provided Argentina a substantial grant that may help to address this historical vacuum, although by now it should be clear to everyone that money is not always the solution people expect it to be. Nor is the Global Fund's attempt the first: the American Foundation for AIDS Research (amfAR), founded by the actress Elizabeth Taylor, entered Argentina in 1992 with what at the time was a hefty sum: $250,000 annually to be divided among five key groups. According to César Cigliutti, the funds were poorly managed, and the planned five-year program ended after only two:

> It's not just a question of honesty. You might be super honest but stupid. Or maybe you did good work, but stole half of it, things like that. I think there were poor criteria [for awarding funds].

In addition, Argentina and especially the capital city of Buenos Aires are notorious for fractious intrigue, and the incipient AIDS world quickly acquired a reputation for conflict and divisiveness. The Global Fund insisted that the nongovernmental sector be included and that groups prove their willingness to join forces through collective efforts. In the ambiance of quasi-official "representatives" who can attend meetings and negotiate with officials and funding agencies, Argentines function with impressive agility. But their battles to reach those positions rarely leave room for compromise. Maulén says the country's AIDS NGOs are now in their fourth attempt to form a coalition:

> Once the AIDS Forum was created, there were a thousand e-mails, 90 percent of them accusations back and forth, permanent fights, and with the Global Fund coming in, things got worse.

Of course, with the sums involved, a certain level of rivalry and distrust is inevitable. The Global Fund went to considerable lengths to organize a transparent process for its competitive grant funding in 2003, even including a pre-competition for the grant evaluators themselves. But after some groups got left out of the hundred-plus subsidy winners in 2003, a lawsuit ensued accusing colleagues of insider influence-peddling.

These sorts of dustups and rivalries are common throughout the AIDS universe and no doubt every other social welfare project known to humankind. Political networks created around the supposed shared goals of the member groups often ignore the fact that the entities are not just ideological allies but also adversaries. Orlov is a total skeptic:

> The Forum will have a very ephemeral life. It will exist as long as they put the carrot of project subsidies in front of people. It's pointless to try to put all the organizations together, it will always break down.

He argues that the remarkable success of Argentina in providing drugs to people with HIV has come at a heavy cost:

> I think that now AIDS is being transformed into a run-of-the-mill disease that is going to end up being a matter between the patients and the health system. The change that people were hoping for, what I was supporting, that gay people could speak up and have their proper place in society, that drug users would be respected in their lifestyle, that people involved in prostitution would start to be called "sex workers" and that it wouldn't just be a semantic change but also one of attitudes—for me those were

pastoral challenges for the churches and for society. I think all that's
been lost.

Everyone can discuss AIDS now, says Orlov; it is safe again because people
are comfortable with sick people and medicines. The Pope could call for lower
prices for AIDS drugs while his morality spokesman, Cardinal López Trujillo of
Colombia, compared condoms with cigarettes and said both should carry warning labels about their danger to your health. There is no hint of radical transformation of social attitudes toward the stigmatized or the outsider.

Mabel Bianco agrees that the tougher questions are off the agenda and that
public opinion has relegated the issue back to the medical professionals. She
believes the organizations, including her own, were not paying attention when
commercial interests "infiltrated" their ranks. Ironically, she says, the civic
groups themselves opened the way for this displacement from prevention to
medicalization because they couldn't mobilize for the former:

> Just as we sued the government for the drug therapies, if we had sued over
> prevention, it would have been much more legitimate and useful. We didn't
> know how to do that and, like I say, we missed the boat. It's a self-criticism
> I make now.

Of course, if activism around the AIDS epidemic has been nudged too far
into the direction of clinical services and away from deeper, knottier social
issues, the fault does not lie with those who have HIV. People seeking essential
medicines to remain alive can hardly be chastised for not focusing on other
things. But other AIDS groups do have broader responsibilities. Ironically, those
earlier groups consistently insisted on elevating persons directly affected as active
protagonists, as people "living with HIV" rather than helpless patients; as
citizens with their human rights intact rather than members of stigmatized "risk
groups." Eventually, the drama of life-saving medicines just out of reach proved
far more potent than subtler issues of sexual culture or social marginalization.
Pastor Orlov may be right, but his more nuanced, integrated view of health and
human rights is no competition for the life-and-death struggles of young adults
with HIV. The nonpatient organizations quickly abandoned any attempt at

even-handedness and to a large extent ceded the ground to those directly affected, thereby quickening their own demise.

Nonetheless, the HIV-positive groups themselves would be well advised to return to a broader view, especially in a country whose economic future is as tenuous and uncertain as Argentina's. Pablo Rosales says Argentines' demands on government to respond to health issues while costs continue to escalate are on a collision course with reality:

> Even now with the crisis we're going through, people are still demanding things as if nothing had happened. This economic crisis is no free ride; it happened because of too many deals, looting, you name it. In health this idea that we can do everything, provide everything, is unsustainable.

Turnpike

Among the tragicomic things that have happened to me, one incident stands out in my mind. The mother of a twenty-three-year-old fellow called me from somewhere way out in Pudahuel to say that he was sick and that she didn't know what to do. It was broad daylight, but I couldn't find the alleyways when I drove out there and ended up in a cul-de-sac. There was something on the pavement there, like lumps, but in fact they were human beings. A woman was standing there too. They all got up and crowded around the car to ask me for a "toll": in other words, it was a holdup. So I decided to use a tactic that could have backfired and gotten me knifed: I got out of the car and said, "Ma'am, you can help me? I'm totally lost."

She looked at me and said, "How much coin are you carrying?" I handed her my purse and said, "Here, take it all, but please help me. I'm looking for a young man who is sick." The woman starts going through my purse and says, "What street is it on?" and starts giving me directions while the two men with faces that would give you nightmares started arguing about whether or not to mug me. But the woman told them no, that I was out helping someone sick. So I left without a nickel in my purse, but I had folding money in my panties and got to the guy's house in the end.

The mother said to me, Come look at my son. He was in a sort of stupor. In those circumstances you don't just walk in and say, Hi, how are ya? You have to invent something else, like Wow, it's hot in here. Shall we have some tea? His mother signaled to me, and we went downstairs. It was a very poor household. She said, "Look, I would offer you tea, but I only have one bag, and I was going to give him a cup." So I said, "Oh, just by chance I have tea and sugar in the car, I'll go get it." Outside I saw a store and went to get a few things to eat, paper towels, toothpaste, and what-have-you. The electricity was cut off, there wasn't a thing to eat. And the kid had broncopneumonia.

His mother was happy to see someone in good spirits because the family was overwhelmed by it all. It was Friday afternoon, and in Chile you don't get sick on Friday afternoon; the emergency rooms ignore you. But I called his doctor on my cell phone, and she said to bring him in. So we set out anyway, and he perked up and started asking me what I did. It was cold as hell. We went to the ER at San Juan de Dios, and he sat there in a wheelchair, the two of us just watching the movement in that place, with the whistle going off constantly, people coming in all cut up, a guy with a knife stuck in his head, accidents, someone else with a heart attack, the doctors running all over and shouting. They didn't pay us any mind at all; since the kid was breathing, I guess they figured he was in pretty good shape.

So after about forty minutes, he says, "This is going nowhere." I called his doctor and told her that it was chaos in the ER, and I didn't dare complain either with everything that was happening. So she says, "I don't know, do whatever you think." I reminded her that she had sent us there, and she said, "No, I didn't, I only suggested it." So I counted to 25 to keep my mouth shut and finally thanked her and hung up. Then the kid says, "I want to have a smoke." "With broncopneumonia?" "Yeah," he says "Apparently, no one in this country gives a shit, so why not?" So we went outside, and he had a cigarette.

A few days later he managed to get hospitalized at the main ER on a gurney in the hallway, but at least there was a very nice doctor looking after him. I went to see him there. So that was my performance, to go get a fellow with broncopneumonia, and the only thing I managed to do was accompany him to smoke a cigarette and then send him home. But he was happy to have the ride in a car. Later he got meningitis and didn't recognize anyone, but the last time I called, he was fine, back at work. He had stopped smoking, but he didn't remember a thing about that day. I had to reintroduce myself.

—Elena Droguett

CHAPTER SEVEN

Brazil: Seductive Models

BRAZIL	
Population	176.3 million
First reported case of AIDS	1983
Total estimated HIV infections (2003)	660,000
Male : female ratio	1.7:1
Estimated number of people needing antiretroviral treatment	180,000
Number receiving drugs	154,000
First AIDS NGO established	1985
First organization for people living with AIDS established	1989
First World Bank loan signed (AIDS I)	1993
Adult women using birth control	77%
Gross domestic product (GDP) 2003	$429.3 billion
Per capita income 2003	$2,710
Annual per-capita spending on health	$271
Unemployment rate	12.2%
New HIV infections (1988)	30,000
New HIV infections (2003)	22,000
Period of military rule	1964–1985
Workers Party candidate Luiz Inâcio "Lula" da Silva elected president	2003

> In the country praised worldwide for getting it right, AIDS pioneers aren't
> entirely convinced.

Brazil registered its first case of AIDS in 1980, and by 1983 the São Paulo gay
rights group Outra Coisa (Something Else) already had handed out informational
leaflets on the new disease. That same year the São Paulo state government established an AIDS program, and two years later activists formed the first nongovernmental organizations dedicated exclusively to AIDS. Elsewhere in Latin America at
that early date, hardly anyone considered the disease cause for local concern.

These facts are readily available because some of the Brazilians involved in
AIDS placed priority from the outset on documenting, describing and analyzing
the epidemic and the social response they themselves were generating. A simple
but detailed chronology of AIDS activism was published in 2002 by anthropologist Jane Galvão who worked for and eventually directed the Rio-based Brazilian
Interdisciplinary Association on AIDS (ABIA). Not coincidentally, ABIA was
founded in 1986 by Herbert de Souza, a well-known opponent of Brazil's military dictatorship (1964–1984), and several colleagues. "Betinho," as he was
known, was also hemophiliac and one of the first Brazilians openly to declare his
HIV-positive status. By 1989 Brazil was holding its first national meeting
among AIDS NGOs in Belo Horizonte, the country's third-largest city.

Even more extraordinary from the viewpoint of Hispanic Latin America
where things evolved quite differently, from the outset ABIA conceived of itself
as a group at the service of a larger social movement, which was or would soon be
in need of intellectual and political nourishment of considerable sophistication.
According to Veriano Terto, executive director of ABIA:

> We thought it was important to create a movement, social mobilization,
> around the AIDS issue, not with the NGOs leading it or not just the
> NGOs, but a broad movement. So [ABIA] would provide information,
> methodology, technology, and it would have to be a professional operation
> in addition to the public criticism and all the activism.

In other parts of Latin America, the earliest expressions of concern about
AIDS more often included finding out some basic information for oneself or

one's friends or possibly getting an HIV test once they became available. Very gradually, some began to think about the need for more organized educational efforts, hardly suspecting the difficulties of constructing a prevention message that involved sexuality. But a social movement built around a disease remained a rather remote concept. True, women had promoted campaigns on breast and cervical cancer as those issues emerged from the feminist movement; others had considered health aspects of environmental pollution. But the most common disease-based models were the practical, mutual-aid groups that sometimes emerged for diabetics or kidney dialysis patients, and these rarely saw themselves as political or social movements except in very parochial and limited terms.

In retrospect, it seems fitting that Brazil, given its stereotypical image as a tropical sex paradise, should have taken the lead on AIDS, in both the negative and the positive sense. Around the continent the first cases were easily dismissed in gay circles by saying it was likely that those infected had "been to Brazil." At the same time, the country's tradition of radical activism in the public health field, coinciding with the excitement of recovering democracy after two decades of military rule, provided fertile ground for innovation, experimentation and critical thinking. It was rare in Latin America for academics to move with such dispatch into grappling with the policy, methodological and cultural issues involved in AIDS (even though some of those Brazilians who did so complain of a degree of isolation among their academic peers). Elsewhere, activists struggled to establish prevention or solidarity initiatives and keep them afloat; the Brazilians did that, but also analyzed them, wrote about them and published the results.

Brazil's sheer size made this vanguard role somewhat inevitable, but in addition the HIV epidemic there included all the most problematic elements: It was at first predominantly homosexual but quickly broke out of the confines of male homo- and bisexual practices and affected a sizable population of straight women and men. Brazil also had a substantial epidemic related to intravenous drug use, especially in the environs of São Paulo and its nearby port of Santos. Brazil's brutal social structure and wildly imbalanced income distribution pattern also provided ample grounds for what later were recognized as important contextual factors for the spread of AIDS: poverty, social marginalization and violence.

The link between the social environment and illness was an area of evident interest to at least a generation of Brazilian health professionals. The public health sector had been radicalized by the long years of dictatorship; in medical schools and local health services, some well-placed people were sensitive to the idea that AIDS was not a strictly technical problem but a social phenomenon as well.

José Ricardo Ayres is a professor of preventive medicine at the University of São Paulo's Medical School. Upon assuming responsibility for a health promotion project involving adolescents, Ayres wanted to "do something more interesting" on sexuality and found the pedagogical materials available to be mediocre. He explains:

> There either was nothing, or it was awful stuff, very dogmatic, like, You can get this disease. Or how to put on a condom. Or else very extreme cases about homeless people, extreme situations. It wasn't what I wanted, something for adolescents from average social environments.

Ayres wanted materials that escaped the usual confines of rigid "risk factor" variables or "risk groups" as objects of public health policy. But traditional epidemiology did not incorporate social dimensions into its abstractions. "Prevention work needed more operational concepts," he says, "and there weren't any."

Simultaneously, Ayres found colleagues at ABIA engaged in just the sort of theoretical work he was looking for. In the mid-1990s Ayres won a Macarthur Foundation fellowship to develop a different approach. When he presented a kit of study materials for schoolteachers in São Paulo based on his concept of *vulnerabilities*, rather than the more traditional *risk* categories, the reaction was unexpected. He recalls:

> It was very funny, actually—when I started to speak, it was as if people went into a hypnotic trance. We have an expression in Portuguese, "The coin dropped." Such a simple thing, to try to place behaviors within a broader discussion that considers the social and economic context.

The idea of people's social *vulnerability* has now gained considerable ground in AIDS prevention programs in contrast with a focus on individual behavior driven by rationality and thus susceptible to modification through the application of the right "health belief" or behavior change model. It is no accident that the particular combination of Brazil's dissident public health traditions and the early attention to the importance of thinking about AIDS—rather than exclusively acting on it—would result in breakthroughs such as this important, but hardly unique, example.

All the same, the advanced thinking suggested by this fundamental insight was far from universal even in the best of environments. The city and state of São Paulo, home to some 38 million people, was the site of the earliest, innovative AIDS projects, eventually influencing national policy. Fabio Mesquita was a young doctor and political radical in the port of Santos when AIDS was first raging through circles of injecting drug users in the 1980s. He soon found treating the new disease both a terrible and an oddly inspiring experience. Mesquita explains:

> The beginning of the epidemic was frustrating for a doctor because you lost the daily battles, you lost many patients with whom you had established warm ties, very interesting people—more so than in traditional clinical work because they were outsiders in their lives, drug users or gays or even the heterosexuals. You would get involved with them, and there wasn't much we could do. The feelings of loss were enormous.

But even in Santos, where some of the earliest needle-exchange programs eventually would emerge, dealing with AIDS was considered the booby prize. Mesquita recalls:

> We had a meeting with the clinic director to decide who was going to handle the AIDS cases. She asked everyone, and nobody volunteered; so since I was the newest on the staff, that was the criterion used, for having the least seniority. It wasn't exactly a popular job.

Even considerably later, AIDS remained a low-status assignment, a punishment detail. After a successful election campaign, the new head of the São Paulo state health department offered Mesquita a job for helping out.

He was a renowned public health specialist. He sat next to me and said, "Okay, I want you on my staff, and you can choose any job in the department." When I told him I wanted to organize an AIDS program, he said, "You don't understand. You can have any job you want."

When AIDS became a huge, national program handling millions of dollars in grant funds and operating with substantial autonomy from the ministry itself, attitudes toward the HIV portfolio would change considerably.

Despite the struggles and obstacles the Brazilians describe, all over Hispanic Latin America we learned from them and looked up to them as political pioneers and savvy analysts. Government support to their sex-friendly prevention initiatives seemed to us unimaginably modern. The resources available also struck us as otherworldly: while we struggled to raise our organization's rent money, Brazil's government was negotiating with the World Bank the terms of a loan program running to $250 million. Our AIDS networks might have one or two NGOs dedicated to the epidemic and had to be fleshed out with a variety of others from the women's movement, human rights defenders or community groups; Brazil's annual AIDS NGO assemblies came to number in the hundreds of organizations, and a single city might have more AIDS groups than most countries west of the Andes.

Even the Catholic church was confined to its corner in Brazil to a large extent. A parish priest in São Paulo who directly supports two AIDS hospices sports a break-glass-in-emergency condom display on his office wall. When I asked him if he had run into trouble for what in Chile would be suicide for a parish priest, he said: "I told the bishop to call me in to argue this theologically. I told them to bring along anyone they wanted to take the other side. They didn't call back."

Eventually, the Brazilian model for handling AIDS would become a shimmering ideal for a resource-strapped, developing country, nearly the best of all worlds with an active NGO sector and a government strongly committed to prevention, guaranteed care and—the radical centerpiece—no-cost medicines for everyone with HIV. Although the country's oversimplified image as free-wheeling and culturally sex-friendly reinforced this view, Brazil also looked courageously independent, daring to go nose-to-nose with the immensely powerful pharmaceutical industry to defend its right to produce generic drug substitutes and thereby force down costs of the key protease inhibitors and other drugs. Rio de Janeiro's city-funded hotline for antigay discrimination complaints still seems worthy of Copenhagen or Berlin rather than Catholic Latin America. In short, the Brazilian approach was dazzlingly appealing to anyone in Peru or Guatemala struggling with recalcitrant bureaucrats or prehistoric reactionaries like the Peruvian health minister who announced plans in 2003 to officially register unborn fetuses. Even Chile's well-considered national program, which included modest and controlled openings to NGO partners, paled as timid and miserly by comparison. And the comparisons, especially in the early years, were inevitable. Says Graciela Touzé of Intercambios in Buenos Aires:

> The government response in Argentina has been deplorable. Compared to Brazil, I just think of the office that the national program has there, versus how many technical staff and the whole organization [*in Argentina*]. We can argue about whether we agree with certain things, but there is an important commitment [*in Brazil*] which you don't see here, no question about it.

The Brazilian government's handling of AIDS was such a point of pride during the 1990s that Health Minister José Serra eventually became the ruling coalition's candidate for the presidency. Although Serra lost to Luiz Inâcio Lula da Silva in a historic election in 2002, the fact that the normally second-tier Health Ministry portfolio could be a trampoline for such ambitions is unusual.

Nonetheless, behind this apparently optimum environment of Brazil as the Promised Land for AIDS policy emerge unexpectedly critical voices. Jane Galvão says:

> I've been very pessimistic about the role of the NGOs for a while now. We have a very strong role for the groups in carrying out tasks—no, for carrying out projects: "the dictatorship of the projects," all very professional and what have you. . . . And it's not just in Brazil and not just in AIDS. It's a crisis for the NGOs, an identity crisis for social projects led by groups from civil society.

It is startling to hear one of the best-known names in the AIDS NGO universe express such starkly skeptical sentiments. But Galvão's conclusion— after two decades of distinguished participation in AIDS nonprofits and all the international planning meetings, NGO committees and networks, debates and seminars imaginable—is curious if not a bit alarming. If discouragement and disillusion have arrived to Brazil, what can other countries expect even if they manage to imitate its apparent successes?

Galvão and others recall the earliest days of the fight against AIDS in Brazil as a period guided by utopian visions, by dreams of social change coincident with the promise of democracy after two decades of military rule. People were drawn to the AIDS issue out of deep personal motivations, concern for relatives or friends, or recognition that the social stigma associated with HIV was both dangerous and an opportunity to address social exclusions programmatically and culturally—crucial in a country with one of the worst forms of economic apartheid in the world. Some were political figures involved in the fight to recover democratic rule; others were distinguished academics. Galvão recalls:

> Now it seems like a simple thing, to have someone like [*Walter Almeida*], a doctor who studied in London, who had a certain social status. But it was important to have an international perspective and to generate a broader debate about AIDS in Brazil, its relation to national, regional and international policies. We're still living off that legacy.

As elsewhere, gay activism and the natural solidarity of gay circles hit hard by the epidemic also played an essential role. According to Marcos Benedetti of the AIDS Support and Prevention Group, GAPA, in Porto Alegre:

> In the beginning of the AIDS movement, at the end of the 1980s, early 1990s, this unity did exist, when it was much more a question of homosexual identity, and also you add this identity of being HIV-positive, which bound people together.

In addition, Brazil's AIDS nucleus also was heavily peopled with political visionaries, as well defined as the Mexicans' but more subtle and inquisitive.

Wildenay Contrera of the first GAPA, based in São Paulo, says:

> We were living under the dictatorship, so little groups formed but not just
> political ones. They were responding to larger, deeper issues of repression,
> with worldwide implications. We were trapped in a symbolic prison; homo-
> sexuals had to hide, to live in very closed circles. The right to the body was
> bound up with the issue of democracy.

The speaker, one of the earliest activists from a pioneer AIDS organization, was not just expounding theory: By the early 1990s, she had lost two brothers to the epidemic. But these were participants with a specific mission that involved not only responding to an emergency outbreak of disease but also examining its implications for Brazilian society. They were not going to be neutralized easily, even by their own successes.

The most extraordinary aspect of Brazil's AIDS program was the bold decision to provide universal access to the life-saving combination drug therapies invented in the mid-1990s. By the end of the decade Brazil was spending some $400 million on medicines alone, despite having fought successfully against the big drug companies for the right to save money by using generic substitutes for the high-priced brand-name medicines. The government now argues that it has avoided 350,000 hospitalizations and 90,000 deaths, as well as saving the country more in productivity, taxes and reduced medical costs than it spends to keep everyone who needs it on HIV drug therapy, now 135,000 citizens. Ironically, the measure that finally established the right to access was known ironically as the Sarney law, after the ultra-conservative transitional president José Sarney who signed it.

The government also argues that the drug-access program is an essential part of its overall prevention strategy and is responsible for impressive drops in sero-prevalence rates among key groups: from 18 percent to 6 percent among female sex workers, 11 percent to 5 percent among gay men and 21 percent to 11 percent among drug injectors. All in all, the national coordinating office on AIDS says 600,000 infections were avoided through actions involving over 2,000 joint government-NGO partnerships. Of course, governments always try to make things look great, and the Brazilian government is no exception. Nonetheless, the sheer scale of the triple-tiered national/state/city programs to address AIDS is impressive. "It's really like a war room, the approach to fighting AIDS," said one academic involved in strategic planning for a state in southern Brazil. "Aside from the criticisms, the inefficiencies and whatever, you see a real effort to mobilize everything they've got."

Mobilization of people facing the disease was always a key part of the strategy to pressure the government toward this now-official stance. An early advocate was Herbert Daniel, the founder of the Rio-based Pela VIDDA (Value, Integration and Dignity of AIDS Patients), the first group of HIV-positive people in Brazil and a pioneer in Latin America. Daniel's pre-AIDS role as an opponent of military rule inevitably marked that group's approach to the issue. One historical review identifies two tendencies in the mobilization of people with HIV in Brazil, one a *universalist* and the other an *AIDS-specific* approach. For Daniel, since AIDS affected all humanity by feeding stigma and prejudice, the main task was to confront discrimination, to combat *social death*, the expulsion of the individual from society on the basis of his or her diagnosis.

Based on this logic, Daniel's group did not exclude non-HIV-positives from its membership, although it pushed for greater visibility and leadership for people affected by HIV and AIDS. As Veriano Terto describes it:

> The important thing was solidarity, full participation by everyone based on respect for differences, fighting for full citizenship, not just for HIV-positive people, but for everyone facing a situation of vulnerability.

Given the glaring social injustices and inequalities existing in Brazil as in all Latin America, such a political, rather than interest-group, approach was natural enough. Eventually, however, this nobly inclusive perspective was bound to clash with a narrower but more urgent appeal. A second wave of HIV-positive organizing focused on the immediate needs of people facing the diagnosis. As the epidemic grew among a cross-section of Brazilian society, these growing thousands must have been somewhat perplexed by discussions of broad and, to them, abstract social issues. Terto continues:

> [*The other HIV-positive groups*] sought to work on the meanings associated with the HIV diagnosis and to face its consequences, a vision much more centered on individual well-being.

It is not hard to imagine which approach would prove most popular with the thousands of HIV-positive Brazilians facing all sorts of needs both before and after learning of their diagnosis. Nonetheless, the fact that the earliest HIV-positive organizations in Brazil steadfastly refused to set themselves apart and insisted on finding common ground with other populations and their problems is extraordinary, as was their implicit rejection of any appeal to public sympathies as AIDS "victims." Although some organizing by people with HIV elsewhere in Latin America may have been inspired by similar philosophies, for the most part interest-group politics have prevailed especially as the treatment-access question grew in importance.

Paradoxically, however, the advent of full triple-combination therapy for everyone with HIV infection in Brazil in the late 1990s tended to blur the boundaries between these two approaches as people with HIV really could return to their normal lives and "living with AIDS" could be more of a reality than a hopeful slogan. It is purely speculative to guess how much influence the universalist approach may have had in the evolution of official policy, and at first glance the Brazilian government's decision to provide universal free access could be perceived as a triumph of the latter position, the satisfaction of specific demands.

But universal access was by no means assured from the beginning; it occurred because AIDS had attracted interest and had stimulated grassroots reaction, because well-informed professionals joined the agitators and backed their personalized demands with cogent arguments. Had the early activists concentrated solely on the solution of immediate needs, such as their own, they might well have been tempted to imitate the Guatemalan example and resolve the problems of their immediate circle, rather than fight for a social right applicable to all Brazilians. That is, the specific demands for triple therapy and care may have been as successful as early as they were not *in spite* of the broader political appeals but *because* of them. Two longtime participants put it this way:

I am old enough to know that the social movement created the political will. It wasn't a gift we received from the government.

—*Mónica Barbosa*

We had a real political movement. Now we've obtained a lot of things and then there was the [*drug*] cocktail. You're afraid to lose that. People thought it was a favor, everyone felt so grateful to the government, and let's work together and—I don't know, all that lukewarm stuff. Now people are starting to reflect a little more.

—*Aurea Celeste da Silva Abbade*

Of course, the World Bank provided key funding that freed the Brazilian national program from financial pressures and made the universal-access decision easier. But as several observers and historians have documented, the World Bank, consistent with its economic calculations, originally did *not* favor the inclusion of drug purchases in its loan program, considering treatment attempts a poor use of resources compared to prevention efforts to avoid future infections. Just a few years later, Brazilian AIDS program officials would be showing their data at world congresses and insisting that universal drug access in fact was saving money.

A vigorous social movement, not official wisdom, had made that happen. Observing the spirited defense of government policy by a spokesman at the Geneva AIDS conference in 1998, one would hardly suspect that strong civic opposition had arisen to denounce the government just a few years before precisely for refusing to countenance this approach. The radical, critical, independent AIDS movement forced the government's hand and also strengthened it in its negotiations with the pharmaceutical companies, opening up the possibilities of mass access to the miracle drugs.

Older veterans of the AIDS battles recall a public health system that could hardly be bothered with "hopeless" cases—attitudes that activists faced everywhere else in Latin America and often still do. Rubens Olivera Duda, now head of the São Paulo State AIDS NGO Network, joined an AIDS hospice as a volunteer long before the life-saving drugs appeared on the scene. He recalls:

I lived in that house for two years when three or four people were dying every week. I would dress the bodies myself because in the hospital they wouldn't do it. How many times I put someone into the coffin—just me!—and then waited for the hearse to arrive. All the residents came because they knew they would be next. I really didn't think there was a solution. And then in 1996 [*when the antiretroviral drugs appeared*], we saw that even in the worst, most impossible situation, you have to keep fighting.

Wildenay Contrera faced similar official indifference as she tried to find services for her brothers and their sick friends in the late 1980s. Her descriptions do not sound like the Brazil of international AIDS stardom. She says:

Treatment was very precarious; there were no beds because the beds were assigned to other diseases, not AIDS. One of our demands was to reserve at least five beds for people with AIDS. That was a big fight because the hospitals said no, we can't because we don't have personnel, it'll be very expensive.

Even the task of assuring an HIV-safe blood supply, quickly and efficiently managed in other countries, turned into a major confrontation with commercial suppliers in Brazil that had long profited from blood shortages and the ready supply of impoverished donors. In fact, problems with safe blood persisted in some states well into the 1990s.

Nevertheless, to see how a pioneer area like São Paulo state is managing AIDS treatment today is remarkable. Public hospitals have created Referral and Treatment Centers (CRTs) for handling HIV cases where patients not only get expedited service but also can call on in-house complaint managers—often themselves HIV-positive—to deal with whatever obstacles arise. Such innovations for dealing with AIDS are particularly impressive considering the continuing problems of health care for other pathologies, which may entail long waits in the clinic and postponements of surgery or other procedures.

We cannot know how well or badly other movements around Hispanic Latin America might have fared on broadening drug access for people with AIDS had the Brazilian experiment not led the way. As it happened, Brazil demonstrated that universal access was possible and even arguably more economical than letting people get sick and die. Ironically, the highly motivated, sophisticated and often indignant grassroots movement that had so much to do with convincing the Brazilian state to adopt and crusade on this issue offers another hint of the dangers inherent in the current atmosphere of apparent consensus, cooperation and success.

The disillusionment certain cautiously skeptical activists hint at in comparing *then* and *now* involves three elements: the relatively early absorption of the NGO human and political potential by the Brazilian state, aided by World Bank funds; the simultaneous professionalization/commercialization of the social movement as NGOs increasingly became subcontractors for prevention and care services; and the third factor that cannot be blamed on anyone: human nature. Roberto Chateaubriand is the president of the main AIDS service and advocacy group in Belo Horizonte.

> I think personal vanity clashed with the political project which transcended individual actors—the protagonism of individuals overshadowed it, and from that point on, things fall apart completely, an impasse is created that cannot be overcome.

Such a diagnosis may be more philosophical than political, but the Brazilian state and the World Bank—institutions presumably aware of the impact of human foibles in social movements—certainly could anticipate the stimulating effects of their impending largesse on amour propre within the world of their NGO counterparts. In addition, without succumbing to simplistic conspiratorial views, the World Bank itself may be assumed to house imperfect beings, capable of filtering their thoughts and actions through the prism of self-interest. Brazilian authors have had plenty to say about that as well.

In any case, the Bank clearly played a crucial role in AIDS in Brazil through its five-year loan programs, known as AIDS I and II, probably to be followed by AIDS III. Negotiations for the first of these loans, which amounted to $170 million matched by another $90 million from the government's own resources, began in 1992, at the time of the short-lived Collor de Melo presidency. Those who recall that brief period say it was a giant step backward on AIDS policy. The top national staff were sacked and positive tendencies reversed in a sort of restoration of the predemocratic ambience of an authoritarian state.

President Collor, however, did not survive a vast corruption scandal and was impeached in 1992. The return of traditional negligence turned out to be temporary, and the head of the Brazilian AIDS program, Lair Guerra de Macedo, came back triumphantly to Brasilia and her old job. According to some accounts, she returned convinced that the NGOs' insistence on joining forces with the state apparatus was an interesting proposition.

The prospects of a large sum of World Bank money dedicated to AIDS implied an important shift, and some of those in the AIDS field had mixed emotions. The Bank's ideological proclivity for neoliberal solutions was well-known and on the surface appeared incompatible with the activists' insistence on the state's constitutional responsibility to guarantee health as a human right, especially in a nation with a huge population of destitute citizens. Furthermore, cooperation with civil society could sound suspiciously similar to privatization, to the Bank's presumed eagerness to dismantle public services and outsource them to the for-profit sector in the name of efficiency. Finally, as already mentioned, the Bank resisted including drug access as part of its funding scheme. All this meant that, at the very least, Brazilians involved in AIDS were facing "a model of state-civil society relations previously unheard of in dealing with health issues," as psychiatrist Wilma Villela puts it.

But according to some accounts, the national AIDS program itself was beginning to take on a very particular life of its own, one quite unlike that of other departments within the Health Ministry. It enjoyed considerable autonomy over its budget, both in generating income and in deciding how to spend it. The World Bank loan was the largest but far from the only chunk of money that these officials were overseeing. From being a low-status specialty in the medical field—dermato-venereal clinics were traditionally dead-end slots where doctors and other staff had to deal with the world of prostitution and other unpleasantness—AIDS was suddenly big business.

The effects of the World Bank's massive entry into the AIDS universe in Brazil included an enormous expansion—"scaling up" in the new jargon—of the country's response to HIV infection and care for people with AIDS. By 1997 some five hundred projects had been carried out by NGOs around the country with World Bank money channeled through the government AIDS program, then called the National AIDS Coordination in the spirit of decentralization. Nor was the government shy about drawing attention to itself as a model in the response to AIDS. Strengthened by the cash, it funded direct interventions by the NGOs on a scale previously unimagined and also supported the NGOs' horizontal links through seminars and assemblies. The partnership eventually appeared to be so seamless that the criticism and battles that had once occurred and in fact had stimulated the official response to AIDS in the first place seemed like a bad dream from another epoch.

These achievements—the services, the treatments, the support networks—were shepherded by a movement that was inspired, visionary, militant and also haphazard, messy, chaotic and often wrong-headed. A few voices see the standard miniproject subcontracted by the government with World Bank loans as gradually "homogenizing" the projects, leaving "little room for real reflection on the process," as Villela says.

One line of criticism is that the two-way, state-civil society mode of cooperation, long touted by the NGO sector in theory, has been reduced increasingly to the distribution of funds. Although this was supposed to be only one aspect of the relationship, it soon became virtually the only one, or the only important one. Unsurprisingly, many actors found this relationship to their liking, and those with a more ambitiously pragmatic approach never fully grasped the doubts expressed in academic papers.

This discomfort with the sudden generosity from the Brazilian state spilled over national borders at one point. An enormous regional blow-up among NGOs occurred in 1996 when a high-profile, non-Brazilian regional activist visiting the country for a seminar flew to the capital city of Brasilia to meet privately with officials of the Brazilian national program about financial aid to a variety of projects—without informing local colleagues. Despite the electronic hailstorm that followed, half the Latin American activists could not figure out why some Brazilians were upset about the meeting: If money is available, they reasoned, why not take it? In the end, that position mostly won out.

The incorporation of new organizations into the AIDS field was another goal of the Brazilian strategy, to mobilize new social actors and spread the prevention and care work more broadly, another aspect of "scaling up." But adding an AIDS project to their portfolio did not necessarily mean real engagement with the issue. Inevitably, the mix of gay-rights militancy and progressive currents in social medicine would be dissipated by the addition of dozens of new groups with vastly different missions. Duda of the São Paulo AIDS network noted in 2001 that of the 250 groups listed in the statewide roster of AIDS NGOs, less than 100 were actively engaged in the more political aspects of the epidemic; the rest kept to themselves. Critics called this the systematic depoliticization of AIDS, in which the NGOs' creativity and energy were channeled into administering state-funded service contracts.

But is this such a bad thing? After all, the more self-critical groups themselves long complained about the NGOs' typical lack of rigor, weak theoretical grounding and fire-engine approaches to the permanent crises that arose in the early years. Politics, it could be argued, is no substitute for technique; belief and passion also require methodology.

One answer from the critics is that the World Bank bounty did not necessarily resolve technical and methodological problems. Although the NGOs now are in less of an emergency-response mode, they are not necessarily carrying out the work or discovering the techniques that will effectively slow or reverse the expansion of HIV infection. In fact, nearly a decade after the first World Bank loan began to operate, evidence of the efficacy of prevention activities is hard to evaluate, despite the national program's boast of significant reductions in seroprevalence rates.

If the NGOs funded by World Bank/Brazilian government funds risk becoming uncritical project executors managing human suffering rather than true advocates of putting an end to it, they did not appear to be overly concerned about this potential loss. At the Sixth National Assembly of AIDS NGOs in 1994 in Vitória—paid for in part with funds from the World Bank loan—two hundred delegates greeted Dr. Guerra de Macedo with a standing ovation. At the same meeting, conflicts among different camps of NGOs resulted in bitter confrontations and at least one fistfight. Three years later, in 1997, the assembly would attract a thousand delegates who had sent their competing abstracts to the conference organizers in imitation of the biennial international congress. For better or worse, project financing directed from the government would determine the shape and character of Brazil's NGO responses to AIDS in the future. Through bank funds and projects, says Galvão, the Brazilian government AIDS program "made itself the centerpiece." Those concentrating on the shortcomings of state action were in a minority.

While the response to AIDS in Brazil was shaped by the recovery of democracy, the World Bank was also facing a defining moment in its own existence.

Fifty years after the Bretton Woods agreements that led to its formation, the Bank found itself the target of a growing critical murmur about its role, especially over its "structural adjustment" loans, which imposed harsh conditions on governments in the developing world. The Bank already had adopted a fall-back position and insisted that its slogan, "A world without poverty," included the promotion of health and other intangibles beyond its notorious dam-building and infrastructural projects. As Terto quips, one can doubt the Bank's role in reconstructing countries but not its skill in reconstructing itself. Although the Bank could hardly admit that its own policies had aggravated long-term poverty, it could certainly lend money to deal with the poverty that existed, whatever its origins. AIDS was a field of action, a pressing social issue that would require a huge infusion of funds and economists and development specialists to manage them. These the World Bank could certainly supply.

The Brazilian groups probably were forced to look more critically at their own praxis due to the rapid spread of the epidemic and the health system's evident incapacity to respond. In the worlds of Roberto Chateaubriand:

> We began to see that it wasn't enough to just help individuals because after those cases would be another and another and another. In fact, we began to see that the help we were giving people was silly—we had one case where a kid wanted to see the ocean before he died, and we organized that! But then we started to think about not offering a service but supporting those who did.

Brazil's size meant that important differences were evolving in the epidemic as well as the social response to it in different parts of the country. In Belo Horizonte, the GAPA acronym stood for Support *and* Prevention of AIDS while in São Paulo, the same initials meant Support *to* AIDS Prevention. Within these subtleties lay important differences of focus and mission; the former included a clear mandate for care-related services while the latter did not, at least not necessarily. In smaller countries of Latin America, the debates raging often had to do with gay liberation versus AIDS awareness; Brazil had plenty of groups to deal with both those topics and a lot more besides.

Aurea Celeste da Silva Abbade is an attorney who almost accidentally became a founding member of GAPA/São Paulo in 1984 and helped push for legal changes to defend people with HIV/AIDS in Brazil, including the Sarney Law that made treatment free of charge. She says:

> We always drew boundaries in GAPA: it is the "AIDS Prevention Support Group," not a sexual liberation group. It may have 99.9 percent homosexuals, but sexuality is discussed in another NGO or another forum. Not here.

A broad spectrum of organizations, talented activists, savvy public health professionals, a rapidly expanding epidemic—Brazil had the full mix of elements for either disaster or a clever response. Given the country's political fragility and vast social problems, things could have gone much worse.

Marcos Benedetti's GAPA was formed in Porto Alegre in the extreme south of Brazil. His group lived through most of the tensions and ambiguities described in this chapter. Although dealing with a predominantly homosexual epidemic, a historical accident—their first meetings took place in a Lutheran church with an outreach project among women in the commercial sex trade—led GAPA/Porto Alegre to get involved early on in the world of prostitution, both female and male-transvestite.

GAPA/Porto Alegre added hospital visits to its mandate and quickly became involved in services and care to people with HIV. In addition, Porto Alegre was one center of a growing political movement, the Workers Party, Brazil's unique combination of traditional leftists, Catholic liberationists and union members, which took over the city government in 1988. President Lula da Silva, finally elected in 2002 after three unsuccessful campaigns, is the historic Workers Party leader.

Porto Alegre is also now the virtual world capital of the misnamed antiglobalization movement and three times hosted the popular World Social Forum to rival the annual meeting of the world's economic powermongers at Davos, Switzerland. The city is admirably well equipped in everything one would expect from a government that emerged from social movements of all sorts, and its process of "participatory budgeting," in which community groups thrash out spending decisions to be ratified later by the city council, is world famous. With this sort of history, Porto Alegre should certainly reflect all the best of how Brazil responded to HIV; if there are still problems with AIDS, they should emerge from this favorable environment with admirable clarity.

Porto Alegre's left-wing city administration promptly moved to establish an AIDS program at a time when many other governments, even national ones, were tut-tutting the entire problem. Furthermore, the first officials in charge were none other than members of GAPA itself. Inspired by the Italian reform of psychiatric care and the movement toward deinstitutionalization, psychologist José Eduardo Gonçalves had already become concerned about AIDS due to the deaths of close friends in New York. He recalls:

> There was nothing organized in Porto Alegre, just a few people with concerns about the wrong way we were going about it, with "risk groups" and all that. But the government apparatus, in the federal, state, city governments, there was nothing, nothing, no response at all.

Nonetheless, the reaction came earlier than most other places as the Workers Party city government pushed its functionaries to involve citizens in governmental actions at all levels. An early member of the AIDS program in Porto Alegre, Uruguayan psychologist Mirtha Sendic, recalls that the peer educator model was snapped up by the city administration. Years later it forms the basis of the city's AIDS strategy. Says Sendic:

> We have 4,500 community leaders around the city talking about this all the time. I think it works better than a campaign on television. We proved that community-based work is better, people learning about it in an everyday environment. You have less resistance to HIV-positive people here among the average person—it's much greater among health professionals.

However, Sendic is not using the term *community* in the same way as others in the AIDS field. She is talking about people in neighborhoods, large numbers of them, often very poor. The traditional NGOs speak of *community* too, but through no particular fault of their own, this can mean fairly narrow circles with considerable socioeconomic and cultural homogeneity. Sendic explains:

> I think the big problem of the NGOs is that they work with a determined sector and social class. We, on the other hand, work with extremely impoverished sectors where the NGOs will never reach.

Sendic is on excellent terms with the NGOs' staff, whom she obviously respects and encourages. But sociocultural gaps in Brazil are so enormous that even when the groups try to open their doors and reach out to less familiar constituencies, they are likely to be frustrated. She says:

> We are talking about people who don't have the cultural wherewithal to understand the importance of organizing into groups or the information they need to become clients, people who don't know they have the right to go to a clinic and get free medicine.

Of course, the founding AIDS NGOs cannot be blamed for not being something they are not or for not having the resources of the state apparatus. But they could be charged with not understanding the limits of their own role. Not surprisingly, the early presence of the government sector and the very openness of the authorities to cooperate led to GAPA/Porto Alegre's most notorious split. Gerson Winckler, one of its founders, objected to the dual roles of some of his colleagues as both city officials and NGO leaders:

> The big identity crisis of GAPA was that in its administration, leadership, there were government people. And we wanted to criticize the government, there they were, inside. . . . It created an abyss. It was terrible.

Although the people identified as the problem gave up their positions, Winckler admits that the conflict was "not resolved until years later." Curiously perhaps, Winckler himself left the group to assume the leadership of Porto Alegre's AIDS program and remained there for eight years.

Meanwhile, the apparently optimum conditions that evolved in Porto Alegre do not stimulate unmitigated praise. Longtime activists like Marcos Benedetti, while recognizing the positive aspects of official policy, are quick to express skepticism about the real depth of the achievements, saying:

> The tensions that should exist between civil society and the state, each with its different role, this was lost when we started getting funding from the World Bank because that's when the professionalization of the NGO work begins, starting from then. Truth is, I don't think this is true only in

Rio Grande do Sul, where we have a leftist government; I think it's true in the whole Brazilian AIDS movement. People started getting paid, and that diminished the tension. The NGOs ended up almost subservient in their relationship to the state.

The preceding conversation, which occurred in one of the dining areas of the World Social Forum at the Porto Alegre Catholic University campus, was interrupted by some of Marcos's activist friends from the local gay group, Nuances, who enthusiastically seconded his critical sentiments. "The government money is only to co-opt and manipulate the social movement," said one, amid considerable camp bantering. It is hard to imagine any country in Hispanic Latin America where the few gay activists aware of official policy would criticize the distribution of money to their own organizations.

At first glance these complaints seem like the nitpicking of perennially dissatisfied *ultras*. Benedetti did not want to fall into facile traps of this sort, but he perceived that the once critical role of GAPA, its function as a monitor independent of the public sector, had been blunted. "They've become more fearful," he said, adding that the explosion of AIDS-related projects has turned the once cutting-edge AIDS-advocacy movement into a series of care-provider projects with little in common and a much diluted vision:

Now you have five hundred new organizations that take care of mothers, children, the homeless, so [*the militancy*] got lost. Now everything is extremely care-oriented, almost like the groups in the churches dealing with the poor, which are not political.

The director of Benedetti's group, Claudia Penalva, also laments the loss of popular response, the snap and buzz of the early militance, replaced by a denatured appeal to "volunteering":

There is a big push in Brazil to encourage volunteering, to be a school friend, for people to "help out." Here in Rio Grande do Sul [*state*] there's an NGO called Volunteer Partners whose objective is to stimulate volunteering. It's a lot of charity work. Their ads show a pretty, blond woman saying, I was unhappy, and then I discovered being a volunteer! And it shows her with children and all that. Then you get a lot of people phoning who want to visit sick people.

Sendic shares this skepticism but from an entirely different perspective:

> I have a critical and political vision of how the NGOs have structured themselves, and it seems to me that it's more friends-of-friends than anything. People know each other, and they end up forming the NGOs, but they don't have our everyday experience. In this government there is a very hard line on social inclusion that is in your face every day, the mayor's office, the department heads. You have to be working with people.

Sendic's comment suggests the limits of the NGO as pioneers and innovators who are too small or parochial really to reconstruct social practices or provide sustainable services. Still, the eclipse of the social movement removes one of the permanent motivations driving the government's more efficient response.

The advent of triple therapy and the partial surmounting of the initial AIDS crisis have made it a little easier to examine the NGO dynamic with greater detachment. But despite the considerable and bitter fights that have occurred, participants tend to couch their critical comments in very general terms and refuse to be drawn into specifics. Everyone involved in AIDS, writes Jane Galvão, "disputed the field," suggesting a pursuit of strategic, institutional and personal interests. Although this may seem self-evident, during the heyday of AIDS activism, with the specter of disease and death all around, the suggestion of *motives* or, heaven forbid, *interests* on the part of groups or individuals would have been insulting. The very gravity of the epidemic to those close by, professionally or personally, obscured the complexity of motivations that were always at work.

Mentor

My first contact with the gay scene in Santiago was in 1995 when I was seventeen. I didn't know anybody, and I didn't know where to meet people. I didn't know anything about AIDS either, just that you had to be careful, whatever that meant.

I happened to go by Santa Lucía Hill with my schoolmates one day and saw a lot of men hanging around, some very feminine or "faggy," you could say. A few days later I went back alone. That's how I started to meet people and have my first experiences, always very uptight about both sex and AIDS.

Once I met a guy there who was two years older, Oscar, and we started going out together. He told me he had to get his HIV test result at the Association, which I had never heard of before. I went along but stayed down on the corner of Vicuña Mackenna and Jofré because I was terrified at the idea of seeing men kiss each other.

After a while I lost track of Oscar, and I went to the Association to find him. A counselor there spoke to me very skillfully and told me to come back, to meet people and talk. He could see my fears, my naiveté at that moment. But he didn't have any news about Oscar.

Then I started to go more often, almost every day, and in March when they had their volunteer course every night for a week, I took it. I joined one program and later several others, including a research project on sexuality. To do the surveys I went back to Santa Lucía and contacted a ton of guys. I was the youngest volunteer at that time. I used to show up in my school uniform.

Years later I worked for the national AIDS program and then for the government hotline, FonoSIDA. One day an operator was shaken up because she had a call from a guy whose boyfriend had committed suicide. We had psychological counseling for the operators, but it was a shock for everyone. Even more for me: I found out that the guy who killed himself was Oscar.

I couldn't look at him in the coffin. At the cemetery his sister told me he was overwhelmed with his problems, his boyfriend, looking for work, no opportunities. But nothing more than that.

Sometimes I think about how thanks to Oscar I got involved in this work, came out of the closet in a good way, with role models that were positive for my development. And yet he killed himself. Luckily, I didn't take that call—it would have been too much.

—Jimmy Esparza

CHAPTER EIGHT

Chile: Seizing Empowerment

CHILE	
Population	15.1 million
First reported case of AIDS	1984
Total estimated HIV infections	26,000
Male : female ratio	7.6:1
Estimated number of people needing antiretroviral treatment	5,700
Number receiving drugs	4,200
First AIDS prevention NGO established	1988
Adult women using birth control	61%
Gross domestic product (GDP) 2003	$72.4 billion
Per capita income 2003	$4,390
Annual per-capita spending on health	$331
Unemployment rate	8.5%
Augusto Pinochet dictatorship	1973–1990
Estimated deaths during military rule	10,000–16,000
Divorce legalized	2004

In a country where public appearances trump private behavior, remedicalizing HIV soothes the conscience; when things *look* fine, they *are* fine.

At a famous incident in the Chilean port city of Valparaíso in 1990, three hundred patrons of a gay nightclub were taken by police armed with submachine guns to a sexually transmitted disease clinic in the middle of the night and forced to take HIV and syphilis tests on the orders of the city's health authorities. As dawn broke, two were found to be HIV-positive. Augusto Pinochet's seventeen-year military regime still had one month to go. The raid had been rescheduled from an earlier date when police discovered that the son of a prominent general was in the bar as a patron and decided to avoid problems. When I later interviewed the doctors who had ordered the mass arrests, one said local gays had to realize the importance of "separating these people [with AIDS] from the community." She remains the director of the local health service there today.

After two decades of military propaganda about the threat of the "Marxist cancer" to the body politic, the danger that HIV infection would be treated as a new invasion of society's physical body, one that would also require a repressive response, was quite real. But as it turned out, although HIV in Chile began and remains the most predominantly homosexual AIDS epidemic in the Western Hemisphere, such heavy-handed tactics were uncommon. In fact, the local media quickly downplayed the homosexual-AIDS connection that accompanied early news of the disease, more out of indifference than open-mindedness.

In 1990 official statistics listed 142 new AIDS diagnoses among men and 5 among women. Over a decade later men still comprise some 70 percent of the total. Nonetheless, in early coverage of the phenomenon, Chilean newspapers focused their worried attention on the threat to married couples and especially the "innocent victims"—newborns with HIV—even when these were hard to find. Government spokespeople frequently noted the increasing "feminization" of HIV infection as the figures for HIV infections among women crept slowly upward despite the fact that in numerical terms men still accounted for most of the cases. On one occasion an assistant health minister even expressed concern about the handful of intravenous drug-related infections while remaining mum on the dozens, later hundreds, of gay men swamping local hospitals. In those years no one pointed out the subtle discrimination in this exclusive concern for anyone not homosexual because no organizations defending gays existed to refine or channel such a discourse. That would eventually change.

Meanwhile, the first cases remained such a novelty that a junior functionary from the Health Ministry could dismiss them confidently in 1986 with the notorious phrase that AIDS in Chile was "under control"—entirely fitting for a military dictatorship. He suggested that the epidemic sprang from dubious sexual practices common in other countries and that well-behaved Chileans had nothing to worry about. I was still making my living as a freelance journalist at the time, mostly watching the progress of the movement against military rule. But I remember sitting at that news conference with the sneaking suspicion that the optimistic doctor had it all wrong.

Once electoral democracy returned to Chile in 1990, the new government slowly geared up to produce a more coherent response. The multiparty Concertación, which emerged from the opposition to Pinochet, won three straight presidential elections and has now been in power for a decade and a half. Today, although no one would describe AIDS as "under control" in Chile or anywhere else, the country is proud of its efforts. Chile has long been a social laboratory for the region, having experimented with the Christian Democrat-led "Revolution in Liberty" in the 1960s as a favorite of President John Kennedy's Alliance for Progress, later with radical, ballot-box socialism led by Salvador Allende and soon after that with the neoliberal counterrevolution engineered under Pinochet's dictatorship. All these experiences reflect the Chilean elite's deep-seated belief that Chile is in many aspects superior to its neighbors, that the country, unlike many in Latin America, "works." They shudder at being lumped in with the "tropical" countries of the Caribbean or Central America.

Irma Palma is a psychologist who recently directed an ambitious sex-education project supported by a raft of UN agencies and the government's science and technology fund. She says that unlike the massive expansion of the availability of contraceptives in the 1960s, the debate today has to focus on sexual rights and individual freedom, a much more difficult battlefield for the weak civilian government. Palma echoes the view that Chile is particularly given to the Latin American tolerance of private rule-breaking as long as it does not challenge official virtues. She says:

> Chile's double standard is comprised of public virtues and private vices, the
> orderly preservation of marriage and the family along with room for quite a
> bit of licentiousness in practice.

This public/private dichotomy does not only apply to individuals but can be understood metaphorically as well. Within the region Chile's AIDS program is rated highly; all the bases are covered, and the reports can boast of important achievements. But the self-congratulatory posture has a dose of collective self-delusion as well: the Health Ministry's epidemiological reports consistently state its figures as fully the equivalent of reality as if the data had been gathered by the Holy Spirit. When things *appear* to be well in Chile, they *are* well. But behind the brave public face, in practice there is room for considerable institutional licentiousness.

While the military dictatorship remained impervious to the AIDS issue, Catholic charities reacted to the new disease in their time-honored way, by providing care for the sick. Caritas-Chile, led by an Italian priest, Baldo Santi, promptly established an AIDS program and in 1988 clashed with Pinochet's appointed mayor of the middle-class Santiago district of Ñuñoa over the charity's decision to place a special residence for people with AIDS there. A neighborhood movement quickly rose to oust the facility, led by angry homeowners who talked of unknown dangers of contagion but whose real fears were of homosexuals and other undesirables passing them on the streets. I met Santi and offered our fledgling group's support to go door to door and explain the issue, but nothing came of it. Caritas remained aloof but continued to publicize its activities to help the sick and dying.

In later years Caritas and another religious outfit, the Sisters of Santa Clara de Asis, refined and perfected their appeals but insisted on dealing with HIV as a strictly medical problem, best resolved by Catholic clergy. The Santa Clara sisters specialized in HIV-infected children, once appealing for donations with a poster of a nun holding an afflicted child under the caption, "They never had a chance to choose"—unlike their adult parents who clearly did have and thus merited less sympathy. In a bizarre 1998 meeting with the mother superior of this prosperous congregation, the newly formed board of Chile's HIV-positive organization sat patiently for over an hour to hear her thrill to recollections of the children taken in by her nuns. "People ask me if I'm frustrated as a woman, but I'm not frustrated," she told us. "I have many children."

I got a glimpse of how the few AIDS infants in Chile were ending up in these sorts of institutions when I received a call on our AIDS hotline in the early 1990s. A woman from one of Santiago's poorest barrios phoned to ask what to do now that her daughter had died of AIDS and left behind an HIV-positive baby. "The nuns are saying I have to sign, but I want to take care of him myself," she told me in evident confusion. "They have a nice house, but I'm the grandmother."

Father Santi dedicated the early 1990s to financing a $2 million private AIDS hospice in the southern zone of Santiago named the Family Clinic, an ironic choice given the number of homosexual men who eventually dominated the patient roster. Well into the 2000s both Catholic entities continue to run their programs although Father Santi has had to reprogram the Family Clinic to accept both AIDS and cancer patients, given the drop in mortality now that HIV medication is widely available in Chile.

Real protagonism by people with HIV was not on the Catholic agenda; nor did doctors offer "their" HIV patients a role in treatment nor did government health authorities broaden planning of their AIDS prevention campaigns to include input from grassroots groups. The government expected activists to support its efforts; doctors expected their patients to obey instructions; Catholic clergy expected people with AIDS to die. All these expectations would be frustrated to a greater or lesser degree over the ensuing decade.

Although Caritas promoted "death with dignity" for people with HIV, it was less interested in keeping them alive: When the battles over treatment access erupted in the second half of the 1990s, Caritas remained on the sidelines. Its clinic has been an important resource for relatives overwhelmed by the dying process, but the place has a ghoulish air that the kindly staff and hygienic surroundings do not dispel. Mass-produced desktop altars are set in front of each bed so that the dying patients can spend their waning lucid moments staring into the face of Jesus. During a visit there to a colleague who died of AIDS in

2001, we encountered former Santiago Archbishop Juan Francisco Fresno making the rounds and commending the patients to the next life. He met us in the waiting area and inquired pacifically, "And you folks are also *enfermitos?*"— a patronizing term used with sick children.

Although Catholic institutions consistently infantilized people living with AIDS, Santi's highly public battles in the late 1980s to insist on humane treatment for HIV-positive people nevertheless were an important precedent for the Chilean populace, highly attuned to appeals to its feelings of Christian charity and compassion. But the good works also obscured what would soon become the next battlefield over HIV: sex. Santi had the church hierarchy's support, and public opinion was solidly behind him in promoting humane attitudes for those with AIDS whose plight echoed those of the lepers in the New Testament parables. But action to prevent people from acquiring the disease in the first place was another matter entirely, especially if it implied acceptance of dissident sexuality.

When Augusto Pinochet finally was forced out of office in 1990, the incoming government began to take more notice of the epidemic. A National AIDS Commission was formed headed by doctors from the opposition political parties, and its background documents contained excellent principles of nondiscrimination, popular participation and respect for individual decisions in the sexual realm.

Dr. Raquel Child is an immunologist who finished her studies in 1981, just when the first cases of AIDS were being reported in the United States and Europe. She ran Chile's government AIDS program throughout the 1990s and was a respected and controversial figure, sometimes liked, often criticized, but rarely dismissed. Child recalls that the excitement of the first years of restored democracy made innovation possible. It was a time of "effervescence and attention to people's rights," she says, as well as a time to take a critical look at Chile's deep-rooted inequalities. AIDS fit into this perspective. She explains:

> A good 60 percent of the country was ready for changes to make the country more just and democratic. I think there was clear agreement on the need for a comprehensive government response on [*AIDS*] prevention and support to infected people. Of course, there were difficulties, especially in the public debate, which are still with us right up to the present.

However, AIDS could not be left to the sphere of private behavior—hidden, unspoken and implicitly illicit—because campaigns to combat stigma and to offer clear guidance to sexually active adults were inevitably public matters. As the government's spokesperson for AIDS for many years, Child did not have an easy job. She had to defend the scientific basis for the official posture, which recognized homosexual and extra-marital relations and promoted condom use, without overreaching her bosses' very tepid willingness to displease the Catholic hierarchy. She often fought with NGOs and was a target of their barbs; she could be aggressive, even hostile, in argument, though she had a sense of humor as well. But her openness to issues of sexuality and the need to engage gay and bisexual men on their own terms provided an official backstop for many of the early efforts, including ours. Eventually the government supported gay prevention work directly; the conservatives generally kept silent about these activities as long as they were confined to gay circles and venues, entirely consistent with the tolerance for the rowdy sex that remained invisible and illicit but, in those terms, accepted.

After laborious studies and planning, the government launched an ambitious public information campaign starting in 1992. One set of TV spots featured a discreet series of illustrative tableaux with dancers in silhouette suggesting sexual relations—images that people still remembered a decade later. But the traditionalists were soon up in arms over the government's cautious ABC campaign in sync with international norms, offering "Abstinence, Be Faithful or Condom use" to prevent AIDS. The "C" of that equation was immediately placed under double-barreled attack.

Child agrees that she and her staff were given considerable leeway to develop "technically appropriate policies," but she could not count on strong support once the controversy erupted. She explains:

> For the government to survive, it has had to make important concessions to
> the right wing, including on the so-called social issues. I believe ideological
> differences within the government have played a role too.

Despite broad, popular acceptance of the tenor of the official AIDS information and Chileans' eagerness to learn about it, conservatives refused to countenance any mention of condom use on two of the three main television channels and turned the entire campaign into a condom-yes/condom-no polemic. To this day, the AIDS prevention debate remains largely stuck in this simplistic and sterile terrain; the condom is now subtly demonized even when put to use— somewhat like Chilean sexuality itself. The retrograde critics and clerics are often the butt of jokes and disdain, but despite their small numbers, they have succeeded in battling public discourse to a dead heat. Catholic traditionalists' resistance to AIDS prevention or any loosening of sexual mores took several other forms as well. They battled the government on every related issue from sterilization norms to emergency contraceptive to the legalization of divorce, finally achieved in 2004. Abortion remains illegal under all circumstances, and no politician will even discuss it publicly; in a recent case a woman was forced to carry an unviable pregnancy to term and watch the infant die while a priest stood by to bless the doomed fetus.

But aside from direct censorship of the public health campaigns and the subsequent well-oiled debates on the impropriety of "encouraging" sexual profligacy among the unravished, the conservative news media also created sex scandals where none existed to discredit sexual liberalization. Two famous incidents provided them with ammunition.

Bellas Artes

Patricia Rivadeneira is a well-known Chilean actress and local sex symbol. She moved in bohemian circles and in 1992 agreed to participate in an avant-garde fashion show to benefit our AIDS project during the slow summer month of February. The producers were a group of young designers and hip bohemians who had lived outside the country and realized that little was happening to stimulate AIDS awareness in Chile. They put together an uneven program with off-beat clothes and a series of tableaux vivants set to music, including one symbolic critique of Chilean prudishness featuring Miss Rivadeneira on a crude cross draped only with a Chilean flag. The right-wing press lost no time in crucifying her in a more substantial way. Not only did hard-line nationalists object to the flag symbolism, but the finale of the event was an even juicier target: a parade of adults and children carrying condoms blown up as balloons. In the headlines this harmless exercise became: "Children Used in Porn Show!"

Over the following ten days, coverage of this supposed "national outrage" was relentless and ruthless, aimed at destroying both the reputation and, if possible, mental health of those involved. Although many people found the reaction extreme, those encouraging AIDS prevention or sex education recognized that the price to be paid could be substantial.

JOCAS

Another episode had a chilling and intimidating effect on the Chilean government's painstakingly slow moves to introduce universal sex education into schools. After years of polite negotiations with Catholic bishops, an ingenious methodology was developed to generate conversations about sexuality within the school environment without, in theory, offending anyone. The one-day activity, called by the acronym JOCAS, meaning "All-Day Workshops on Sexuality and Intimacy," incorporated the entire school environment, with the key innovation of using students' own questions as the core material. Despite the lack of a curriculum, textbook or any sort of "party line" on what constituted legitimate sex education, all the controversial issues quickly emerged from the adolescents' avid curiosity.

The conservative media could not attack the JOCAS study materials because none existed. Instead, they focused on the final portion of the JOCAS methodology in which participating youth produced skits or drawings to illustrate their knowledge. As these ad hoc works of art were sometimes explicit, the JOCAS could be targeted for "promoting obscenity." The government backed down and agreed to eliminate the exercise while also explicitly allowing each school to censor the content of the replies provided to students' questions. Although the JOCAS continue, the government's latest sex education pilot program was renamed "Responsible Sexuality," more in line with traditional teachings. Despite its careful groundwork to bring everyone along, the government's approach proved no match against the tight boundaries established by militant Catholicism.

While the government attempted to loosen the tight laces of Chilean sexual culture with these very tepid results, AIDS was slowly expanding and settling into the population of men with homosexual practices. An AIDS epidemic among gay and bisexual men involves not only the particular risks of their sexual practices but an enormous set of sociocultural and psychological issues as well. Gays face stigma, secrecy and incomprehension and barriers to their sexual and emotional development related to all three. If men are stressed, hidden or ashamed, they are unlikely to find services or feel motivated to take care of themselves. A prevention campaign sensitive to these factors and employing a variety of creative strategies can play a crucial role for vulnerable gay men of all ages, although there is no guarantee that the strategies will work for everyone.

Many methods have been developed over the past two decades for involving vulnerable gay men, but at the time we began our efforts, we were laughably clueless. The evolution of a coherent prevention and support program from that early landscape reveals much about the state of affairs today, both the pioneers' legitimate grounds for satisfaction and their parochial resistance to innovation.

Gay-oriented organizing in Chile traces its origins to the creation of the AIDS Prevention Association sometime in 1987. Before then, nothing existed to deal with either AIDS or gay issues, and the Sunday-afternoon meetings in a downtown apartment were full of heated debates on whether the main focus of the group should be the epidemic or social equality. On one hand, the motive for attending these meetings and the excitement they generated had little to do with AIDS or any other disease—they were conclaves of gay men who wanted a better life and thought that forming an organization might help them to obtain it.

But others were concerned that the epidemic, which had appeared in Chile in 1984, would soon be an emergency affecting them and their friends. The latter group won out, in part because enthusiasm for creating a gay-rights movement quickly waned over the lack of a willing public spokesman. Organizing around AIDS in 1987 was virtually the same as declaring oneself homosexual, but in the context of Chilean cultural idiosyncrasy, ambiguity was more comfortable. At one of our first news conferences, a sympathetic reporter once pulled me aside and asked in a worried tone, "How do you want us to describe your organization?" meaning "Do you want us to call you gay?" We said it was not necessary.

Our ramshackle Santiago offices near Avenida Matta, a grimy commercial zone dotted with auto repair shops and furniture makers, opened in 1988. Volunteers were needed and welcomed, given responsibilities, listened to, "empowered." There was little alternative, given the complete lack of resources and the vague desire to respect internal democracy, to treat people equally and make them agents for change and to subvert the strict class lines that usually divided "professionals" from "beneficiaries" in social projects. The operation could function only after 6 P.M., when people arrived from work to receive visitors or answer the telephone. The Chile AIDS Prevention Association, to the extent that it existed at all, was mostly an idea in our minds; legal papers authorizing our operations took nearly four years to be finalized, what with waiting for our volunteer lawyer to take action and the slow wheels of the Justice Ministry bureaucracy.

There was no real plan, barely a structure and no budget; making the monthly rent by hustling donations, collecting dues from charter members and holding fundraising parties on the premises occupied at least half our attention. We knew something about HIV and that the use of condoms protected against it, but we had little or no idea of how to disseminate this information or promote these practices, aside from handing out pamphlets or distributing free condoms to people who asked for them. (Few did.) In fact, we had no idea that such a thing as "health education" even existed as a discipline. Although we eventually became "peer educators," we did not think of ourselves in that way at all; we were just a group of guys trying not to get sick and die.

Esteban was an amiable lad in his early twenties who began to show up regularly when we started to meet earlier in the afternoon. Like so many young guys in Santiago, he had time on his hands, no work prospects and a need for a regular social outlet that did not cost money. He would always grab a broom and try his best to make our frigid headquarters cozier or do minor errands. Old Chilean houses often are built around an inner courtyard, a nod to the Spanish and probably Moorish custom of protecting the family—that is, females—from the gaze of outsiders. The front door typically opens directly onto the street, with the household compound occupying the entire lot; no space is wasted on a decorative outer yard. We rented three small rooms on the first floor; for meetings with more than twelve people, we had to move to the open-air patio. We often held our training courses there in the middle of the Santiago winter, with temperatures in the forties and our trainees huddled in their coats. Upstairs lived a friendly, hip family that ignored our hilarious gatherings, which we appreciated and only understood much later when we realized that they were drug dealers with more important things on their minds.

Friday and Saturday nights were the main events at the association, in part due to the proximity of one of the city's three gay bars just a few blocks away. People would come early to see what was up, meet their friends and accidentally hear about HIV. Many critics dismissed the association as "not serious" because so many mildly curious or bored gay men used it as a waiting room until the club opened its doors at midnight, but we defended the modality, unaware that we had inadvertently created a "drop-in center." Our program consisted of discussions, sometimes presentations from doctor friends or psychologists, or reports from the latest pamphlets we had obtained from Spain or the United States.

At least once a month the activity was strictly social-commercial, a fundraising café-bar show, emceed by a drag queen introducing humorous skits and amateur lip-syncers, that generated about a third of the rent money for the following month. One night we set Esteban at the door to collect the donations. When the evening was over, the "stage" and dressing room cleaned up and the chairs put away, we looked for him to count the proceeds and could not find him anywhere. He had left with the kitty and never came back.

In retrospect, it is sad to realize how much valuable time was lost and how much skill and insight on AIDS prevention existed even then, had we known where to look. But those potentially useful contacts were consistently frustrated or sidetracked in a number of ways, aside from the challenges presented by volunteers like Esteban. Friendly gay doctors, including two from the Health Ministry itself, were resourceful allies, often on hand to provide educational lectures. After some months, one of them brought back a safe-sex workshop manual from a visit to the United States. Reading it provided an insight into why our previous didactic exercises were having no effect, and the workshop format, including participatory discussion and amusing exercises and games, revolutionized the association's strategy.

Soon afterward, the workshop manual was somehow filtered to a participant who took it to a friend at a teacher's union. Without telling us, the two of them applied for cash from the World Health Organization in our name and almost got it. When we wrote to Geneva to denounce the scam, I was called onto the carpet by a local NGO bigwig and told not to be a troublemaker.

In this and other incidents, Chilean class dynamics played an important role. These professionals, like others who came to observe or participate in our operation, had their own dubious notions of "empowerment." Many of those with academic backgrounds could hardly hide their disdain for the low-end social milieu from which our group had emerged. They tended to arrive on the scene ready to assume leadership; when it was not offered to them, or when they felt jealous hostility from the earlier arrivals, they did not stick around. A respected university professor took a shift on our hotline and once attempted to hold a workshop with the volunteers. But the group, bristling at his impenetrable, academic discourse, was suspicious and resentful. After a few months, he set up his own NGO in another part of the city.

Two doctors offered us their clinical services in those years. One was a sympathetic gay physician who convinced us to set up a makeshift clinic in our offices, buy some rudimentary equipment and print prescription pads for him with our scarce funds. In no time, we had a steady stream of patients taking advantage of this discreet, free service; the last appointment sometimes ended at 1 A.M., and we gladly waited for him week after week to finish his service and close the office. A few months into this arrangement, the doctor published a booklet about treating people with HIV (our organization was not mentioned) and began to appear on television as an "expert." As he was an amateur thespian as well, we agreed to organize a performance of a Molière play in which he played the leading role—anything seemed worth the trouble to be able to keep such a self-sacrificing individual and to sustain an alternative to the grim public hospitals. But one day the doctor stopped showing up, without a word to the patients left in the lurch; we never got an explanation or heard from him again.

But an even more common obstacle was the enormous difficulty in keeping our own people from interpreting "empowerment" to mean personal gain. As we functioned only at night, almost anyone might pick up the messages on the answering machine or open the mail that arrived during the day. One letter contained an invitation to the 1989 International AIDS Conference in Montreal. The person who read it promptly sent in his own name, received the invitation and went, despite not speaking a word of English or French. He was unable to bring back any useful information.

Another invitation came by telephone to attend a UN-sponsored meeting on AIDS to be held in the Santiago headquarters of the Economic Commission for Latin America and the Caribbean (ECLAC). One member of our temporary leadership committee, who arrived first each evening, took the message, phoned back in secret and later went to the international meeting as our representative, without a clue as to what to say. (In the late 1990s he resurfaced as a middleman in the local black market for AIDS drugs.) Our space heaters and answering machines also disappeared almost as soon as we could scrape together enough donations to buy them.

Some years later another young medical student offered to volunteer. He promptly began to handle and catalog the drug donations that sometimes reached us, "disposing" of any that had expired. He also disappeared without a trace, along with hundreds of dollars' worth of AIDS medicines. His name and telephone number turned out to be false, and no doubt his medical credentials were as well. So in spite of the urgent need to strengthen our work with intellectual skills, volunteer professionals just never seemed to work out.

Despite all these irritants, the association again and again produced programmatic innovations in those early years, often by accident and always based on its proximity to the people directly affected by HIV. One initiative involved preparing people for the HIV test, known in the jargon as VCT, "voluntary counseling and testing." As we had unconsciously created one of the first AIDS hotlines in Chile by opening our offices and installing a telephone—and by further accident finding it listed on page 2 of the telephone directory, along with the fire and police departments' emergency numbers—we received a deluge of calls, more and more often from anguished men recently diagnosed with HIV. It was immediately clear that the public services providing the blood test had no clue about how to handle either homosexuals or an HIV diagnosis.

Furthermore, given the disease-detection bias of the public health services, those receiving a negative test usually were dismissed and sent home, wasting an opportunity to delve into what lay behind their risky practices. Gay callers reminded us that they were uncomfortable discussing their sex lives with nurses or clinic staff who were either hostile or at best sympathetically mystified. We knew we could do better.

I had had an AIDS test at the Whitman-Walker Clinic in Washington, D.C., in the mid-1980s, surrounded by friendly gay fellows drawing blood and handing out the test results. Although the procedure could hardly be termed "counseling" as we understand it today, it was superior to anything existing in Chile. Whitman-Walker processed us fifty at a time with a short course on the meaning of test, then gave us our results a few days later one by one in a large meeting hall. A positive test result was not such a big deal at the time; people still thought that only a certain percentage of those with the virus would eventually develop AIDS.

In Santiago I had once used the public sexually transmitted disease clinic for a case of gonorrhea. The doctor in charge made no effort to hide his repugnance. The experience was laughably inhumane, and there was every reason to suppose that things had worsened with the advent of HIV. Through an employee of Planned Parenthood, I found a friendly psychologist at the Academy for Educational Development in Washington who handed me an enormous HIV test-counselor's training manual free of charge. (This client-centered model, later adapted by the Chilean government's AIDS program, remains the frame-work for HIV test counseling in the Chilean public health services today.)

With the help of a distinguished Chilean psychologist, we decided to train our own volunteers as HIV test counselors and turn HIV testing into an educational and care service. A public sexually transmitted disease clinic cooperated by allowing us to send our blood samples to their lab. Because we consistently had HIV-positive rates of around 10 percent among our clients, it made the clinic look as if it were concentrating its resources at the epicenter of the epidemic. Hundreds of straight couples and individuals eventually came for the service as well, a curious reversal of the old stigma: they said it made sense that homosexuals should know what to do about AIDS. By the mid-1990s we were counseling and testing 1,000 people a year. Eventually the national AIDS program set up courses throughout the country on HIV test counseling, even using one of our peer educators as a trainer.

Our volunteers consistently detected new problems and suggested program-matic innovations. We inaugurated bar and sauna interventions, took condoms and counselors to cruising parks and brought the first discussions about anti-retroviral drugs to public attention after the landmark Vancouver International AIDS Conference in 1996. Our volunteers and student interns fanned out into other organizations, academia and government consultancies, taking over the contract for the AIDS hotline and joining research projects. For all its miscues, bungling and inexperience, the association started from nothing and made an important mark.

In the early years the Chilean news media committed all the crimes and misdemeanors familiar worldwide in sensationalizing and misrepresenting the realities of AIDS. They focused on the drama of HIV cases appearing in different parts of the country, were careless about privacy issues and accepted uncritically the early use of raids on gay bars and topless clubs as AIDS prevention strategies.

But the newspapers also forced sensitive issues into the public debate. Once a gay-rights organization decided to go public, the very stigma of homosexuality made it a journalist's dream, and the news was guaranteed automatic coverage. In addition, many journalists were concerned and sympathetic to the AIDS problem and did their best to be even-handed, despite headline writers who often sabotaged their efforts. But the industry wanted, above all, faces, people with HIV. Eventually it got them.

One of the first programs on Chilean television about AIDS was an hour-long special in 1989 aired on the Catholic University channel. It was comprised of packaged interviews and short bits to be followed by a live panel discussion. Father Santi was one guest; I was another. Although I had resisted taking a formal role in the new AIDS association, no one else wanted to go on TV to discuss the subject; doing so was virtually equivalent to declaring oneself homosexual in front of 14 million compatriots. Caritas already had an infrastructure and needy beneficiaries; Father Santi's lead-in featured footage from his work with AIDS-affected toddlers, and his comments were in fact measured and nonjudgmental.

Although our group's president had refused to appear on the program, he did introduce me to a man who might be willing to talk about his HIV diagnosis anonymously and in silhouette. César was inclined to cooperate, but his new boyfriend was nervous about anonymity. I went to the liquor store where César worked to accompany him to the studio and found him reluctant to go, afraid of losing his new job. I suggested that we go to the studio and discuss it with the producer to see if we could find a way of keeping his identity secret. Eventually he agreed to the interview and went ahead with the program.

Journalists then and now were eager to beef up their stories with what they called "impact"—a news item or a documentary did not have the same "impact," they would always tell us, if no one with HIV or AIDS appeared in it. They rarely thought to ask whether "impact" was useful for AIDS prevention or care or whether the person with HIV could handle yet more "impact" in his own life. For years we got calls asking for interviews about AIDS but always with the condition that the speaker be HIV-positive. Later this elementary fact of journalism indeed provided a potent tool for people living with HIV to push their public leadership to center stage. But in 1989 the risks were still enormous.

César's appearance was my first experience in facilitating this ambiguous relationship between HIV-positive people and the news media. We clearly wanted and needed to get our message out, but the single-minded focus on people directly living the experience felt all too much like soap opera. As part of an organization that would support and even protect him, I had some credibility and could try to bring the two sides together even when skepticism about the news media remained high. Without me, Channel 13 probably would not have had a person with HIV on their program that night.

César's testimony was admirable: entirely free of self-pity, determined to move forward in his life, valiant. His appearance provided material for debate for those of us on-camera, the priest smiling kindly and the reporters raising the inevitable issue of "innocent" children, providing me a chance to ask if adults like César were then guilty for getting HIV. In the midst of our contradictory positions, we collectively showed a calm, supportive face and repeated that there was no reason to fear or shun people with HIV infection.

At worst, I had to face sidelong glances and wisecracks at my apartment building later, and no doubt the other panelists went on with their lives as well. César, however, was not quite so lucky. Someone from his hometown in northern Chile recognized him despite the scrim, and his HIV anonymity was over. After that episode, we lost track of him entirely and never knew if his cooperation with my pressure to appear publicly, to testify and show "the human face of AIDS," had wrecked his life.

Ten years later, when the fight over access to HIV treatments took off in Chile and the HIV-positive community—by then much larger—came together to lobby for it, the new leadership pushed each other to go public, to "come out" as HIV-positives and make their case. They saw themselves as trailblazers, the first people to do what really had to be done. In the first months they would march through downtown Santiago, sometimes blocking traffic and guaranteeing coverage in the evening news.

Luis was a fifty-ish employee at a finance company who took our volunteer training course and later got involved at the HIV self-help group at the hospital where he was treated. Then he became an officer of the newly formed coalition of HIV-positive groups, later to call itself Vivo Positivo (Positive Living). He was courageous as well, chaining himself to the Health Ministry and eventually going on television to talk about his diagnosis. No one stopped to ask whether Luis should prepare the groundwork with his adult children before he was turned into a true-story drama on evening TV.

Luis was also involved in a personal development movement. It offered free courses for HIV-positive people and had an enormous impact on the early organizers with weekend seminars for sharing deep emotions and building what seemed to be a powerful and close-knit community among those coming to grips with their diagnosis. When invited to seminars to discuss HIV policy, Luis and other newly involved people with an HIV diagnosis sometimes turned their presentations into a curious mix of argument, anecdote and group-therapy exercise. This was a stylistic mélange I recognized from our own early attempts to produce effective HIV education that went beyond handing out pamphlets and dictating classes on the immune system. It was understandable but also a pity to see people reinventing the wheel; nevertheless, all the hugging and testimonials seemed quite harmless, part of a process of turning personal crises into a political movement.

Still, I was dubious about the rush to go public by people who had little organizational experience or previous exposure. Popularized and often for-profit therapeutic movements impress people by dredging up deeply held feelings, and when done in groups the experience can be thrilling and cathartic.

But unleashing such powerful emotions is fairly easy compared to the job of managing them afterward. Mixing the therapeutic techniques with the complex and conflictive process of organization-building struck me as unwise, especially as Vivo Positivo would soon experience a messy crisis of leadership, resulting in the overthrow and replacement of the first president, a process in which Luis played a key part.

But HIV-negative people were not very welcome in those second-generation efforts of the late 1990s: The first NGOs had been surpassed by the dynamic new movement whose participants sensed an end to their despair and isolation. We were considered vaguely suspect for "not doing enough," and any hanging back at protests or other tactics was considered just the timidity of people who did not understand what living with HIV infection really meant.

Luis disappeared for a couple weeks in 1999 after the leadership shake-up and failed to appear at Vivo Positivo planning meetings. When friends went to his apartment to inquire, they found that he had hanged himself several days before.

As the government AIDS program finally cranked into gear and prepared to launch its mass media campaigns, it contracted experts in social communication to map attitudes about AIDS in Chilean society and especially among the key target groups. These included homosexual men, but the uptown consultants had little idea about who belonged to this mysterious group or where they might find its members. Naturally, they turned to our association. In the early 1990s we had little notion of social research and had never heard of focus groups or other qualitative techniques to study attitudes and opinions. When the market study consultants called us to ask for help, we thought it was an opportunity to influence the government's messages on AIDS and agreed immediately.

Our job was to assemble two groups of gay or homosexually active men from different socioeconomic strata. We arranged one evening meeting in a gay bar that attracted the middle class and another with street hustlers in our own office. The latter was pulled together virtually single-handedly by Víctor, a now-deceased Peruvian drug dealer whom we had met through our program of jail visits to HIV-positive inmates. He was grateful for the help we had provided him during his prison term and was always ready to lend a hand. These contacts were not ones that uptown sociologists were likely to have in their research arsenal.

The experts came to the meetings, served sandwiches and asked their questions, took copious notes and taped everything. They did not explain to us the logic of their techniques or discuss their impressions of the conversations. Later we realized that the going rate to produce one of these groups was in the range of $500, but the agency did not offer us a peso for our collaboration, despite our desperate financial straits. Nor did it occur to us to charge the experts for our work.

However, when they phoned back a few weeks later to urge us to assemble another group for them in twenty-four hours, the relationship began to feel unbalanced. The woman in charge was even bold enough to ask our part-time secretary, "Are all the guys at that organization homosexuals? Is the director a homosexual?" We refused.

We never knew what the conclusions of their opinion research were, nor did the government AIDS program share their findings. When the next round of AIDS educational messages finally appeared on television, one of the HIV risk behaviors highlighted was phrased as "sexual relations between men," rather than "unprotected sexual relations" or "unprotected anal sex." Even the gay doctors inside the ministry had not noticed the gaffe until all the posters and other literature had been printed. The phrase—which could have been caught in an hour review session with a half-dozen gay disco patrons—had to be blacked out of thousands of official materials with Magic Marker.

I often recalled the incident years later when we faced questions about our study of men having sex in parks, saunas and gay cinemas—the heated controversies among ethicists about how far you can go in observing the intimate behavior of people who do not know they are being studied. In our introduction to social science, entrepreneur consultants had casually exploited the only gay-oriented prevention project in the country to produce half-baked conclusions, which then were used to further complicate the prevention work itself. But this ruthless, for-profit behavior was never questioned in ethical terms.

More important, because the academic disciplines seemed to offer only ambition and mediocrity, we failed to see that they also possessed useful research tools. Nevertheless, the experience introduced us to social science procedures and made us realize that we had valuable resources at our fingertips. Years later the Ford Foundation would support our efforts to conduct this research directly through our nonprofessional health promoters, the results of which were published in 1997 as *Loves and Shadows*. In it, 75 percent of the men surveyed said they had used condoms at least once, light-years ahead of the similar population group of heterosexual men. Despite the years of frustrations, we could chalk up a major achievement.

Other approaches to political influence sprang from more strategic differences. Those more interested in gay emancipation created a sexual rights workshop and eventually formed their own organization, known as MOVILH, the Homosexual Liberation Movement, in 1991. After a period of consolidation, it went public and caused a sensation, both in public opinion and among gay-identified Chileans themselves. Interested gays and lesbians flocked to their new offices a few blocks from ours; fifty people sometimes attended their planning meetings, and several times that number went to their parties. Despite its decision to shun the AIDS issue in favor of overtly gay politics, MOVILH promptly inaugurated an AIDS program of its own, and the conflict over mission that had marked the association's early years shifted over to MOVILH's. One public spokesman was particularly adamant about eliminating AIDS as an issue for gay politics and campaigned relentlessly to suppress the group's AIDS activities, finally forcing yet another split.

Chilean author Juan Pablo Sutherland was among MOVILH's founders and supported its decision to distance itself from the AIDS issue, a position he criticizes today. A lanky and kindly man who was pilloried by the right-wing press when the government gave him an arts grant for one of his gay-themed books, Sutherland tries to promote cultural activities around sexuality and eroticism. He keeps a hand in gay politics but considers it too influenced by the left-wing habits of the 1980s. Sutherland says MOVILH quickly decided to move beyond AIDS and tolerated little internal dissent:

> Eventually we realized the impact of the epidemic among our own people, but even then there wasn't really much reflection, just Hey, this is affecting us, and then that one, and that one, and that one. We came from a fairly uniform political style, and that led to big mistakes, which we realized later because our people were getting hit by what was happening.

In parallel and despite their conflicts, all the associations and splinter groups constructed symbiotic prevention strategies directed at gay men; these eventually included magazines, a permanent presence in nightclubs and cruising areas, HIV testing, workshops of all sorts, alliance-building, lobbying and participation in public debates. Thousands of men received basic information about AIDS, and condoms gradually began to be part of Chilean gay sexuality. At the same time, AIDS forced a public debate on homosexuality, and MOVILH took advantage of the opening. Opinion surveys confirm that social attitudes have shifted markedly in Chile during the last decade, and in 1999 a nineteenth century antisodomy law finally was eliminated from criminal statutes.

But participants on both sides of the issue today wonder why the two currents, gay politics and AIDS prevention, could not have evolved in a more cooperative spirit. Alejandro Guajardo was a teenager when he first participated in both organizations and, much later, joined Vivo Positivo where he ran a drug-adherence program until 2003. He recalls trying to convince his colleagues at MOVILH not to dismiss AIDS:

> The gay movement pushed aside the people with HIV because supposedly that wasn't part of the political fight. So today you have a gay movement working on AIDS and living off it, applying every month for survival through AIDS work. The gay radio program wouldn't have any funds without the AIDS subsidy.... [*The two issues*] should never have been separated. Had there been [*unity*] from the beginning, I think the homo-bisexual population would have lowered the HIV curve a lot more because the intervention strategies would have been more similar rather than two different things.

By the late 1990s, as the numbers of people living with HIV continued to grow, the centrifugal forces became even greater. Having been in all three camps—gay rights, AIDS prevention and HIV-positive groups—Guajardo sees little collaboration and synergy among the different activist currents:

> Next we're going to have the homosexuals of the La Pintana district, the people with AIDS of La Pintana, then the women of La Pintana, the nonhomosexuals of La Pintana. Identity is essential, but it's clearly the collaborative, collective fight that can bring about positive changes.

It would be easy to pin the blame for this fragmentation, the splits and the subsplits, the carving out of political territory, on the oversized egos or misplaced desires for the spotlight of a few individuals. But any attempt to keep issues like homosexuality, AIDS and HIV seropositivity together as a set of integrated phenomena probably was doomed from the beginning. The appeal of identity brought people together and in fact forms the basis of much HIV prevention and solidarity work relying on peer educators, on people who can bring the message to others defined as somehow "like themselves."

These initiatives make no sense detached from a focused, slightly selfish perspective. Gay men woke up to AIDS and gathered to take action not as public health educators but as gays. Once people with HIV found their voice, they would do the same thing: they were not stirred to action by abstractions but by their own needs and crises, which gave their demands real force and persuasive appeal. More altruistic postures to promote public well-being might make good copy but lousy institutional glue. Any nuanced, integrated approach is destined to be overshadowed by an unapologetic pursuit of clearly defined group interests that interprets the fight for "empowerment" in narrower but more attractive ways. Articulating this essentially self-interested approach in the most seductive and emphatic fashion may not be particularly generous or statesmanlike, but as politicians know, it works.

Although the frequent disappointments with academics and professionals were exasperating and did not endear our hardworking volunteers to potential newcomers, the cost incurred to the work itself was even more considerable. In those crucial early years our ad hoc programs were rarely guided by examples of successful AIDS prevention work, nor were experienced sociologists or anthropologists on hand to add their contributions.

From her job as head of the government AIDS program, Dr. Child also noticed that skilled gay professionals tended to shy away from participation. She says:

> I think they are still afraid of discrimination and stigma, and this is one of the reasons why the organizations don't grow. This fear is more relevant in upper-income social groups where people have intellectual training, and I think that is a significant loss. You see very few people participating in the organizations, which generally have well-meaning people with little

training. This makes their work harder and also keeps the issue marginalized from the rest of society because people say, I don't feel represented by these groups.

Class in Chile is not as sharply defined as in Peru or Guatemala, but it was strong enough to keep many potential allies in separate camps. The earliest toilers in the AIDS fields learned to be jealous and protective of their modest but sustained labors; the lettered classes tended to keep their distance or form their own groups. Both prevention and care services suffered as a result.

In addition, class society has its own set of unspoken rules, which are sometimes hard for naively Jeffersonian outsiders to grasp. When options for work and advancement are few, a clan mentality takes over: one either has the good luck to be born into a well-connected social group or one spends one's youth and early adulthood constructing an alternative. One consequence is the proliferation of an entire subset of mini-brotherhoods whose members rely on and support each other as if their lives depended on it—which they often do.

On one occasion the government AIDS program decided to produce a video on HIV for a gay audience. But when officials could not produce an appropriate script, officials turned to the organizations for assistance. I contacted a video producer friend who wrote up a story line that I then shared with our regular volunteers. Despite my best efforts to convince them, they hated it, and we had to inform the ministry that the idea would not float. When the producer got wind of our negative review, he phoned me in a fit, incredulous that a "friend" could have blocked him from getting the contract. We never spoke again after that.

Another incident occurred years later when the hospital-based mutual support groups for people with HIV were coalescing into a citywide coalition to fight for the new AIDS drugs. One leader who would later achieve worldwide fame in the AIDS field asked me to lunch one day. I assumed it was to discuss work plans, but instead he sounded me out about forming a strategic coalition between his fledgling group and our NGO, to be based on a personal understanding between the two of us. He pointed out the cultural weight of his two surnames, which showed that he came from prominent families on both sides. "It makes a difference when *I* call someone in the government," he said. Boosting participation was all very well, he seemed to be suggesting, but the untrained, impoverished people living with HIV in Chile needed a more traditional power broker, and he knew just the person to fill that role.

At the 1989 Montreal AIDS Conference, NGOs from around the world were coalescing into international and regional alliances, something that the Brazilians and others thought should be replicated within each country. In Chile, after four years of scratching the sand and considering the option of closing our association's doors for lack of funds, the Panos Institute in London invited us in 1991 to organize a seminar on AIDS to encourage joint action among a range of potential allies. The idea of building a coalition or network around HIV/AIDS eventually became standard practice worldwide: experts believe that the complex nature of the AIDS epidemic requires a multipronged approach and broad, horizontal cooperation among defenders of human rights, women's and youth groups, religious entities, medical professionals, gays and grassroots groups of all kinds including, where possible, sex workers and drug users.

The 1991 seminar was not the first attempt to pull together a civil movement around the issue: a Chilean exile in Norway came to Santiago in 1989 and advertised in the newspaper for a meeting of interested parties, which took place in a downtown hotel. He assured the participants that a Norwegian agency was willing to put $75,000 toward the establishment of an AIDS coalition in Chile, a remarkable sum at the time. But once again ambition sidetracked the effort at the starting gate. A local doctor who had created an AIDS foundation lobbied hard to get himself elected president of the barely existing entity and promptly went public with a front-page criticism of the Chilean government in the name of all its members. The coalition was mortally wounded and ended up as one more NGO, retaining only the word "front" in its title as a reminder of the abandoned collective dream.

This was our first hint that a cooperative attempt to create urgently needed mutual support could be a site of conflict and even usurpation. Networks are not simply combinations of groups; as time and energy are spent in building up these coalitions, they quickly become valuable entities in and of themselves, extremely useful and even lucrative to their "owners." Despite the obvious imprudence of snatching at power and headlines, veterans of other social movements nodded their heads knowingly: coalitions create intangible products, which are very difficult to defend. Nonetheless, it made no sense to address AIDS in isolation, given the difficult range of issues involved.

Unlike the ill-fated Norwegian visitor's experience, Panos had a more methodical and eventually successful approach. A coordinating committee emerged, and more than two hundred people attended a follow-up conference two years later in 1993, including city government officials, police, teachers, health professionals and a key senator. The featured speakers covered the major bases—sexuality, gender, discrimination—and even included a woman sex worker from Uruguay who left the audience speechless. Despite a brief scandal over homoerotic art in the hallway, the event marked another high point of cooperation and mobilization. Even the government was impressed.

Sonia Covarrubias is a social worker with Popular Education for Health (EPES), a twenty-year-old health promotion project that concentrates its efforts in the poor neighborhoods of Santiago and Concepción. She eventually became a co-coordinator of the AIDS network, at a time of "few resources and high motivation." The experiment was wildly successful at first, praised for openness and consistently provocative debates. The May Candlelight Memorial march attracted five hundred people at its peak in 1993, including important figures from the human rights movement. But informality was the Achilles' heel: Covarrubias explains:

> In all the networks in which we participate, historically people don't want rules or formalities, not even minutes with the agreements. They just operate on the basis of goodwill. But when conflicts arise, you need structure.

Formal agreements are harder to ignore than verbal ones, and the AIDS network's vagueness about rules and commitments left more room for participants to exploit the coalition for personal or institutional gain rather than share their successes with the entire group. But in the midst of the heady early achievements, it was easy to ignore this potential for conflict. Juan Pablo Sutherland recalls the early 1990s as inspired by common visions of an unusual need:

> [*The network*] brought together all these organizations around the idea of an epidemic that carries such a stigma, an absolutely social aspect that other

diseases didn't have. That forced us finally to join forces to pressure the state to do something.

The vigorous AIDS Network became a trademark, and Chile's record in bringing disparate groups together was noticed internationally: one of its co-coordinators later was recruited to represent all Latin American NGOs on the newly formed UNAIDS advisory board in Geneva. Despite considerable grumbling, the coalition held together for the next couple of years. Its eventual breakdown came, however, from none other than people with AIDS themselves.

The first regular public face of AIDS in Chile was a sharp-spoken individual who liked to say he did not pass out "hypocritical smiles" just to get along. Through his take-no-prisoners approach, he pressured medical staff to consider their behavior and reform their practices. His group of people with HIV struggled to establish itself as a coherent voice for those affected, but they were relatively few. Even fewer were willing to go public in the early 1990s.

At that time not many of us could imagine the everyday obstacles and abuses that people with HIV faced in Santiago, and the presence of someone willing to describe and denounce these barriers was illuminating. However, we often found ourselves lumped into the same category as hospital staff or government officials if we did not agree to their demands, including those related to our joint efforts. This situation would prove enormously debilitating to efforts to build a coalition.

The AIDS Network decided to organize the first national meeting of people living with HIV, pooled resources and pulled together people from both Santiago and Concepción to an assembly in a borrowed schoolyard in 1994. The HIV-positives' group chaired, and a follow-up event was scheduled for the next year. But a year later the group organized its second assembly in secret with selected allies, hand-picked the participants and left out people they did not like—even if they were HIV-positive as well. Their explanation was that people living with HIV had the right to do things however they liked. At the time meetings restricted to people with HIV were common enough and understandable on some level; discrimination, however, was not.

This apparently minor incident went to the heart of what "empowerment" for stigmatized minorities was to mean: either a change in their status and their capacities or permission for their leadership to dictate terms to everyone else. Human beings, when oppressed, abused or discriminated against, obviously must accumulate the power they need to realize what is happening to them and fight back. But when individuals act in concert and generate leaders to represent their demands, the phenomenon is no longer a personal drama. When individuals awaken to their situation, they do what they decide is best for themselves; when an organization seeks to empower itself in the same way, the logical outcome is dictatorship. Furthermore, representatives of these movements inevitably face difficult situations in which the line between their constituents' interests and their own becomes extremely murky. A particularly stark example occurred in subsequent years when leaders of the HIV-positive groups had to decide whether, as leaders of their hospital associations, they would accept offers of drug therapies that their fellow patients could not obtain. If they were sick, doctors sometimes said, they could not work to defend the rest; on the other hand, if they took advantage of the offer, someone else in their group would be deprived. There was no easy answer.

A pithy definition of empowerment was circulated years ago by an HIV-positive AIDS leader from the United States who described it as "the realization that you can do something; then you do it." I often celebrated this phrase until I witnessed this same leader launch a stinging, racially-tinged attack at the Durban International AIDS Conference in 2000. "My daddy always told me that the pig who squeals the loudest is the one that got stuck," he answered belligerently when asked to consider the tone of his remarks. This was empowerment not as personal development but as slash-and-burn identity politics at its worst. As Mao Zedong might have phrased it, "Empowerment is not a dinner party."

In the inevitable battles over resources and influence in a complex arena such as that presented by the AIDS epidemic, it was hardly surprising that people living with HIV would resent the first groups that focused on education and prevention rather than services to people like themselves. They sometimes saw the prevention groups that gained influence or attracted funding as "living off AIDS" while those with the virus suffered the consequences.

Reading and listening to the Brazilians' accounts of the pulling and tugging that occurred when they tried to form an AIDS NGO network, it is apparent that a common AIDS fault line ran between the older, more established groups with a few resources or paid staff and the less fortunate newcomers, who saw themselves as more grassroots or closer to the grit and struggle of the daily dramas of HIV/AIDS. Heated conflicts erupted.

However, an important difference in the Chilean case was that the underlying conflict was control over the HIV-positive "franchise." Unlike the politicized HIV-positive organizations that sprang up in Brazil, the Chilean version was conceived and operated in the earliest years as an interest group concerned exclusively with protecting and improving conditions for its members, not even "persons living with HIV/AIDS" as a class but those persons with HIV/AIDS sitting in the next room. After the incident over the Network-sponsored gathering, many hours were spent attempting to iron out differences, but in the many meetings and discussions, all that was clarified was the determination of the HIV-positive groups and their backers not to budge an inch. For them, the AIDS Network was to be utilized when convenient and ignored at will. With this level of institutional loyalty, the ideal of a common front collapsed. It would take the advent of the AIDS miracle drugs to rejuvenate the HIV-positive movement several years later, albeit with its original outlook intact.

In retrospect, it would have been prudent to rethink and restructure the AIDS Network as a loose informative body with a much more limited mandate. Just as the Brazilians discovered, the idea of a diverse social movement around AIDS that could act in concert was largely utopian given the far more categorical impulse for institutional and personal survival. Like associations of shoe manufacturers, AIDS NGO networks have common interests and can lobby to defend them; they are also fierce competitors. By acknowledging this dual reality, the relevant actors in a given country can hang together. In the Chilean case, eventually the rewards would prove enormous.

As occurred throughout Latin America, the 1996 Vancouver International AIDS Conference sparked interest among people living with HIV in Chile to obtain the new miracle drug therapies and eventually set off a movement in favor of obtaining them for everyone. Suddenly the same elements that had made AIDS a nightmare for those affected—the stigma, the hopelessness, the scorn and rejection—could be turned on their heads. The clinical options meant that people with HIV could no longer be painted as living on borrowed time, but rather as people fighting for their lives. Going public would be their most potent weapon.

One day shortly after the Vancouver meeting a doctor visiting from Miami phoned our organization to see about an HIV test for his Chilean boyfriend. Although we had heard vaguely about the new combination drug treatments, he was the first expert to tell us that the products were within reach and that we could hector the government into providing them. He agreed to address a public meeting organized for the purpose.

Over a hundred people turned out to learn about the viral load test and the efficacy of triple combination therapy to drive the virus into a state of latency. (However, HIV does not disappear from the system and is known to lodge in the lymph nodes and elsewhere, even when it is undetectable in the bloodstream.) Although it was not realistic to expect the Chilean government suddenly to fund these costly therapies, hope was on the horizon. Then the race against time began for people with HIV, as they sought somehow to get hold of the drugs before it was too late through contacts, donations, friends overseas, the black market or emigration.

Without expecting immediate solutions, we invited people with HIV to meet weekly to formulate a strategy on treatment access and to share the past week's events. The meetings gradually grew and sometimes reached forty participants. Enrique Vargas, a rotund, bespectacled businessman, attended on occasion. He enjoyed the comradeship of the weekly meetings despite the unfamiliar social environment. Vargas, who came from the growing group of upper-middle-class professionals ruined economically by the need to finance their disease, explains:

> My real estate business was deteriorating because of the country's economic situation, and I realized that I couldn't keep buying my medicines, the money was running out. We had sold apartments and properties to sustain the monthly cost. And when I saw that it was getting more and more difficult, I found out about the public health program that we saw as so remote from the our way of life.

Vargas entered the Arriarán Foundation that runs the AIDS program at one of Santiago's public hospitals and obtained AZT while continuing to pay for his other medicines himself. He also joined the foundation's AIDS support group. All the hospitals had these loose associations, which soon would reach critical mass and spawn the potent movement for access to medicines. At the Arriarán Foundation and elsewhere, a few lucky patients were receiving some medicines based on a macabre lottery system. Vargas recalls how it worked:

> Everyone who had fewer than three hundred CD4 cells, they would put our charts in a basket, and whoever was picked, got their meds. I didn't win.

But one day even that system broke down. Vargas says:

> In April of 1997 Dr. Wolff called together the few people who received drugs to tell us that donations of even those few medicines were discontinued. They were out of stock, and there just weren't any more. One woman cried because she asked if the medicine for her one-year-old daughter with HIV would be cut off too, and they said yes, there isn't any, there isn't any. It was the same problem at Salvador, at Sótero del Río, at San Juan de Dios, in all the hospitals with an AIDS program. I couldn't sleep that night thinking about the reaction, the crying, it all kept resonating in my head.

At that critical moment the hospital-based groups of people with HIV pulled together as an openly political coalition to insist on a more coherent government policy on HIV treatments. Vargas generated confidence and became the coalition's leader and first elected president. As the coalition had no resources or physical space, his business provided the infrastructure. He says:

> It was a period of horrendous economic deterioration. First of all because my face was recognized, I was on television, in the newspapers, as the official spokesman of this movement, and that cost me a lot. I lost clients, my business sank further, plus [the cost of] my medicines. Plus for almost two years I maintained the organization with my secretary, fax, telephone, meetings in my home. There was no other way.

Despite the enormous obstacles, people living with HIV became a political force in Chile, at first shyly, using masks and disguises, and later more boldly. But despite the hardships and the continued pressure of the disease itself, Chileans with HIV had turned weakness into power. They gave interviews, held news conferences, blocked traffic and dogged top health officials to deal with their plight. From defenseless figures forced into hiding their diagnosis, the leaders of people living with HIV and AIDS overwhelmed and dominated the public discourse; today they overshadow the official government spokeswoman herself. Despite delays and administrative problems, by 2003 coverage for the AIDS combination therapy in Chile's public health system was approaching 100 percent.

Just like the gay-emancipationists five years before, people with HIV felt more comfortable operating as an identity-based movement and addressing public opinion from that standpoint—certainly a legitimate choice in both cases and a brilliant public relations strategy. Like the early organizers of MOVILH who saw other gay groups as a bit lily-livered for not "coming out," people with HIV could not understand why AIDS-related organizations had not dedicated more of their institutional energies and resources to meeting the needs of those affected—that is, to them. Both of these criticisms had merit; both were also slightly demagogic. Neither offered any guarantee that *their* representation of the groups mentioned in their titles would be more consistent, democratic or altruistic than that which had gone before.

César Herrera owns a corner store in the northern zone of Santiago served by the San José Hospital. When Roberto, his longtime partner, fell ill and was hospitalized for HIV-related causes, César witnessed discrimination firsthand. He recalls:

People were left to themselves, the doctor rarely came around. Roberto ended up weighing twenty-eight kilos [*sixty-two lbs*]. Behind my back, his family came and took him to Loncoche in the south, but he got worse. I went right away, and in the hospital I had to insist that they operate on him even though they didn't want to.

Then a weird thing happened. His sister and I went to a church nearby although I'm not religious, and suddenly I felt that Christ came down from the crucifix and touched me. I don't know if it was the madness of my desperation, but I asked Christ that if the situation didn't improve, that I be the one to die instead of Roberto. And that if he did get better, I promised I would go to work for others.

When we got back to the hospital, he wasn't there. We assumed he had died. But no, he was in the operating room. It lasted eight hours, but he recovered. He's still okay—you can see him around here, plump as ever.

Herrera, who soon received his own HIV diagnosis, later became the president of Vida Optima representing the eight hundred registered HIV patients at San José Hospital. It concentrates on direct aid and provides lunch for forty people daily, home visits and other types of assistance. Herrera was a founder of the Vivo Positivo coalition that led the drug-access fight and applauds its handling of that lengthy struggle, which meant the difference between life and death for many.

At the same time, Herrera laments the transformation of the coalition into a super-NGO that concentrates power in its own hands. His criticism echoes the same resentment that the nascent HIV-positive groups felt towards the first-generation AIDS organizations. Herrera explains:

We formed [*the coalition*] to provide help to people, but we never received even a sheet of paper from it. To feed forty people every day, I go to the produce market to beg. We live off charity, week after week. It's tiring.

Of course, Vivo legitimately identified its priority as providing drug access to its beneficiaries, and in that it was wildly successful. Writer Juan Pablo Sutherland has worked with hospital-based HIV-positive groups and describes the single-minded focus on drug access.

I did a writing workshop in six hospitals with people from the organizations, and I was struck by how instrumental the whole relationship was, how focused it was on direct aid. People came to see what help they could get, and of course they had a lot of needs.

Ironically, Herrera's criticism of his own movement is precisely that the focus of HIV-positive organizing was too narrowly concerned with their immediate needs:

> Now that the antiretroviral drugs are available, the [*hospital-based*] groups are dying, they're disintegrating. Most people, what were they looking for in an organization? Access to the drugs. Once they get it, they go back to their lives or back to work and leave the organizations.

Herrera's group is only one out of dozens around the country, and his experience may not be mirrored by others. Still, the San José Hospital where Vida Optima operates is one of the largest, and its HIV program is one of the best. If Vida Optima cannot pull more regular resources toward its admirable direct-aid programs, groups of people living with AIDS in the remote provincial cities are unlikely to fare better.

If the hospital-based HIV-positive groups find themselves unable to develop the long-term services that their beneficiaries need, they may be reaping the success of their own strategy. Those living with HIV/AIDS were the only individuals who could turn stigma and discrimination on its head and express their demand to live and receive treatment. They had a unique voice that echoed with concrete experience and direct, personal interest, and they used it with enormous skill to obtain their demands. At the same time, the leadership's domination of the scenario encouraged members—including their own people—to redefine AIDS in terms of clinical care and, implicitly, their own immediate needs.

The original social movement around AIDS responded to other concerns; it had arisen from people *not* directly affected, who had joined in *without* receiving a diagnosis, out of concerns over people's rights to be informed, to live their sexual and intimate lives as they chose, to receive services *and* to be treated humanely and properly when sick. These sidelined actors are now expected to fulfill a supporting, backup role to demands from those with HIV, and in large measure they do. But the work emerging from the AIDS epidemic is inevitably poorer as a result.

Enrique Vargas did not remain in Chile to witness the triumph of the movement he had helped to generate. After an internal power struggle in 1998, he lost the presidency of the nascent group by one vote and soon after fell seriously ill. (He had refused offers of antiretroviral therapy while heading the group, offers that dried up once he became just another patient.) Eventually Vargas abandoned his home and sought help in Miami. He lived in a homeless shelter there and nearly died from HIV-related illnesses while trying to obtain his immigrant papers. Upon recovery, he worked as a volunteer at the public hospital, leading workshops for Latino and Haitian residents with HIV in Spanish and French. Vargas was employed as a case worker for a Miami AIDS service organization and is in the process of obtaining U.S. citizenship. He has never returned to Chile.

Raquel Child, who left the national AIDS program in 2003, says the Chilean state assumed responsibility for AIDS as a public health issue, eventually committed itself to providing modern treatments and opened up a needed debate. She also welcomes the new actors who arose to grapple with health issue. But she sees stagnation setting in as well:

> The response in Chile has fallen off; the initiatives and creativity have declined. I would have expected a stronger public presence, more development, more growth, more capacity to mobilize people, and this hasn't happened. I think that the organizations have become entropic entities that aren't visible. I suppose they are doing things, but you don't see what we had at the beginning of the 1990s. I won't say it doesn't exist, but I don't see it.

One area where initiatives are sorely lacking is the slowly increasing impact of HIV on Chilean women. After early work with women sex workers and some consciousness-raising among scattered communities using women health promoters, the attention to women dropped off. Women with HIV reentered the public debate in demand of their clinical needs, but despite regular references to the "feminization" of the epidemic in Chile and the less lopsided male : female infection ratios, no coherent prevention program addressing how to prevent AIDS among women or their male partners emerged. The shift of attention from the highly charged debates about sexuality education and reproductive health services for adolescents to the focus on drug access has left the country without a clear point of orientation for addressing heterosexual transmission.

I left my job as the director of the Chile AIDS Prevention Association in 2000 over differences about strategy and internal practices. Inevitably these divergences became personalized, and the long professional cohabitation and friendship with my cofounders came to an end. Curiously enough, one contentious point during this final breakdown was "professionalism" despite our historical posture in favor of boosting the weak and reining in the strong, of encouraging the nonprofessional and not relying on formal university credentials.

Although our group had started out with few university-educated collaborators, some of the staff and volunteers pursued their studies over the years, in some cases with our assistance. We tracked down and funded English courses to expand their access to research and conferences and encouraged people to accumulate all-important credentials, even when not taking them too seriously. But the increase in the number of university degrees did not lead to greater internal democracy.

Differences of opinion emerged in our association in the late 1990s around two issues: women and people with HIV/AIDS. Despite its origins as a gay-oriented project, the association was not an explicitly gay entity, and our group could have expanded its services and its discourse to the area of sexual and reproductive rights; it chose not to. A women's program I instituted did not survive my departure, and by 2002 the association was reiterating that its target population was "male homosexuals." Women were discouraged from seeking its services.

A second area of conflict was our role in the fight for antiretroviral access and services to people with HIV/AIDS, a long-standing conundrum. Although our approach to HIV diagnosis was nondiscriminatory and upbeat, there was little institutional capacity to troubleshoot for people with HIV or to expand casework services to confront the complex problems that faced these individuals aside from obtaining their drugs, the sorts of situations reflected in the anecdotes interspersed among these chapters. Without depoliticizing or overpersonalizing the epidemic along the lines of the Catholic charities, I believed the AIDS association should develop direct services for those affected. Many cases reached us through consultations to our hotline or our testing service; they were time-consuming and hard to fit into a programmatic framework.

Our seventy-year-old secretary, Elena Droguett, was always assigned to handle these tough cases due to her willingness and skill at handling difficult situations. But some of Elena's key coworkers believed her lack of formal training made her incapable of assuming this responsibility. Our empowered young gay professionals, fresh from the university, campaigned relentlessly to "professionalize" these activities, and she resigned in November 2000, one month after I did. Given the weaknesses of the hospital-based HIV-positive groups and the main HIV-positive coalition's dedication to the political side of the AIDS epidemic, these services have never been created in Chile, and probably never will be.

Meanwhile, is prevention education on AIDS for gay and homosexually active men in Santiago effective today? Our own 1997 study suggested that condom use was common although inconsistent among at least half of self-identified gay men at that time. HIV seroprevalence rates are hard to estimate, but some 12 percent of men who report homosexual practices turn up HIV-positive at the city's sexually transmitted disease clinics. The figure has not risen in recent years, but it does not need to; at those rates, any sexually active, unattached gay man who is not extremely careful has a good chance of acquiring the infection over the course of his life. Some close observers fear that the momentum is now being lost and that the younger generation of gays is less likely to take precautions than their older peers. Vicky Braga is a bar owner who says she lost an entire generation of clients in the first wave of AIDS. She explains:

> The young kids don't go to the organizations, they disdain them. Their attitude is that nobody is going to tell them what to do, that they're grown up and know what's what. They're very "lite." Nobody is surprised at the death of the next guy, he just died, and that's that. It doesn't mean a thing.

Just as the lengthy treatment access debate shifted public attention away from sexuality issues to clinical ones, the government's decision to shift funds to drug purchases and away from public information lowered the general level of awareness about the continued risk. Dr. Child thinks society is generally more comfortable with a traditional, doctor-patient approach to the whole business. She says:

> The viewpoint has changed, and you can see it in the way the issue is handled by the news media. Preventive behaviors and probably the whole

AIDS phenomenon in all its dimensions are less important. Treatments exist, so what are we worried about? You see how society medicalizes every subject. It's the easiest way out and furthermore a solution that is not up to me. I take a pill, and that's that.

Child suggests that in AIDS and in many other areas, the promise of the post-Pinochet period and the enthusiasm of the populace to make meaningful changes has dissipated; Chilean society has settled back into much more traditional patterns. Her argument is a familiar one: that the country's age-old power brokers—the armed forces, the business elite, the right-wing press, the Catholics bishops—although a minority, have neutralized the weak, liberal state and forced it to administer, rather than solve, social problems. The forms of popular sovereignty are respected, but the underlying reality is glacial change, if any. Meanwhile, those who have no choice but to survive under this system look for ways around it as best they can.

At the same time, the shift of the locus of public debate around AIDS from sexuality to medicines imperceptibly removed the entire issue from polemics about morals and mores and placed it in the realm of good administration and government budgetary decisions. AIDS could now be discussed not as a wrenching issue of sexual culture and human rights but a disease to be resolved by doctors—and of course, their patients. Child continues:

> I would say that this lesser activity, lower profile from society, has to do with the demoralization of people and our lack of a critical spirit, where the media dish it up, and we consume it. People and society in general don't act today unless the mass media put something on the agenda. The other issues don't exist.

The success of placing access to medicines on the public agenda forced the government's hand and rewrote policy. If Child is right, however, the clinical solution has neutralized other aspects, including prevention efforts. Nonetheless, Child herself characterizes the country's response to HIV as a partial success, and that half-full glass is what agrees with the national idiosyncrasy. Technical competency, rather than lingering looks at the roots of social problems or audacious solutions for them, is the watchword. Indeed, the overall coherence of the Chilean response has attracted new resources: Chile was among the first countries to win a five-year grant from the Global Fund to Fight AIDS, Tuberculosis and Malaria—an impressive $38.1 million. The expressed aim of this radical injection of funds is to "scale up" national efforts: to take the experience accumulated and the institutional resources already existing and reduce the curve of HIV infection in the country. Doing this will require real ingenuity and broad-based mobilization of all Chilean society, not merely well-executed projects and their accompanying optimistic reports.

But the entrenched, conservative social attitudes that still characterize Chilean sexuality and block reproductive health services and sex education for future generations make the triumphalism and complacent management of the Global Fund largesse slightly absurd. The three main actors—government, HIV-positive groups and the other NGOs—now rarely criticize each other in public and have their hands full managing all their funded projects. The news media are far less curious about AIDS than before, now that controversy and the easy narratives of conflict and personal tragedies cannot stir the same "impact." Today the obstacles to deeper successes—beyond the initial goals of raising public consciousness, improving services and buying medicines—are reinforced by the country's congratulatory self-image. Enormous programmatic gaps belie the sanguine forecasts. But for the time being, things in Chile look fine.

Epilogue

Latin America is rarely on the radar in discussions of AIDS; the epidemic arrived there somewhat later than in the wealthier countries of the North, and the devastation caused is incomparably less than that afflicting Africa. The infection rates among adults remain below 2 percent for most countries of the region, far from the 20 to 30 percent rates estimated for Botswana or Zimbabwe. The total numbers of people likely to acquire HIV in Latin America pale when set against the hundreds of millions of Asians now at risk.

Yet the suggestion that the region somehow has been "luckier" than others is reprehensible. "Is AIDS a big problem in Chile?" people often ask me, to which the only possible response is yes: If you get AIDS in Chile, it is a big problem. "Only" some 250,000 people acquire HIV infection in the Latin American and Caribbean region every year, while "only" another 120,000 die of AIDS-related illnesses, mostly for lack of access to modern medicines. If all comparisons are odious, this one is surely right near the top of the list. Examining successes and obstacles to future progress is far more useful than ranking human tragedy on a scale.

Despite the considerable success of some governments and public health systems to respond systematically to the epidemic, in many situations foot-dragging and incompetence still reign. A quantitative leap has occurred in the levels of funding available to address HIV prevention and care issues just in the years I have taken to research and write this book. But the exasperated tone of many of the electronic communications I see describing events in Honduras, the Dominican Republic and Bolivia is almost the same as before. Even when governments cannot plead poverty, they often seem unable to organize what should be fairly straightforward administrative services to get drug warehousing and delivery systems in place. Where the performance is better in terms of care and services for people living with HIV, prevention often seems to lag behind. The fact that HIV has not spread faster through heterosexual transmission in Latin America probably is more the result of happy accident than wise public policy. We seem to have learned how better to administer and manage, rather than to undermine, HIV disease.

In criticizing failings due to administrative dysfunction and narrow self-interest, there are many easy targets; pharmaceutical companies and incompetent bureaucrats top the list. But all human institutions have strong tendencies to seek comfort and continuity rather than risk and renewal. This is as true of NGOs as of governments, and we excuse our heroic social movements from that analytical lens at the risk of abandoning our first responsibility, which is to the purported beneficiaries of our labors.

As the preceding chapters should have made clear, I am concerned about several tendencies within the varied social responses to HIV/AIDS in the countries observed and in which I participated. It is true that we resisted attempts to box us into the role of "vectors of infection" or "risk groups" and defended the population groups to which we belonged; that was good. But it was not good enough. HIV infection cannot be combated simply by more self-esteem workshops and pamphlets produced for carefully segmented interest groups of sex workers, drug users and gay men. We need radically new preventive strategies and more determined assaults on phony "conservative" social mores that mask indifference to people's urgent sexual health and reproductive health needs. We must know whether the activities and projects that have worked in the past are still working or will work in the future rather than simply repeating them because that is what we have always done and what we have always gotten paid for doing.

The increase in heterosexual transmission of HIV and the resulting new cases of AIDS among women and their male partners is accompanied in most countries of the region by a thin and not entirely cordial alliance between women's health advocates and the largely gay first-generation leaders of the AIDS organizations. These two fields of action have much to learn from each other, but the lessons will be obscured if each side succumbs to temptations to push its respective constituency to the top of the AIDS tragedy honor roll and fight over who is "more vulnerable" or "more affected" or the "principal victims," all phrases that repeatedly roll off the tongues of activists.

Similarly, we struggled with some success against the stigmatization of people living with HIV and encouraged them to be protagonists of the epidemic. But they cannot be the only ones. Those who have acquired HIV infection have an essential message to transmit; those who have avoided it have another. Both partake of the sexual culture in which they live, and both have a stake in the conditions of autonomy, privacy, human rights and solidarity that obtain there.

In the long run, I am skeptical of the HIV prevention and care strategies that do not look beyond the disease or the subpopulations affected to question broader issues, including reproductive health and sexual rights, the status of women and the rampant push to privatize health services in the region. The agencies pouring funds into the region err if they allow AIDS-related activities to operate in isolation from these pressing contextual concerns.

By its very nature, AIDS created an atmosphere of crisis and even desperation. It is no accident that one of the oldest AIDS service groups, the pioneering New York organization, is named Gay Men's Health Crisis. But disease cannot mobilize human energy into social movements in the long run because it is inherently negative. Early gay groups did not attract their armies of volunteers out of fascination with an illness but with the community that was under assault by it. If sex workers and intravenous drug users organize and achieve important gains, they do so not because they feel motivated by a virus but by the social links and the opportunities that the virus's presence generates. We need a long-term vision of our own work free of the straitjacket of "preventing" a bad situation and capable of imagining a good one.

At the same time, getting beyond the crisis mode should not lull us into the mistaken notion that we are winning the fight against AIDS. We may be losing it. A Herculean worldwide effort is underway to bring life-saving medicines to three million people by 2005 while another five million new infections are added to the world total annually. We are still far from reversing those numbers, and meanwhile a vaccine seems as remote as ever despite the worthy and somewhat unsung efforts to find one.

For now, of course, access to treatments for HIV is still an emergency issue for Latin America and the Caribbean, and the agitation dedicated to it is a good thing. But those countries that provide near-universal access face other problems that the clinical focus has not resolved. As speakers from different countries noted, movements to obtain drugs run the risk of collapsing after the drugs are obtained. In parallel, we need to generate additional services that overburdened public hospitals are unlikely to provide to help people with the many issues of living with or avoiding HIV infection that a steady drug supply does not resolve.

The consistent dismay and disappointment reported in country after country at the squabbles and breakups of AIDS networks, the nongovernmental coordinating bodies formed to join forces against the scourge of the epidemic, now seem to me a result of wrong-headed optimism. One need not be a cynic to realize that these groups and their members have both shared and competitive interests. But there is no reason to be ashamed of ambition just because AIDS causes suffering and death. Our work can aim at alleviating human misery and still provide professional advancement and institutional growth. Donors and UN agencies know that networks flourish while they serve as conduits for contacts, influence and cash, and there is nothing wrong with them performing that role; nor does self-interest prevent them from acting as advocates for sound public policy. Rivalry and opportunism are inevitable and should be taken into account. However, if the goal is to expand a national response, neither governments nor the established NGOs and HIV-positive groups can be permitted to exercise monopolistic control over the process, control that, in the natural pursuit of their institutional survival, they inevitably will seek to acquire.

Doctors who came to AIDS work from their clinical practices sometimes insist on continuing to see patients after taking on administrative jobs. These physicians say that something crucial is lost when dealing only with policy and epidemiological statistics. The anecdotes of my personal experiences and those of my colleagues interspersed among the preceding chapters are offered in the same spirit. I once scoffed at the "AIDS soap opera" as disrespectful to those affected; now I realize that the epidemic requires narrative to communicate key facts. Few governments would have agreed to spend money on AIDS medicines without the skilled recourse to publicizing the dramas faced by individuals with the disease. Ideally, personal stories such as those shared here do not replace but rather anchor political pressures for sound programs and improved services; they are reminders of the complex human needs behind the public statements and private negotiations.

Illogical as it may seem, I found that the effort to provide direct aid to individuals in addressing the myriad problems that arise in their lives related to HIV and AIDS was highly controversial. The activity stirred enormous practical, if not ideological, resistance among my peers. It was considered fine to challenge governments, insist on funding, denounce abuses, pursue changes in cultural attitudes, fight for sexual emancipation and even reveal personal dramas. But in my experience, there was little interest in generating systematic social services or dedicating institutional resources to individuals in need. Sometimes this approach was called "paternalistic" or dismissed as "charity." More frequently it was applauded from the sidelines but given no institutional framework or real backing. It is ironic to realize how many of the organizations dedicated to AIDS are incapable of responding to the individuals affected by it, with or without the virus in their bodies. My withdrawal from the day-to-day world of AIDS service provision and advocacy in 2000 occurred over precisely this point. At that time I believed that by continuing to focus on individuals and their real struggles to avoid HIV or to deal with the diagnosis, we could better understand the conditions that diminish their well-being and our own performance in changing those conditions. Nothing I saw or heard during my visits and interviews in Latin America and the Caribbean has led me to abandon that conviction, and I hope circumstances permit me in the future to contribute once again to the effort to combine prevention and care services with strategic public health thinking.

Index